AN INTRODUCTION TO
QUANTITATIVE ANALYSIS
IN HUMAN GEOGRAPHY

McGRAW-HILL SERIES IN GEOGRAPHY

EDWARD J. TAAFFE AND JOHN W. WEBB, *Consulting Editors*

**McGRAW-HILL
BOOK COMPANY**

New York
St. Louis
San Francisco
Düsseldorf
Johannesburg
Kuala Lumpur
London
Mexico
Montreal
New Delhi
Panama
Rio de Janeiro
Singapore
Sydney
Toronto

MAURICE YEATES

*Queen's University
Ontario, Canada*

An Introduction to Quantitative Analysis in Human Geography

This book was set in Times Roman.
The editors were Janis Yates and James R. Belser;
the cover was designed by Pencils Portfolio, Inc.;
and the production supervisor was Leroy A. Young.
The printer and binder was Kingsport Press, Inc.

Library of Congress Cataloging in Publication Data

Yeates, Maurice
    An introduction to quantitative analysis in
human geography.

    (McGraw-Hill series in geography)
    Published in 1968 under title: An introduction
to quantitative analysis in economic geography.
    Bibliography: p.
    1. Geography, Economic—Methodology. I. Title.
HF1025.Y4   1974   330.9   73-8771
ISBN 0-07-072251-X

**AN INTRODUCTION TO
QUANTITATIVE ANALYSIS
IN HUMAN GEOGRAPHY**

234567890 KP KP 7987654

ACKNOWLEDGMENTS

The author and publisher wish to express their thanks to the following for permission to reprint or modify material from copyright works:

Annals of Mathematical Statistics for extracts from pp. 86 to 92 from "A Comparison of Alternative Tests of Significance for the Problem of *m* Rankings," Volume 11, by M. Friedman; pp. 117 and 118 from "The 5% Significance Levels for Sums of Squares of Rank Differences and a Correction," by E. G. Olds; and extracts from pp. 133 to 148 from "Distribution of Sums of Squares of Rank Differences for Small Numbers of Individuals," by E. G. Olds, 1938.

Barnes and Noble, New York for Table 10 from *Tables for Statisticians*, 1962, by H. Arkin and R. R. Colton.

Dr. S. Brunn, for pp. 200 to 206 of "Changes in the Service Structure of Rural Trade Centers," 1968, in *Rural Sociology*, Volume 33.

The editor and the authors for the following from *Geografiska Annaler*: Tables III, IV, and V, p. 55; and the price models on p. 56 from "Concept of Potential Applied to Price Formation," 1966, by B. Tegsjo and S. Oberg.

Hafner Publishers Co., New York for Tables 3 and 4 from *Statistical Tables for Biological, Agricultural and Medical Research*, 1943, by R. A. Fisher, and F. Yates.

Professor T. Hagerstrand, Lund, Sweden for the Table on p. 190 and map on p. 62 of "Innovations forloppet ur korologisk Synpunkt," Gleerup, 1953; and the diagrams on pp. 17 and 23 of "On Monte Carlo Simulation of Diffusion," in *Quantitative Geography, Part I*, by W. L. Garrison and D. F. Marble.

Holt, Rinehart and Winston for data from p. 34 from *The Northern Colonial Frontier*, 1966, by E. D. Leach.

Iowa State College Press for the table on pp. 222 to 225 from *Statistical Methods*, 1946, by G. W. Snedecor.

Dr. A. Shachar, Jerusalem, Israel for extracts of information on p. 203 from "Some Applications of Geostatistical Methods in Urban Research," 1966, in *Papers of the Regional Science Association*, Volume 18.

The authors and the University of Chicago Press for data from *Mental Disorders in Urban Areas*, 1939, by R. E. L. Faris and H. W. Dunham.

Yale University Press for Table 3.8, pp. 64 and 65; Table 4.3, p. 96; and Table 4.4, p. 98 from *Changes in the Location of Manufacturing in the United States Since 1929*, by V. R. Fuchs.

Mr. K. A. Yeomans, Birmingham, England for Figure 77, p. 278 from *Applied Statistics*.

To my parents

CONTENTS

PREFACE

This book is *not* merely a revised version of *An Introduction to Quantitative Analysis in Economic Geography* (New York: McGraw-Hill, 1968), for only about 15 percent of the material contained in that little book is also contained in this. Rather, this book is an outgrowth of that volume and two semester-length courses that have been offered to second-year undergraduate students at Queen's University since 1966. The first of these courses is designed to be a general introductory survey of the application of certain statistical models in geography. It has no prerequisites, other than an introductory course in human or economic geography, and it covers, in essence, the material contained in the first four chapters in this volume. Associated with the course is a series of practical problem-solving exercises, and the students manipulate the data, using electronic calculators or a typewriter terminal linked to a large computer that uses APL (*a p*rogramming *l*anguage).

The second course, which is also semester-length, covers most of the material contained in the last six chapters, and has the first course as a prerequisite. It also requires a higher level of mathematical competence. The students usually experiment with the techniques with their own data, though occasionally some exercises are provided by the instructor, and, of course, they make use of the skills they have developed in computer programming. Those students who wish to continue to graduate school are encouraged to participate in courses in theoretical statistics, the calculus, linear and matrix algebra, and so forth, in the department of mathematics.

Associated with the two undergraduate courses are several required texts in statistics. In the first course the students appear to enjoy Moroney (1965), and are quite content with Mills (1955), Blalock (1960), Hoel (1960), or Freund (1967). In the second course considerable use is made of the monograph prepared by the School Mathematics Study Group (1961) on matrix algebra, and also Kemeney et al. (1966) along with the excellent discussion of statistical techniques in geology by Krumbein and Graybill (1965), and the very good survey presented by King (1969). For both these courses a book of mathematical tables, such as that prepared by Arkin and Colton (1962), is vital. Additional references can be found in the recent bibliography prepared by Greer-Wootten (1972).

The last two chapters are included because at the end of the second course the instructor frequently presents a few introductory lectures in factorial analysis or linear programming, or both, in order to satisfy the demand for some information concerning these procedures. These lectures are useful because they also lead toward graduate-level courses concerning these methods. If factorial analysis is the concern, then Fruchter (1954), Harman (1960), and more recently, Rummel (1970) may be suggested. If linear programming is the focus of interest, then Dorfman et al. (1958), Ficken (1961), and Simonnard (1966) may be suggested as basic information texts, and the review of dynamic programming by MacKinnon (1970) and combinatorial programming by Scott (1971a) can be suggested for their spatial interest.

Thus, the present text is an outgrowth of some years of practical experience in teaching quantitative methods to undergraduate students in a Canadian university and, parenthetically, from shorter survey courses offered at the University of California at Los Angeles in 1969 and Berkeley in 1970. There are, of course, a number of techniques and methods that have been ignored, such as the whole class of models concerned with point processes (Dacey, 1969; Rogers, 1969a and b; and King, 1969, pp. 32–59), graph theory (Kansky, 1963 and Werner, 1968), and the theory of games (Williams, 1954 and Gould, 1963). For these omissions, and many others that have been glossed over, the author can only apologize and trust that one day a volume for all men can be produced.

This book was one of four tasks completed during a sabbatical leave from Queen's University, 1971 to 1972, during which period I also had the financial assistance of a Canada Council Leave Award. But even with that kind of splendid support my objectives would not have been fulfilled without the continuous encouragement and interest of my wife, Marilynn. My young children, Maurine and Harry, and their friends, usually left me alone while I was at my desk, because they were under the impression that I was writing a new version of *Puss in Boots*. I wish that I were that able!

MAURICE YEATES

AN INTRODUCTION TO
QUANTITATIVE ANALYSIS
IN HUMAN GEOGRAPHY

1

INTRODUCTION

Geography can be regarded as a science concerned with the rational development, and testing, of theories that attempt to explain and predict the spatial distribution and location of various characteristics on the surface of the earth. The role of geography as a science is discussed at great length by Harvey (1969), who is obviously greatly stimulated by the earlier provocative statements made by Schaefer (1953), Hartshorne (1959), Bunge (1962), and the National Research Council Ad Hoc Committee on Geography (1965), concerning this particular role. The important point, as far as the beginning researcher in human geography is concerned, is that if this role is accepted, it leads to the application of a widely used approach to research, which, for the sake of brevity, can be referred to as the *scientific method*. The great advantages of this approach is that it is logically problem-solving, it permits replication and therefore cross-checking, and most importantly of all, it instills into the geographer the lingua franca of the sciences. The last aspect is emphasized because no discipline, and particularly geography, can exist in isolation of others, and any common language, whether it is the result of the use of similar research procedures, techniques, or tools (such as computers), that breaks down disciplinary barriers is important of itself.

It is, of course, recognized that the scientific method can be oversold. Among geographers, this has been recognized by Gould (1970), who suggests that a myopic use of the scientific method results in research which concentrates solely on using statistical procedures which have been developed for the application of this particular philosophical view. He points out, for example, that many of the classical procedures of parametric statistics developed during the past 100 years are based on assumptions of independence and randomness, and when these procedures are applied to social and behavioral data the results can be quite meaningless. As the discussion in this volume does focus at some length on these particular techniques, a word of caution is appropriate.

The scientific method for, or approach to, the analysis of the spatial distribution and interrelation among a number of characteristics involves two components which are equally important. The first is the collection of facts or data, and the second is the drawing together of these facts into meaningful general relations which can be called theories. The theoretical, or analytical, component should precede the empirical, or data, component in the design and execution of any research procedure; for the theory usually indicates the type of data that needs to be collected, and it focuses the direction of research. In fact, the "quantitative revolution" in geography (which occurred during the early 1960s) was not simply an innovative situation involving the application of statistical and mathematical techniques, for the real "revolution" suggested a complete change in approach to geographic research. This change was a shift in emphasis from a descriptive-inductive approach to a theoretical-deductive approach (Burton, 1963). Acceptance of the latter point of view should not, however, imply complete rejection of the former, but just recognition of its drastic limitations.

THEORY AND THE SCIENTIFIC METHOD

A *theory* is a general statement that defines and explains the interrelation among a number of variables. It can be "the creation of a scientist's imagination, the distillation of a scholar's experience with the subject matter, or a tediously built structure slowly erected on a foundation of numerous experiments, investigations, and findings" (Rummel, 1967, p. 454). Whatever the source, the essence of the word "theory" is that the form of the interrelations that it specifies can be explained by abstract deduction. A tenable theory can be substantiated by *empirical verification*. The phrase "abstract deduction" refers to a reasoning process whereby one can infer a general conclusion from a set of premises that are themselves internally consistent. An example of such an abstract deduction is Weber's theory of industrial location's relating to weight loss (Conkling and Yeates, 1974). From a set of specific assumptions (premises), the only variable being a raw material that incurs different weight loss in the manufacturing process, Weber is able to determine where the manufacturing process will occur. The term "empirical verification" refers to the process of collecting data to support, or perhaps negate, the abstract theory that has been deduced.

The Scientific Method

The *scientific method* refers to the procedure by which theories are established, developed, and refined. Haring and Lounsbury (1971) present rather a good introduction to the application of the scientific method in geographic research; so in this section our discussion will focus upon the fundamentals. The first step in the procedure is the definition of a problem, which is followed by the formulation of hypotheses (Kerlinger, 1964). Hypotheses form the cornerstone of quantitative analysis; consequently, the definition of the problem is extremely important.

Presentation of problems   Scientific research always starts with a problem, for the problem sets the tone of the whole research. Problems are best expressed in the form of interrogative statements. To express the problem as "the purpose of this study is . . . " or "the problem is . . . " is somewhat unsatisfactory because a statement of this kind is not precise. The question must inquire into the relation between two or more variables, and it should be presented in such a way that the conclusions may be verified by empirical testing. Thus, value judgments are avoided in scientific research.

　　An example of a research problem in human geography may be, What factors influence the distribution of cash-grain farming in the Midwest of the United States? This is a rather general problem, because many factors may influence the distribution. In order to break the problem down into a series of more specific problems, the geographer will have to develop some theories concerning what might influence the spatial distribution of cash-grain farming. These can be based on known agricultural location theories, such as Thunen's theory of land use, or other theories, such as those relating to physical determinism. If the theory is not very well formulated, then certain statistical "search" procedures may be applied to a set of data, such as linkage analysis (Chap. 4) or factorial analysis (Chap. 9), from which some hypotheses, and perhaps theoretical structures, may be derived. Cattell (1966, p. 15) refers to the creation of hypotheses from the data as the "inductive-hypothetico-deductive spiral," and Wilkie (1973) refers to it as the "Process Method."

　　If there is some tenable theory, then it is usually possible to break the problem down into a series of more specific problems, one of which could be, To what extent do land forms influence the distribution of cash-grain farming in the Midwest of the United States (Hidore, 1963)? Once the problem has been stated this way the geographer can formulate a hypothesis to help solve it. This solution may be achieved in many different ways. If the theory is fairly strong, it may be possible for a researcher to specify the exact form of a relation, for example, that Y is a linear function of X. These, and certain nonlinear functions, may be evaluated by simple regression (Chap. 4), and multiple regression (Chaps. 5 and 6). These statistical models are, however, highly deterministic, and the researcher may be more inclined to test the hypotheses with pseudodynamic stochastic models of the kind using simulation procedures or Markov chains (Chap. 7).

Hypotheses

The hypothesis is very important in the scientific procedure since it guides the course of research. Hypotheses are always expressed in a declarative sentence in which the relation between two or more variables is presented as a possible solution to a problem. Such a declarative sentence could be, The spatial distribution of cash-grain farming in the Midwest of the United States is related to the distribution of flat land. It will be noted that this statement has been formulated in such a way that the relation may be tested, though the exact form of the relation has not been hypothesized. Furthermore, the rather vague term "landform" has been defined as the spatial distribution of flat land, and the area Midwest can be defined according to some geographic consensus.

"Flat land" is, in fact, an operational definition for "landform." Landform is difficult to measure, but flat land can be measured by referring, for example, to a degree of slope. This measurement is a surrogate, for it stands in place of the general term landform. Operational definitions of this kind are used frequently in quantitative analysis because many concepts are difficult to define mathematically. For example, the concept "stage in the life cycle" as it pertains to families or individuals is very difficult to measure. Several measures could be used—age of head of family, size of family, number of children, ages of children, and so forth, all of which are indicators of the concept, but none, by themselves, actually measure it. However, it may be possible to combine all the scalings into a common calibration by using principal-components analysis (Chap. 9), and in this case the principal component would be the operational definition for stage in the life cycle. The important point to remember is that whenever operational definitions are employed, they must be explained carefully when the variables are discussed.

When formulating hypotheses, the researcher takes special care to indicate their relation to other empirical studies of the same or a similar phenomenon. In some cases, the researcher is duplicating work done in other geographic areas, in order to indicate the wider generality of the previous studies. This type of study is often called a *comparative study*, and the researcher should make clear the degree to which the studies, and therefore the conclusions, are comparable. In other instances, the researcher may be undertaking a reevaluation or a retesting of a study completed at an earlier date in the same geographic area. This type of study is frequently referred to as a *revisited study*, and again, the researcher should make clear the degree to which the studies are comparable. One advantage of the scientific method is that it does permit replications of this type. The only way in which a researcher can be aware, and demonstrate that he is aware, of studies of the same type that have been undertaken in the same or other areas is through a good *knowledge of the literature*. Furthermore, a good knowledge of the literature will, of course, also provide the researcher with refinements for his hypotheses and will also help in the design of his research problem.

Although hypotheses are the building blocks of theory, it is very difficult in geography ever to have a theory that can be completely proved, for it is difficult to envisage a situation where a theory can be verified under all possible conditions. As a consequence, one does not try to prove that a hypothesis is true; one tries, instead, to reject the general statement that the hypothesis is not true. This general statement is called the *null hypothesis*, and it states that there is no relation between two or more variables. The *research hypothesis*, on the other hand, states the exact aim of the research, that A is related to B, or that A is positively related to B, or that A is negatively related to B, and so forth. The roles of the null and research hypotheses are explained at greater length in Chap. 3 with respect to sampling, and tests of significance for various statistics are discussed frequently throughout the entire text.

These tests of significance are important in the context of the possibility of making a Type I or Type II error (mistake). A Type I mistake can occur if, on the basis of his results, a researcher rejects a hypothesis that is, in fact, true; and a Type II mistake occurs when a researcher accepts a hypothesis that is, in fact, false. These mistakes can occur because the data may be based on samples that are not really representative of all the information in the area pertaining to the characteristics being measured. Also, there may be errors in the measurements themselves, which can lead to misleading results. It is for these reasons that hypotheses analyzed by using information derived from samples are tested at a particular confidence level, a procedure which is explained in greater detail in Chap. 3.

Whenever hypotheses are tested, a number of *assumptions* are involved. Measurement itself is an assumption, and the various types of scales are discussed in the ensuing section. In hypothesis testing, assumptions of a randomly drawn sample from a normally distributed population (Chap. 2) are frequently made and need to be substantiated. Many statistical techniques require data that are measured in a particular way (interval or ratio scales) for which particular parameters can be calculated (Chap. 2). If the data are not available in this form, then some kind of nonparametric statistical technique should be used (Chap. 8) for which especially derived significance tests have been developed. All these various assumptions concerning the data and the techniques used are referred to frequently in the ensuing chapters. The researcher should, however, be cautioned at this stage to keep the number of assumptions in any study to as few as possible, and to explain them with sufficient detail for the reader to appreciate the limitations that they may place upon the conclusions.

Models   The quantitative analysis of problems in human geography often makes use of models (Chorley and Haggett, 1967*a*). Models can be classified into three types (Ackoff et al., 1962, pp. 108ff.), which represent increasing degrees of abstraction. The first type, the *iconic model*, represents the properties of the real world and involves only a change in scale. An aerial photograph is an iconic model of reality since it maintains the same spatial relations between phenomena, but at a reduced scale. The second type is the *analog model*, in which one property is represented by another (Chorley, 1964). In a topographic map, for example, the contours are used to show a third dimension of relief. The third type of model is the *symbolic model*, in which the properties of objects are represented by symbols. When the symbols are measured, this type of model is called a *mathematical model*. Models of this kind can be expressed in the form of an equation in which the relation between the variables can be mathematically determined.

Models of various kinds can, therefore, be used in all aspects of research in human geography. Iconic models and analog models have been used frequently in the past, particularly in the form of maps. Symbolic models and mathematical models are introduced into geographic research through the use of quantitative analysis, for the measured symbols are the variables. The relations between the measured symbols or variables can then be expressed in the form of an equation, and the model can be used to describe reality and to predict future events. Mathematical models are, therefore, particularly important to the scientific method because they enable the researcher to predict, which is a major aim of science.

DATA

In any defined area over which numerous characteristics are distributed spatially, a primary task of the human geographer is to measure the characteristics and record their spatial distribution. The choice of the characteristics and the way that they are defined depend upon the form of the hypotheses and the theory to which these pertain. The process of measurement involves the use of numbers, which permit the application of arithmetic manipulations. The recording of the data involves special problems in geography, one of which is scale and level of aggregation.

Measurement

There are three basic kinds, or levels, of measurement, which are, from the simplest to the most complex, *nominal, ordinal*, and *interval*. Frequently, the last level is subdivided into two kinds depending upon whether the scale has a zero base, in which case it is referred to as a *ratio* scale, or does not have a zero base, in which case it is referred to as a *nonzero-based interval scaling*. Very nearly all qualitative (that is, verbal) description can be subsumed in one of these levels of measurement, particularly the nominal and ordinal. One of the themes that is emphasized continually throughout the ensuing chapters is that the level of measurement that has been accomplished immediately restricts the kind of quantitative work that can be done.

Nominal scales The nominal scale of measurement simply records a fact as present or absent, male or female, good or bad, and so forth. Qualitative descriptions of this kind can be represented numerically by the numbers 1 and 0. For example, the male category can be assigned the number 1, and the female, 0. Examples of the use of this kind of measurement in human geography are included in many of the following chapters. For example, the theoretical sampling distribution of binary-coded data for which the probability of a 1 is .5 and of a 0 is .5 is discussed with respect to the binomial distribution in Chap. 2. Techniques making use of binary information for determining coefficients of association from contingency tables are discussed in Chap. 8. In a different vein, methods for including and interpreting nominally scaled variables in multiple-regression models are presented in Chap. 6.

Ordinal scales The ordinal system of measurement ascribes a rank order to a series of qualitative expressions, such as good, average, poor. In this case a numerical sequence 1, 2, 3 could be applied to the qualitative expressions. This form of measurement can be applied only if it is possible to develop a qualitative descriptive sequence in which it is logical to place one statement before another. For example, if houses are to be qualitatively scaled according to their living condition, the following adjectives may be applied: adequate, comfortable, blighted, run-down, luxurious. A rank-ordering scheme cannot, however, be applied to the sequence, for there is no logical sequence among the statements; for example, adequate implies a condition that is not better than comfortable, but comfortable implies a condition that is better than blighted. If the conditions were expressed in the order luxurious, comfortable, adequate, run-down, blighted, then a living condition ranging from extremely good to very poor can be inferred. In this case a numerical rank order of 1, 2, 3, 4, 5 can be ascribed to the expressions, and the numbers can then be manipulated in the most appropriate way. Techniques specifically developed for rank-ordered data are discussed in Chap. 8.

Although rank-ordered variables are very useful for research in human geography, two basic problems must be noted. The first, and most important, is that the intervals between the ranks are not equal. Thus, it is not possible to say that the living conditions of blighted homes are one-third as good as those of adequate houses, or that luxurious houses are twice as good as comfortable houses. For this reason parameters such as the mean and standard deviation have no meaning with respect to rank-ordered variables. As a consequence, the second problem with rank-ordered data is that its use is, theoretically, confined to nonparametric statistics and therefore limited. Unfortunately, many researchers have found that while some of the variables that they wish to use in a particular study are suitable for parametric techniques, others are rank-ordered. Rather than transform their intervally scaled data to ranks, they have assumed the rank-ordered data to be intervally measured, and have used nonparametric techniques for the entire system of variables. Obviously, there is a conscious trade-off in choice of technique in this type of decision, and it behooves the researcher to make clear the kind of trade-off and the limitations it places upon the results.

Interval scales   Interval scales, as the label implies, consist of measures for which there are equal intervals between each discrete measurement. Thus it is possible to take the difference between two scores and present it as a measurement, or to compare differences between a number of pairs of scores and say that one difference is so much greater than another. As a consequence, intervally scaled variables can be added and subtracted, and the parameters calculated for them will have a specific meaning, providing that the data conform to the theoretical distribution to which the parameters apply (see the discussion of the normal distribution in Chap. 2).

The difference between nonzero-based interval scales and ratio scales is that with the latter it is possible to locate a zero point. Therefore, it is possible to compare scores not just by looking at their differences, but also by comparing their absolute values. Thus, if we are looking at the density of persons per square mile, a density of zero implies no people, and a density of twenty persons per square mile implies twice as dense a population as ten persons per square mile. If there were no zero base, it would not be possible to assume that 20 is twice as "something" as 10. But, as Blalock (1960, p. 15) points out, for all practical purposes this distinction between nonzero-based interval scales and ratio scales is "purely academic," for it is extremely difficult to find an interval scaling that cannot be converted in one way or another into a ratio scale. Furthermore, as most parametric statistical analyses require manipulations of data with respect to their means, the division between these two forms of measurement is likely to confuse far more than it clarifies.

Recording the Data

There are two methods in geography for recording the data: maps and tables. Maps are most commonly used because they preserve the spatial nature of the characteristics. Since the map is a scaled representation of reality, the data usually have to be grouped or modified in some way. If the concern is to analyze the spatial distribution of people in a large city, a single dot on a map must represent a large number of people, perhaps 1,000 people; for if one tried to plot the exact location of each person, a map almost the same size as the urban area would have to be used. Thus, the items usually have to be aggregated into general units, termed *recording units*, each having not only a location but also an area and a shape (quantitative measures concerning shape are discussed in Chap. 2). Many of the items (facts or data) at the disposal of the human geographer are aggregated to some level, such as the block, parish, enumeration area, census tract, county, state, province, or country.

Aggregation   The problem of *aggregation* in human geography is an extremely important one, and its effect on the calculation of means and standard deviations is illustrated in the ensuing chapter. Ideally, the level of aggregation depends almost entirely on the scale of the study. For example, if one wishes to analyze the spatial distribution of income throughout the world, and per capita income data for comparative purposes is available only at the country level, then the level of aggregation would be very high. However, the study can be undertaken because the whole world is being analyzed, even though the size of the countries varies considerably. If one wished to analyze the spatial distribution of income in North America, and the data were available only at the country level, then such a study would be inappropriate because the only variation one could show would be the difference between Canada and the United States. To study the spatial distribution of income in North America, the highest level of aggregation acceptable would be at the state and provincial level.

One unfortunate aspect of much of the information available to geographers is that it is aggregated to some set of census units, such as counties. This is done in order to prevent disclosure of census information pertaining to individual persons, manufacturing plants, and so forth, a right which is protected by law. Unfortunately, census units frequently vary greatly in size; for example, the largest county in Florida is over ten times as large as the smallest. As a consequence, geographers have to transform the data to a unit area basis, such as density or percentages. In many cases, even if this transformation is undertaken, the data can be next to meaningless. This is particularly the case where census units embrace a wide variety of geographic conditions within the same area. For example, in eastern Ontario, counties extend in relatively long strips north and south, whereas most of the population is clustered in towns and villages like beads along an east-west string in the far south bordering Lake Ontario. The result is that data aggregated to the county level yield a picture that is really nowhere existent within the area. If census units were all of equal size and the same shape, the data could be compared with little or no trans-formation, and they could be aggregated (and disaggregated) easily according to the areal scope of the study.

Tables   Both the recording units and the characteristics can be recorded in tables, where the recording units form the rows, and the characteristics the columns. Assume that for the whole world there are n rows and m charac-teristics. For any ijth cell ($i = 1, 2, 3, \ldots, n; j = 1, 2, 3, \ldots, m$) there is a fact. The geographer is not really interested in the facts per se, but he is interested in the spatial distribution of the facts. In Table 1-1 each row has a location; therefore, each characteristic or column has a spatial distribution. If each fact is a measured number, the columns can be called "variables." A *variable* can be defined as a set of measurements on a particular characteristic that do not have constant values, but variations in value. To the geographer, the essential property of the variables is that the variations in value are distributed over space. Therefore, the concern of geographic study at this elemental level is with the

Table 1-1   AN ABSTRACT INFORMATION TABLE

Recording unit location	Characteristics or variables						
	Total population	Population density	Total employment				
	1	2	3	$\cdots$	j	$\cdots$	m
1				$\cdots$		$\cdots$	
2				$\cdots$		$\cdots$	
3				$\cdots$		$\cdots$	
i				$\cdots$	ij	$\cdots$	
n				$\cdots$		$\cdots$	nm

spatial variation in the distribution of the values and with the causes of the spatial variations. This tabular approach has been suggested by Berry (1964a) as a possible avenue for synthesis in geography, and the utility of its model-based inverse has been demonstrated with considerable ingenuity by Chorley and Haggett (1967b).

Quantitative analysis in human geography therefore requires a variety of statistical and mathematical techniques. The reader is introduced to some of those that are used most in geographic research in the following chapters. The discussion commences with a brief review of various methods of data description; continuing with a discussion of various sampling techniques, it uses this to introduce the reader to hypothesis testing. With this base, the discussion focuses upon parametric techniques in simple and multiple correlation and regression, with some necessary matrix definitions and operations being introduced to explain the multiple-variable models. Various applications of these models are discussed in Chap. 6 along with analysis of variance, and the curve-fitting and matrix procedures are developed further with respect to time in the following chapter. Nonparametric methods are discussed in some detail in Chap. 8. Finally, the last two chapters introduce the student to some more complex methods with factorial analysis and linear programming, which, it is hoped, may act as an appetizer to further detailed studies of these subjects.

2

THE DESCRIPTION OF GEOGRAPHIC DATA

The human geographer is commonly confronted with a mass of data pertaining to data units at different levels of aggregation distributed over space and referring to various periods of time. One of the foremost tasks of the researcher is to reduce these data to manageable form so that he may answer the hypotheses posed. At the outset this requires methods concerning data description, which, though they may be simple, are vital precursors to the more complex methods of quantitative analysis, particularly those of a statistical nature. This chapter will therefore be concerned with various methods of summarizing the distribution of data in both a mathematic and geographic sense, and describing the shapes of the sometimes complex areas to which the data all too frequently refer.

DISTRIBUTIONS

The "spatial" distribution of a particular variable is different from its "mathematical" distribution. The examples discussed in this section concern the spatial distribution of per capita income throughout the countries of the world and the threshold values of business types in central places in rural northwest Ohio, but the properties of the distributions that are discussed refer to the mathematical distributions of these variables. In other words, the spatial aspects of the per capita income and the threshold value data are not emphasized, and this is true for most of the conventional statistical techniques used by geographers. However, later in the chapter, certain applications of quantitative measurements to the spatial properties of geographic data are discussed, and this theme recurs throughout the text.

The Data Array

In Table 2-1 the threshold values [or the minimum number of people required to support the first establishment of a given business type (Thoman, Conkling, and Yeates, 1968)] are listed for thirty-nine business types found in a random sample of thirty-two small central places in rural northwest Ohio in 1940. It is to be noticed that the threshold values vary considerably for the thirty-nine business types, and so therefore the list can be described as *variable*. In fact, to

Table 2-1 THE THRESHOLD VALUES FOR THIRTY-NINE BUSINESS TYPES FOUND IN A RANDOM SAMPLE OF THIRTY-TWO SMALL, CENTRAL PLACES IN RURAL NORTHWEST OHIO

Business type	Threshold value	Business type	Threshold value
Filling station	338	Sheet metal shop	741
Food store	342	Plumbing and heating	743
Auto repair shop	352	Bank	762
Restaurant	420	Family apparel store	778
Hardware store	489	Jewelry store	788
Auto dealer	509	Men's clothing store	802
Tavern	514	Furniture store	837
Animal feed store	579	Hotel	843
Undertaker	586	Bakery	845
Farm implement dealer	589	Electric repair shop	854
Construction materials	635	Printing shop	886
Feed mill	635	Dry goods store	888
Appliance dealer	636	Dairy products	892
Auto parts dealer	636	Florist	910
Drugstore	645	General store	929
Fuel oil dealer	679	Shoe store	1,033
Confectionery	724	Variety store	1,091
Lumberyard	725	Dry cleaner	1,250
Meat market	728	Women's apparel	1,277
Paint and glass store	734		

SOURCE: Brunn (1968, p. 204).

be even more precise, the list appears to be a *discrete variable*, for there is a definite jump from one value to another. This is true of many variables in human geography, for example, the number of people in various towns in a country or the value of a plot of land. But in many cases the variables are really *continuous*; that is, an observation can take on any value between two limits, such as the density of population in different census tracts in a town, though they are almost always converted to a discrete form by rounding to a convenient unit of measurement. The only way in which infinitesimally small differences between observations can be measured is by the differential calculus. Therefore, it is apparent that our threshold example is theoretically a continuous variable that has been rounded to a discrete one for practical and commonsense reasons (there is no such thing as a fraction of a human being).

A first step in describing the mathematical distribution of the data is to rank the information in an array from highest to lowest (or vice versa). This array (Table 2-2) can then be used to determine the mode, median, quartiles, and deciles of the distribution. The easiest to obtain is the mode, which is the most frequently occurring value, and in this case there are two modes, 635 and 636. The median is the value that divides the observations in the distribution into two halves—the 50 percent of the observations that exceed that value and the 50 percent that are less. Similarly, the quartiles demarcate those values that mark the 25th percentile, the 50th percentile, and the 75th percentile, the second quartile being the median. The deciles are those values that mark the 10th, 20th, 30th, and so on, percentile values in the data array. From the example in Table 2-2 it can be observed that the median is the twentieth ranked business type, for there is an odd number of observations. Thus the value 734 divides the number of observations in the data array into exactly two halves—50 percent of the observations have values less than this and 50 percent have more. The quartiles are at 854, which separates the top 25 percent of the observations from the lowest 75 percent; 734; and 589, which separates the lowest 25 percent of the observations from the highest 75 percent. The deciles are at 420, 579, 635, 679, 734, 778, 843, 888, and 1,033. It must be noted that in this case interpolation has not proved necessary, but in most cases it is, and for this purpose (among others) graphs are very useful (Alexandersson, 1956).

Graphs of Variables

From the data array a *frequency distribution* can be obtained which indicates the frequency of occurrences of observations in a particular class interval. The magnitude and number of classes can be determined externally by some rule of thumb, but usually a reasonable interval and manageable number of classes are chosen after perusal of the ranked array. Croxton and Crowden (1955), for example, suggest that most frequency distributions should have between six and

Table 2-2   RANKED ARRAY OF THRESHOLD VALUES, PERCENTILES, AND
STANDARD SCORES FOR THIRTY-NINE BUSINESS TYPES IN THIRTY-
TWO NORTHWEST OHIO SMALL TOWNS, 1940

| Observation business type | Threshold values | | Rank | Percentile | Standard score |
	X	X^2			
Filling station	338	114,244	39		−1.82
Food store	342	116,964	38		−1.80
Auto repair shop	352	123,904	37		−1.75
Restaurant	420	176,400	36	10th	−1.44
Hardware store	489	239,121	35		−1.12
Auto dealer	509	259,081	34		−1.03
Tavern	514	264,196	33		−1.01
Animal feed store	579	335,241	32	20th	−.71
Undertaker	586	343,396	31		−.68
Farm implement dealer	589	346,921	30	25th	−.67
Construction materials	635	403,225	29		−.45
Feed mill	635	403,225	28	30th	−.45
Appliance dealer	636	404,496	27		−.45
Auto parts dealer	636	404,496	26		−.45
Drugstore	645	416,025	25		−.40
Fuel oil dealer	679	461,041	24	40th	−.25
Confectionery	724	524,176	23		−.05
Lumberyard	725	525,625	22		−.05
Meat market	728	529,984	21		−.03
Paint and glass store	734	538,756	20	50th	.00
Sheet metal shop	741	549,081	19		.03
Plumbing and heating shop	743	552,049	18		.04
Bank	762	580,644	17		.13
Family apparel store	778	605,284	16	60th	.20
Jewelry store	788	620,944	15		.24
Men's clothing store	802	643,204	14		.31
Furniture store	837	700,569	13		.47
Hotel	843	710,649	12	70th	.50
Bakery	845	714,025	11		.51
Electric repair shop	854	729,316	10	75th	.55
Printing shop	886	784,996	9		.70
Dry goods store	888	788,544	8	80th	.71
Dairy products store	892	795,664	7		.72
Florist	910	828,100	6		.81
General store	929	863,041	5		.89
Shoe store	1,033	1,067,089	4	90th	1.37
Variety store	1,091	1,190,281	3		1.64
Dry cleaner	1,250	1,562,500	2		2.37
Women's apparel shop	1,277	1,630,729	1		2.45
Total	28,644	22,847,226			

SOURCE: Threshold data from Brunn (1968, p. 204); calculations by the author.

sixteen classes, and Blalock (1960, pp. 34–37) makes the obvious point that the frequency distribution should not obscure some of the basic variability in the data. A reasonable interval for the data in Table 2-2 would seem to be 100, which would give ten class intervals.

The frequency distribution of thresholds is presented in Table 2-3. It is to be noted that the true intervals are recorded with respect to the discreteness of the data and that the *modal interval* is 700 to 799. A frequency distribution can be presented diagrammatically as a *histogram*, where the class intervals are along the *abscissa*, or *horizontal axis*, and the number of observations (business types) in each class interval are represented by solid bars to be read off on the *ordinate* or *vertical axis* (Fig. 2-1). The tops of the bars can be joined by lines, and when the line diagram is presented by itself, the graph is known as a *frequency polygon*. Another common method of presenting frequency data is to accumulate the bars successively from lowest to highest (as is illustrated in the third column of Table 2-3) and then connect the upper limit of each bar by a line (Fig. 2-2). A diagram of this kind is known as an *ogive curve*, or a *cumulated-frequency curve*. The frequency polygon and ogive curve are sometimes smoothed, which suggests a continuum rather than discreteness. This is often done when there are many class intervals, but even in this case the fact that the data are discrete should not be forgotten.

The Binomial and Normal Distributions

Of the many types of distribution that can be derived from empirical data, some have recurred so many times that they are referred to as "normal curves." This is particularly true of psychological, biological, and intelligence measurements. The importance of the normal curve does not rest, however, in the fact

Table 2-3   FREQUENCY AND CUMULATED-FRE-QUENCY DISTRIBUTION OF THRESHOLD VALUES

Class interval	Number of occurrences	Cumulated number of occurrences
300– 399	3	3
400– 499	2	5
500– 599	5	10
600– 699	6	16
700– 799	9	25
800– 899	8	33
900– 999	2	35
1,000–1,099	2	37
1,100–1,199	0	37
1,200–1,299	2	39

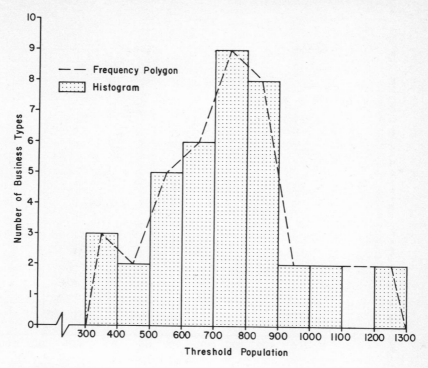

FIGURE 2-1
Histogram and frequency polygon of threshold values in rural northwest Ohio, 1940.

that it seems to reappear in many circumstances, but that it can also be derived theoretically. As a consequence, it is a standard expectation with a theoretical base for its form, and as such provides the basis for sampling theory and tests of significance.

The theoretical basis can be explained most simply by using coin tossing, and this will lead us into elementary probability theory. Let us presume that two unbiased coins A and B are tossed simultaneously. What are the likely combined outcomes? The combinations equally likely are one head, one head; one tail, one tail; one head, one tail; one tail, one head. Grouping these, we find that there is:

1 chance in 4 of two heads
2 chances in 4 of one being heads and the other tails
1 chance in 4 of two tails

If four coins are tossed simultaneously, the combinations of heads (H) and tails (T) equally likely to occur are HHHH, HHHT, HHTH, HTHH, THHH,

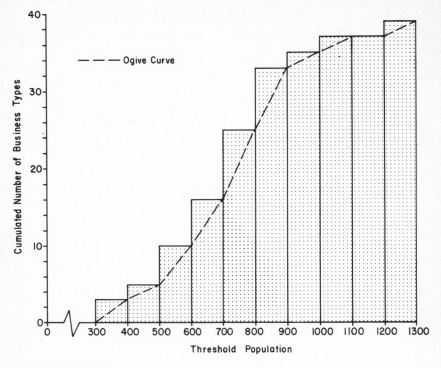

FIGURE 2-2
Ogive curve or cumulated-frequency curve for threshold values in rural northwest Ohio, 1940.

HHTT, HTTH, TTHH, HTHT, THTH, THHT, TTTH, TTHT, THTT, HTTT, TTTT. Grouping these, we find there is:

> 1 chance in 16 of four heads
> 4 chances in 16 of one being tails and three being heads
> 6 chances in 16 of two being tails and two being heads
> 4 chances in 16 of one being heads and three being tails
> 1 chance in 16 of four tails

It would obviously be a very long and time-consuming procedure to work these combinations out for five, six, seven, and so on, coins tossed simultaneously, but it is quite easy with use of the binomial expansions. For example, the binomial expansion of

$$(a + b)^2 = a^2 + 2ab + b^2$$

and of

$$(a + b)^4 = a^4 + 4a^3b + 6a^2b^2 + 4ab^3 + b^4$$

The sum of the coefficients gives us the number of all possible outcomes, and the individual coefficients indicate the number of each combination likely to occur. The coefficients for the binomial expansion for tossing 2, 3, 4, ..., 10 coins at a time are listed in Table 2-4, where a and b have both been set equal to unity, for a head is as likely as a tail. The distribution of these possible outcomes for eight coins tossed simultaneously 256 times is graphed in Fig. 2-3a.

It is to be noted that the binomial distribution has discrete quantities. If, however, the number of coins tossed is allowed to get larger and larger, the number of possible combinations of outcomes $k + 1$ will be continually increasing, and if the binomial expansions of these outcomes are plotted on the

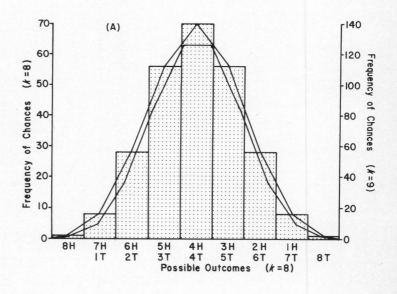

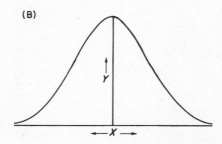

FIGURE 2-3
(a) The binomial expansion (histogram and frequency polygon) for eight coins tossed simultaneously 256 times, with the binomial expansion (frequency polygon) for $k = 9$ superimposed on the same base; (b) the normal curve.

Table 2-4   PASCAL'S TRIANGLE: EXPANSIONS OF $(1 + 1)^k$, WHERE $k = 2, 3, \ldots, 10$

k	Expansion											Total number of possible outcomes
2					1	2	1					4
3				1	3	3	1					8
4			1	4	6	4	1					16
5		1	5	10	10	5	1					32
6	1	6	15	20	15	6	1					64
7	1	7	21	35	35	21	7	1				128
8	1	8	28	56	70	56	28	8	1			256
9	1	9	36	84	126	126	84	36	9	1		512
10	1	10	45	120	210	252	210	120	45	10	1	1,024

same base (see Fig. 2-3a), the curves will define a set of distributions which can be smoothed into a normal curve. This curve is bell-shaped, and as it is smoothed, it defines a continuous relation between two variables, for the frequency is on the ordinate, or y axis, and the independent variable on the abscissa, or x axis (Fig. 2-3b). The statistics of this distribution can be discussed in the ensuing section.

DESCRIPTIVE STATISTICS

A complete set of data referring to a real-world situation is described as a *population*, for it contains all the data available concerning a particular characteristic being measured. Thus, if the spatial distribution of per capita income at the country level of aggregation were a variable to be examined, the population would be a set of per capita incomes for every country in the world. A *parameter* is a derivable number distinguishing that particular population, two examples of which have been previously described—the mode and the median—while other examples include the mean, variance, and standard deviation. The last three parameters will be defined subsequently. A *sample* is a subset of a population, and distinguishing characteristics of a sample are referred to as *statistics*. Thus a series of statistics, such as a mean $\bar{X}$ calculated from a number of samples drawn from a particular population, should cluster around the respective parent population mean μ. The use of Greek letters for parameters and Latin letters for statistics simplifies the symbolic language.

The Mean, Variance, and Standard Deviation

Whereas the mode and median are determined easily from the ranked array and frequency distribution, the mean, variance, and standard deviation are derived from simple arithmetic manipulation of the set of data. The *mean* is the arithmetic average or "expected value" for all observation units, with each observation unit's being given the same weight. This qualification is important, for when observation units of different magnitudes are being used (such as countries), the average of, for example, per capita incomes of the countries is not the same as the average per capita income for all persons incorporated within all the countries being used.

The mean is defined as

$$\mu = \frac{\sum\limits_{i=1}^{n} X_i}{N} \qquad (2\text{-}1)$$

where N = number of observation units
X = variable concerned
Σ = operation term meaning "the sum of"
$i = 1, 2, 3, \ldots, n$

The expression

$$\sum_{i=1}^{n} X_i$$

means that all the data should be summed from first to last, the nth being the last observation in the ranked array. Using the threshold data for an example,

$$\overline{X} = \frac{\sum_{i=1}^{39} X_i}{N}$$

$$= \frac{28,644}{39} = 734.46 \approx 734$$

where $\overline{X}$ = sample mean, because the threshold data are estimated from a random sample of small northwestern Ohio settlements

Thus one measure of central tendency, the median, indicates that 50 percent of the business types had a threshold value of 734 or more, and 50 percent had less; and another measure, the mean, also indicates that the average threshold value for all the business types is 734. The histogram, frequency polygon, and ogive curve indicate that a considerable amount of variability exists. For example, the threshold value of the lowest-order business type in the sample is 338, while that for the highest is 1,277. Although the quartiles and deciles are statistics measuring the dispersal of the distribution, the most commonly used are the variance and standard deviation.

The *variance* (σ^2 for the population variance, s^2 for the sample variance) is defined as

$$\sigma^2 = \frac{\sum_{i=1}^{n} (X_i - \mu)^2}{N} = \frac{\sum_{i=1}^{n} d_i^2}{N} \tag{2-2}$$

where $\sum_{i=1}^{n} d_i^2$ means the sum of the squared deviations. For samples, where statistics are being calculated as estimates of unknown population parameters, μ is replaced by $\overline{X}$, and the denominator in the variance equation becomes $N - 1$ in order to account for any error that may occur when a statistic already estimated, $\overline{X}$, is used to calculate another statistic. Thus

$$s^2 = \frac{\sum_{i=1}^{n} (X_i - \overline{X})^2}{N - 1} \tag{2-3}$$

It is to be noted that the sum of the deviations about the mean, which sum to zero, is frequently referred to as the "first moment" about the mean, and the variance, or the mean sum of squared deviations, is referred to as the "second moment." The *standard deviation* (σ for population standard deviation, s for sample standard deviation) is simply the square root of the variance. Thus $\sigma = \sqrt{\sigma^2}$, and $s = \sqrt{s^2}$, and each is described as the "root-mean-square deviation."

Computationally, the variance is more easily obtained from the formula

$$s^2 = \frac{\sum\limits_{i=1}^{n} X_i^2 - \left[\sum\limits_{i=1}^{n} X_i\right]^2 \Big/ N}{N - 1} \tag{2-4}$$

providing that the numbers are small, for with large numbers there is a danger of overflowing computers and Eq. (2-3) is preferable. The variance for the threshold data is

$$s^2 = \frac{22{,}847{,}226 - \frac{28{,}644}{39}}{38} = \frac{22{,}847{,}226 - 21{,}037{,}916}{38}$$

$$= \frac{1{,}809{,}310}{38} = 47{,}613.4$$

Therefore, the standard deviation is 218.2.

The Parameters of the Normal Distribution

The mathematical equation for the normal curve, an example of which is presented in Fig. 2-3*b*, is

$$y_i = \frac{1}{\sigma\sqrt{2\pi}} e^{-(X_i - \mu)^2/2\sigma^2} \tag{2-5}$$

To the average geography student (or for that matter, students in the other social sciences) this is a horrendous equation. As e is the base of the natural logarithms, and π is a constant, the parameters of the curve are the variance, standard deviation, and mean. Thus, in the continuous case it is possible to determine the ordinate value of y_i for any value of X_i as long as the μ, σ^2, and σ have been calculated. Also, it is possible to estimate the value y_i for a sample if the $\overline{X}$, s^2, and s have been estimated.

Because the normal distribution is used so frequently, tables of the curve have been calculated for data in standardized form. The tables used most frequently indicate the area under the curve between the mean and a specific standardized value. The standardized value for a set of data is obtained by,

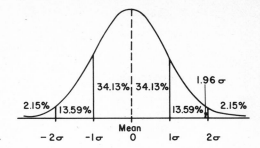

FIGURE 2-4
Areas under the normal curve.

in effect, scaling the data with respect to its mean and standard deviation. For example, the standardized threshold value for filling stations is

$$Z_i = \frac{X_i - \overline{X}}{s} = \frac{338 - 734}{218} = -1.82 \tag{2-6}$$

The *standard scores* for the data are listed in Table 2-2. It is to be noted that the standard score for the mean is, of course, zero, and that all the data are expressed in terms of their dispersal (positive and negative) around the mean. Also, it can be observed from the standard-score equation that there will be no upper and lower limits for the values of the standard scores, the implication being that it is never theoretically possible to enclose 100 percent of the area under the normal curve no matter how many standard scores are calculated. It is well to remember this point, even though we may at times assume that 100 percent of the observations are included beneath the estimated curve.

A table of areas of the normal curve is given as Table 2-5 for various standard scores (or standard deviations) corrected to two decimal places. The table lists only half of the curve, because the distribution is symmetrical. This is apparent from Fig. 2-4, in which the standard score for the mean is zero and that of 1.96 is marked. Table 2-5 indicates that .4750 of the area under the normal curve lies between zero and 1.96σ. In other words, 47.5 percent of the observations should lie between the mean and a standard score of 1.96. This, of course, implies that 97.5 percent of the area under the normal curve is at and to the left of 1.96, or that 97.5 percent of the observations should have a standard score of 1.96 or less. Thus the area under the curve between the mean and one standard score, 1σ, is 34.13 percent, between 1σ and 2σ it is 13.59 percent, and greater than 2σ it is 2.15 percent.

The table of areas under the normal curve can therefore be used for calculating the number of observations that would be found in a given class interval if the data were distributed normally. For example, Table 2-3 lists the actual number of threshold values found in a series of class intervals. What would be the number of observations in each class interval if the data were

Table 2-5 AREAS UNDER THE NORMAL CURVE

$\frac{d}{\sigma} = z$	.00	.01	.02	.03	.04	.05	.06	.07	.08	.09
.0	.0000	.0040	.0080	.0120	.0159	.0199	.0239	.0279	.0319	.0359
.1	.0398	.0438	.0478	.0517	.0557	.0596	.0636	.0675	.0714	.0753
.2	.0793	.0832	.0871	.0910	.0948	.0987	.1026	.1064	.1103	.1141
.3	.1179	.1217	.1255	.1293	.1331	.1368	.1406	.1443	.1480	.1517
.4	.1554	.1591	.1628	.1664	.1700	.1736	.1772	.1808	.1844	.1879
.5	.1915	.1950	.1985	.2019	.2054	.2088	.2123	.2157	.2190	.2224
.6	.2257	.2291	.2324	.2357	.2389	.2422	.2454	.2486	.2518	.2549
.7	.2580	.2612	.2642	.2673	.2704	.2734	.2764	.2794	.2823	.2852
.8	.2881	.2910	.2939	.2967	.2995	.3023	.3051	.3078	.3106	.3233
.9	.3159	.3186	.3212	.3238	.3264	.3289	.3315	.3340	.3365	.3389
1.0	.3413	.3438	.3461	.3485	.3508	.3531	.3554	.3577	.3599	.3621
1.1	.3643	.3665	.3686	.3718	.3729	.3749	.3770	.3790	.3810	.3830
1.2	.3849	.3869	.3888	.3907	.3925	.3944	.3962	.3980	.3997	.4015
1.3	.4032	.4049	.4066	.4083	.4099	.4115	.4131	.4147	.4162	.4177
1.4	.4192	.4207	.4222	.4236	.4251	.4265	.4279	.4292	.4306	.4319
1.5	.4332	.4345	.4357	.4370	.4382	.4394	.4406	.4418	.4430	.4441
1.6	.4452	.4463	.4474	.4485	.4495	.4505	.4515	.4525	.4535	.4545
1.7	.4554	.4564	.4573	.4582	.4591	.4599	.4608	.4616	.4625	.4633
1.8	.4641	.4649	.4656	.4664	.4671	.4678	.4686	.4693	.4699	.4706
1.9	.4713	.4719	.4726	.4732	.4738	.4744	.4750	.4758	.4762	.4767
2.0	.4773	.4778	.4783	.4788	.4793	.4798	.4803	.4808	.4812	.4817
2.1	.4821	.4826	.4830	.4834	.4838	.4842	.4846	.4850	.4854	.4857
2.2	.4861	.4865	.4868	.4871	.4875	.4878	.4881	.4884	.4887	.4890
2.3	.4893	.4896	.4898	.4901	.4904	.4906	.4909	.4911	.4913	.4916
2.4	.4918	.4920	.4922	.4925	.4927	.4929	.4931	.4932	.4934	.4936
2.5	.4938	.4940	.4941	.4943	.4945	.4946	.4948	.4949	.4951	.4952
2.6	.4953	.4955	.4956	.4957	.4959	.4960	.4961	.4962	.4963	.4964
2.7	.4965	.4966	.4967	.4968	.4969	.4970	.4971	.4972	.4973	.4974
2.8	.4974	.4975	.4976	.4977	.4977	.4978	.4979	.4980	.4980	.4981
2.9	.4981	.4982	.4983	.4984	.4984	.4984	.4985	.4985	.4986	.4986
3.0	.49865	.4987	.4987	.4988	.4988	.4988	.4989	.4989	.4989	.4990
3.1	.49903	.4991	.4991	.4991	.4992	.4992	.4992	.4992	.4993	.4993
3.2	.49931									
3.3	.49952									
3.4	.49966									
3.5	.49977									
3.6	.49984									
3.7	.49989									
3.8	.49993									
3.9	.49995									
4.0	.49997									

SOURCE: Herbert Arkin and Raymond R. Colton, "An Outline of Statistical Methods," 4th ed., New York: Barnes & Noble, 1950.

distributed normally? Table 2-6 illustrates the series of calculations used to ascertain these values. Column 1 indicates the upper limit of each class interval; and column 2, the standard score for each number. The proportion of the area under the normal curve to the left of that standard score is determined from Table 2-4 and listed in column 3. For example, Table 2-5 states that .4767 of the area under the normal curve lies between the mean and -1.99; therefore $.5000 - .4767 = .0233$ of the area under the curve lies to the *left* of that standard score. Thus 2.33 percent of the observations (thirty-nine) should lie between a threshold value of 0 and 300. The interval 300 to 399 is bounded by standard scores (in the continuous case) of -1.99 and -1.53, and from Table 2-4 it can be determined that .0233 of the area under the normal curve lies to the left of -1.99, and .0630 lies to the left between -1.53 and -1.99, and consequently 3.97 percent of the observations should lie in this interval. These calculations can be continued to ascertain the expected frequency in each class interval.

Lognormal distributions   The parameters $\overline{X}$, s^2, s, median, and mode therefore have a distinct interpretation when applied to the normal distribution. The mean, median, and mode all coincide if the data are normally distributed; also the percentiles can be derived directly once the mean and the standard deviation have been calculated. If the data are not normally distributed, the mean and standard deviation tell us very little, and this is the chief statistical

Table 2-6   STAGES IN THE CALCULATION OF THE EXPECTED FREQUENCY OF OBSERVATIONS IN GIVEN CLASS INTERVALS, ASSUMING THAT THE POPULATION IS NORMALLY DISTRIBUTED

Upper class limit (rounded)	$Z = \dfrac{X_i - \overline{X}}{s}$	Proportion of area under normal curve up to class limit	Proportion of area in class interval	Expected frequency (rounded)
300	-1.99	.0233	.0233	.9
400	-1.53	.0630	.0397	1.5
500	-1.07	.1423	.0793	3.1
600	$-.61$	.2709	.1286	5.0
700	$-.15$	.4404	.1695	6.6
800	.30	.6179	.1775	7.0
900	.76	.7764	.1585	6.2
1,000	1.22	.8888	.1124	4.4
1,100	1.67	.9525	.0637	2.5
1,200	2.14	.9838	.0313	1.2
1,300	2.60	.9953	.0115	.4
∞	∞	1.0000	.0047	.2
Total number of observations				39.0

objection to Nelson's (1955) urban classification. For example, in Table 2-7 are listed the frequency and cumulated-frequency distributions of per capita income for as many countries in the world as data can be estimated for in 1961. From this table it is to be noticed that there are far more poor countries than rich ones, and the fact that the mean is $428 and the standard deviation $493 tells us very little. Quite obviously the countries are not distributed symmetrically with respect to their wealth around the value for the average country, and 34 percent of the countries do not lie between the mean and one standard deviation ($428 + $493 = $921). The median, however, does tell us something about the data as a whole. The median in this case is $222, which indicates that 50 percent of the countries in the world had a per capita income greater than this figure and 50 percent had that or less.

The kind of distribution discovered above occurs frequently in human geography—there are many poor countries and few rich ones; there are many poor people, fewer rich ones; and there are many small towns, fewer large ones. Many of these distributions can be "normalized" by a transformation of the measurements pertaining to the observations, and one of the most commonly used is a transformation to common logarithms. If a logarithmic transformation normalizes a distribution, the variable is described as *lognormal*. This is illustrated in Fig. 2-5, where it can be observed that per capita income by country is distributed almost lognormally.

Skewness Distributions that are highly affected by extreme values are described as "skewed," and whenever a distribution is highly skewed, the median is preferable to the mean as a measure of central tendency. Data may be positively skewed or negatively skewed. If there are a number of observations

Table 2-7 FREQUENCY DISTRIBUTION OF PER CAPITA INCOME, 1961

Class interval	Number of occurrences	Cumulated number of occurrences
$0– $299	56	56
300– 599	17	73
600– 899	9	82
900–1,199	3	85
1,200–1,499	6	91
1,500–1,799	2	93
1,800–2,099	1	94
2,100–2,399	0	94
2,400–2,699	0	94
2,700–2,999	1	95

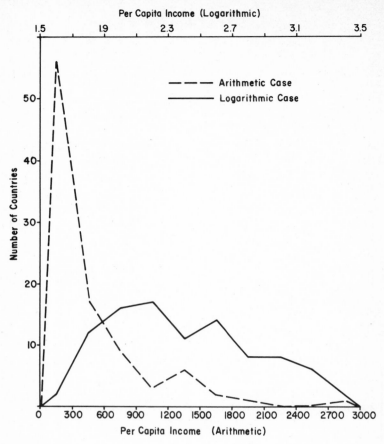

FIGURE 2-5
Frequency polygon of per capita income: arithmetic and logarithmic cases.

with very large values that result in the mean's being much larger than the median, the distribution is positively skewed; such is the case with our per capita income example. On the other hand, if the mean is smaller than the median, that is, adversely affected by an abundance of observations with very small values, the distribution is negatively skewed. One measurement of skewness takes advantage of this interrelation between the median M and the mean, and measures skewness as

$$\text{Skewness} = \frac{3(\overline{X} - M)}{s} \tag{2-7}$$

Positively skewed distributions will result in a positive number, and negatively skewed distributions will result in a negative number. For our threshold data the skewness number is zero, because the mean and the median are the same, but the per capita income example yields a large measure of skewness

$$\text{Skewness} = \frac{3(428 - 222)}{493} = 1.25$$

Mills (1955, p. 132) suggests an alternative measure of skewness based on the difference between the upper quartile and the median, q_2, and the lower quartile and the median, q_1

$$\text{Skewness} = \frac{q_2 - q_1}{q_2 - q_1} \tag{2-8}$$

The value will vary between ± 1. For distributions with perfect symmetry, $q_1 = q_2$ and the measure is zero; but if the median and one of the quartiles coincide, either q_1 or q_2 will equal zero, and the value of the measurement will be $+1$ or -1. For our threshold data, this measure of skewness yields

$$\text{Skewness} = \frac{120 - 145}{120 + 145} = -.094$$

whereas for the per capita income data, the measure is

$$\text{Skewness} = \frac{311 - 117}{311 + 117} = .45$$

It is suggested that a value of $\pm .1$ indicates a moderate degree of skewness, and a value of $\pm .3$ a very marked skewness.

CONCENTRATION AND DISPERSION

Our discussion thus far has concerned univariate distributions—data which are, in effect, aspatial. Human geographers are, however, beginning to develop descriptive statistics for data distributed spatially, and some of these are simply bivariate extensions of basic univariate statistics such as the mean and standard deviation, and as a consequence include similar assumptions in their interpretation. These and many other geostatistical measures are described in detail in Bachi (1962) and Neft (1966), and the derivation of these measures including numerous examples are presented in Lee's (1967) analysis of residential segregation using census tract data. Shachar (1966) in a study of population and land use in Tel Aviv, Israel, has presented the results of applying such centrographic measures as the mean to indicate the general location of nodal spatial distributions; the "standard distance," "mean distance," and

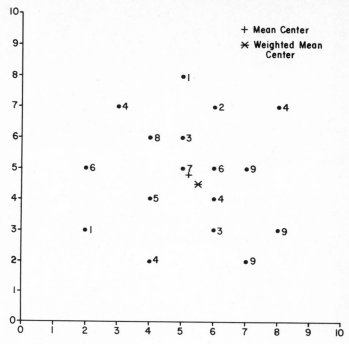

FIGURE 2-6
The bivariate mean center: distribution of points and associated values.

"equidistribution rings" around a mean center; and the "main direction" of a distribution. In this section we shall concentrate on those geostatistical centrographic measures that are direct extensions of the univariate measures already discussed, and shall also introduce nearest-neighbor analysis as another method of describing the form of a pattern.

Centrographic Measures

There are computer programs available that have been developed by geographers (Tobler, 1970; Hultquist et al., 1971) to determine a variety of centrographic measures. The most commonly used are the mean and standard distance. The *mean center* is directly analogous to univariate mean and is defined as that point on a plane which minimizes the sum of the squared distances to all other points on the plane. Consider the distribution of points in Fig. 2-6; each of these points has a location on the X and Y coordinates defined as x_i and y_i. Each point has a value (the number of people living at that location, or the number of stores in that retail nucleation), and the x_i and y_i coordinates and the values (or weights) are presented in Table 2-8. The mean center for the distribution of points is simply the average for each coordinate

$$c\overline{X} = \frac{\sum\limits_{i=1}^{n} x_i}{n} = \frac{88}{17} = 5.2$$

$$c\overline{Y} = \frac{\sum\limits_{i=1}^{n} y_i}{n} = \frac{82}{17} = 4.8$$

and is therefore $c\overline{X}, c\overline{Y}$. If, however, the values (or weights) of each point, w_i, are taken into account, the weighted means are

$$c\overline{X}w = \frac{\sum\limits_{i=1}^{n} x_i w_i}{w_i} = \frac{469}{85} = 5.5$$

$$c\overline{Y}w = \frac{\sum\limits_{i=1}^{n} y_i w_i}{w_i} = \frac{385}{85} = 4.5$$

It is to be noted that the high values at the periphery of the distributions pull the weighted mean center significantly away from the mean center.

Table 2-8 DATA FOR THE CALCULATION OF THE MEAN CENTER OF THE DISTRIBUTION OF POINTS IN FIG. 2-6

x_i	y_i	Weight	$w_i x_i$	$w_i y_i$
5	8	1	5	8
3	7	4	12	28
6	7	2	12	14
8	7	4	32	28
4	6	8	32	48
5	6	3	15	18
2	5	6	12	30
5	5	7	35	35
6	5	6	36	30
7	5	9	63	45
4	4	5	20	20
6	4	4	24	16
2	3	1	2	3
6	3	3	18	9
8	3	9	72	27
4	2	4	16	8
7	2	9	63	18
88	82	85	469	385

The *standard distance* (Bachi, 1962), "standard-distance deviation" (Neft, 1966), "dynamical radius" (Stewart and Warntz, 1958), or "standard radius" (Lee, 1967), as it is variously called, describes the dispersion of points around a particular point, which is usually defined as the mean center. It is directly analogous to the standard deviation in the univariate case and can be calculated as

$$cs = \frac{\sum_{i=1}^{n} (x_i - c\overline{X})^2 + \sum_{i=1}^{n} (y_i - c\overline{Y})^2}{n} \qquad (2\text{-}9)$$

The *cs* for our example is estimated to be 2.53, which implies that 68 percent of the points should lie within a circumference defined by a radius of that value.

The standard-distance measure can be used for a variety of purposes, for example, to identify business types or industrial activities which are spreading out throughout the city as a result of decentralization. Standard-distance measures can be calculated for numerous business types and industrial activities, and the rate of increase in size of the measure can be compared between the different types. For example, Table 2-9 presents a series of standard-distance measures for eleven different commercial activities in Tel Aviv in 1964. From these data it appears that insurance and marketing companies are the most centralized, and barbers and cinemas are the most decentralized.

The use of the standard-distance geostatistic can be carried even further by calculating the *relative dispersion* of a particular economic activity. This is defined as the ratio of the standard distance of an economic activity to the standard distance of the urban area being analyzed. The measure is thus

Table 2-9   STANDARD-DISTANCE MEASURES FOR ELEVEN DIFFERENT COMMERCIAL ACTIVITIES, TEL AVIV, 1964

Commercial activity	Standard distance, meters
Insurance companies	740
Marketing companies	1,070
Engineers' and architects' offices	1,130
Headquarters of industries	1,150
Hotels	1,300
Banks (including branches)	1,830
Restaurants	1,970
Laundries	2,020
Pharmacies	2,090
Barbers	2,230
Cinemas	2,630

SOURCE: Shachar (1966, p. 203).

invariant with respect to population size, and can be used to compare the rates of dispersion of different economic activities over time and between urban areas of different sizes. For example, in Table 2-10 relative dispersion measures are presented for Jerusalem, Tel Aviv, and Rome, and the measures are remarkably consistent. The only great difference in relative dispersion is for finance and insurance companies in Tel Aviv and Rome, and here one would ask the process question, Why?

Nearest-Neighbor Analysis

Apart from estimating the geostatistics of a spatial distribution, human geographers are also interested in finding a method of analysis that discerns objectively between clustered and dispersed spatial distributions, and that also distinguishes between degree (or intensity) of clustering or dispersal. An approach to this has been derived in the study of plant ecology by Clark and Evans (1954) with the use of *nearest-neighbor analysis*. This method quantitatively defines a scale which measures the degree of departure of an observed spatial distribution from a theoretical random distribution. The maximum departure at one end of the scale is absolute clustering (all points falling at the same place), and at the other end of the scale is absolute dispersal (all points distributed in a hexagonal pattern, each point being equidistant from six other points). Thus there are three benchmarks: absolute clustering, absolute randomness, and absolute dispersal.

The nearest-neighbor scale (R scale) and the individual R values can be calculated as

$$R = \frac{\bar{r}_A}{\bar{r}_E} \tag{2-10}$$

Table 2-10   THE RELATIVE DISPERSION OF COMMERCIAL ACTIVITIES IN JERUSALEM, TEL AVIV, AND ROME, 1964

Commercial activity	Standard distance, meters			Relative dispersion		
	Tel Aviv	Jerusalem	Rome	Tel Aviv	Jerusalem	Rome
Population, thousands	2,870	1,800	4,180	1.00	1.00	1.00
Groceries	2,440	1,650	3,850	.85	.86	.92
Apparel	1,300	770	.....	.45	.43	
Barbers	2,230	1,470	.....	.78	.80	
Finance and insurance	780	.....	1,520	.27	....	.36
Doctors	1,560	910	.....	.54	.51	

SOURCE: Shachar (1966, p. 203).

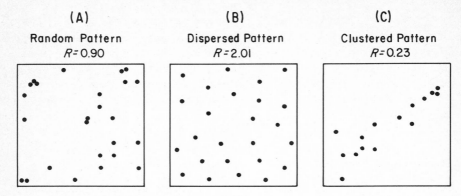

FIGURE 2-7
Three spatial point patterns: random, dispersed, clustered.

where

$$\bar{r}_A = \frac{\sum\limits_{i=1}^{n} r_i}{N}$$

which defines the mean of the series of straight-line distances of each point to its nearest neighbor, r being the distance from each point to its nearest neighbor (A meaning actual); and

$$\bar{r}_E = \frac{1}{2\sqrt{p}}$$

or the expected mean distance $\bar{r}_E$ to a nearest neighbor in an infinitely large random distribution of density p (E meaning expected); and

$$p = \frac{\text{number of points, } N}{\text{total area}}$$

The individual R scores can, therefore, take on any value between zero, signifying absolute clustering, to 2.1491, signifying maximum dispersion, with unity indicating the presence of a random observed distribution.

Three spatial patterns have been generated to illustrate randomness, dispersal, and clustering (Fig. 2-7). It must be noted that in each of these patterns the R value is influenced by the presence of a boundary and the size of the area, a problem that has been noted by Getis (1964). A visual examination of Fig. 2-7a suggests a number of "loose" clusters, but the nearest-neighbor analysis $R = .90$ indicates that randomness predominates overall. The second pattern (Fig. 2-7b) presents a distribution of points that lie very close to absolute dispersal, $R = 2.01$. In a few places, arrangements of points very similar to a hexagonal pattern are evident, but elsewhere the arrangement is quite dissimilar to such a pattern. It is noticeable, however, that all the points are quite distant from their nearest neighbors, and this is the situation that the term "dispersed" implies. The third synthetic pattern (Fig. 2-7c) presents one of many forms of clustering. This distribution can best be described as a "linear clustering," a situation that is quite common in settlement geography. The R value .23 indicates that the pattern is approaching a true cluster.

Interesting examples of the use of nearest-neighbor analysis in human geography are available in studies by Dacey (1960, 1962), King (1962), and Getis (1964). In Table 2-11 are listed nearest-neighbor indices for a number of different commercial activities in the central business districts of Jacksonville, Florida, and Kingston, Ontario, in 1965. These indices were calculated on the basis of central business districts defined by the Murphy-Vance (1954) method, ground-floor land uses classified according to the same code, and distances measured as straight lines between doorways along streets. It could be hypothesized that certain activities such as clothing stores and financial concerns should be clustered as a result of external economy forces, and this appears to be the case, especially in the Kingston central business district, for clothing stores. On the other hand, a number of land-use activities are widely dispersed, particularly offices. Of course, this picture would change if first, second, third, and so on, floors were analyzed separately.

Table 2-11   NEAREST-NEIGHBOR INDICES FOR VARIOUS COMMERCIAL ACTIVITIES IN CENTRAL BUSINESS DISTRICTS OF JACKSONVILLE, FLORIDA, AND KINGSTON, ONTARIO, 1965

Commercial activity	Jacksonville	Kingston
Household goods	1.47	.84
Offices	1.44	1.41
Automotive sales	1.43	.77
Personal and public services	1.14	1.15
Variety stores	.96	.78
Food stores	.90	.95
Miscellaneous	.88	1.01
Parking	.84	1.19
Finance, insurance, real estate	.82	.67
Clothing stores	.81	.34

SHAPE

Geographic data are always enclosed in an area which is defined by a boundary or zone of some kind, and as a consequence it has some shape. Where the boundary is clear, the area will have a definite shape; but where the boundary is difficult to define, the shape may be quite amorphous. In human geography the shapes are frequently well defined, for the data usually pertains to urban areas, census tracts, countries, counties, provinces, and so forth. Bunge (1962) suggests that shape is of intrinsic importance in geography because it is implicit in much of our theory, such as central-place theory, which is very much concerned with the shape of market areas. The limited volume of research involving analysis of shapes in human geography is related, perhaps, to the difficulty of providing concise, meaningful measurements, for it is often impossible just to measure shape alone. Two methods that have been developed by geographers for measuring shape will be discussed in this section, the simplest being that proposed by Boyce and Clark (1964), and the most complex, that by Bunge (1962).

The Boyce-Clark Method

The Boyce-Clark method for measuring shape is based on a formula that calculates an index which varies between 0 and 175 regardless of shape or size of area concerned. The index can be represented mathematically as

$$\text{SBC} = \sum_{i=1}^{n} \left| \frac{r_i}{\sum_{i=1}^{n} r_i} 100 - \frac{100}{n} \right| \tag{2-11}$$

where SBC = the Boyce-Clark shape index
r_i = the length of the ith radial
n = number of radials
$| \ |$ = mathematical expression meaning the "absolute value of," that is, ignore the signs

The major problem is to determine the point within the shape from which the radials are to be drawn. Boyce and Clark suggest using the center of gravity of the area, but the point can be any *meaningful* center (in a theoretical context) derived by any acceptable method. In the example of a hypothetical urban area in Fig. 2-8a, the center is the mean center of all commercial activities within the city, which is the center of the central business district. The perimeter of the area is defined as the population density isoline of 2,000 persons per square mile (a reasonable lower limit of dense urbanization in North America).

Figure 2-8b and Table 2-12 indicate how the Boyce-Clark index is calculated for this hypothetical urban area. The steps are as follows:

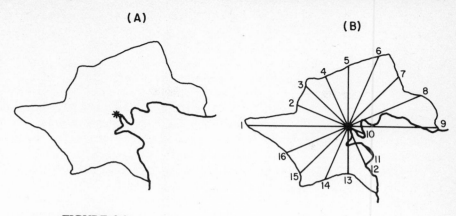

FIGURE 2-8
Hypothetical urban area used for calculation of the Boyce-Clark measure of shape.

1   Determine the center of the shape.

2   Construct a series of *equally spaced* radials to the perimeter from this center. The number of radials used depends upon the complexity of the shape to be measured. The more radials used, the more satisfactory the measure. In our example, sixteen radials are probably quite satisfactory.

3   Measure the length of each radial in any unit of measurement (row 2 of the table).

4   Calculate the percentage of each radial to the total length of all radials used. For example, for r_4 this is $\frac{0.7}{12.1}(100) = 5.78$ percent.

5   Determine the expected percentage for each radial of the total length of all radials used. This is simply $\frac{100}{16} = 6.25$ percent, and it represents the average contribution of each radial to the total length of all radials if the shape were a circle.

6   Calculate the difference between the actual proportion and the expected proportion for each radial. For r_3 this is $6.62 - 6.25 = 0.37$, and for r_4 it is $5.78 - 6.25 = -.47$.

7   Sum the figures in row 4, ignoring the signs; the total is 29.7, and this is the SBC.

The question that arises at this juncture is how to interpret the shape index. If the measurement SBC is zero, the shape being measured is a circle. In a series of experiments, Boyce and Clark found that the index for a square is approximately 12; a cruciform shape has an index of around 18; a star shape, one of around 25; and a rectangle which is twice as long as it is wide, one of about 28. As the length of the rectangle increases proportionate to its width, the index

Table 2-12   WORK TABLE FOR THE CALCULATION OF THE BOYCE-CLARK MEASUREMENT OF SHAPE

		1	2	3	4	5	6	7	8	9	10	11	12	13	14	15	16	Total
1	Radial number																	
2	Radial length r_i	1.3	0.7	0.8	0.7	0.8	1.0	0.9	1.0	1.1	0.2	0.1	0.5	0.6	0.8	0.8	0.8	12.1
3	$\dfrac{r_i}{\sum\limits_{i=1}^{n} r_i}100$	10.75	5.78	6.62	5.78	6.62	8.26	7.43	8.26	9.09	1.65	0.82	4.13	4.95	6.62	6.62	6.62	100.0
4	$\left\|\dfrac{r_i}{\sum\limits_{i=1}^{n} r_i}100 - \dfrac{100}{n}\right\|$	4.50	0.47	0.37	0.47	0.37	2.48	1.18	2.48	2.84	4.60	5.43	2.12	1.30	0.37	0.37	0.37	29.7

gets larger and larger, and an upper limit of 175 is reached for measurements from the center of a straight line. In the example in Fig. 2-8*b* the SBC index is 29.7, which suggests a general rectangular shape.

The Bunge Method

The Bunge method is much more complex than that explained above; but it does measure certain extreme shapes with greater accuracy, and it does not require the prior determination of a center. The method is based upon two theorems (Bunge, 1966, pp. 73–76):

1 Any simply connected shape can be matched by a polygon of any number of sides in which the lengths of each side are equal, but the lengths can, of course, vary from shape to shape.

2 If the distances between all vertices of the polygon lag 1 are summed and then squared and summed, lag 2 are summed and then squared and summed, and so on, there will exist a unique set of sums that define the shape of that polygon.

Thus the first step is to define, for any given shape, an abstract polygon which adequately represents the shape to be defined. In our example (Fig. 2-9), it is assumed that a seven-sided polygon (each side being of equal length) adequately describes the hypothetical urban area discussed previously. The urban area is shown in Fig. 2-9*a*, and the polygon superimposed on that area, in Fig. 2-9*b*.

The unique set of sums which describe that polygon can then be calculated with respect to the vertices. In Fig. 2-9*c* the distances between all the vertices, lag 1, are indicated diagrammatically. The measurements are presented in Table 2-13, in which the measurements are in inches for each connection. Thus the distance between vertices 2 and 4 is 1.30, and the square of that is 1.69. The lag 1 distances summed are therefore 10.30, and the sum of the squared distances is 16.14. The lag 2 distances are indicated diagrammatically in Fig. 2-9*d*, and the distances and the squares, in Table 2-13. The sums and sums of squares of the lag 2 measures are 12.25 and 23.07. The lag 3 sums and sums of squares will produce the same totals as in lag 2, and the lag 4 situation would repeat the lag 1 measurements. Thus four unique sums describe the seven-sided polygon in Fig. 2-9*b*.

The problems with using this method are many. As with the radials in the Boyce-Clark method, it is difficult to determine the number of sides in a polygon which will adequately define an area. Complex shapes require many-sided polygons, and these in turn yield larger sets of unique sums. For example, an eight-sided polygon (used by Bunge, 1966) yields six sums, but when sixteen vertices are used, fourteen shape sums are produced. This proliferation of

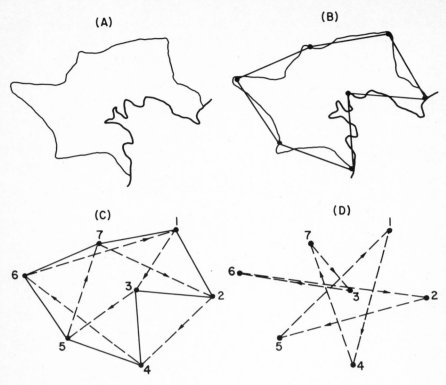

FIGURE 2-9
The calculation of shape by the Bunge method.

Table 2-13   WORK TABLE FOR CALCULATION OF THE BUNGE MEASUREMENTS
OF SHAPE

Lag 1 measurements			Lag 2 measurements		
Connections	Distance of edge	Distance squared	Connections	Distance of edge	Distance squared
1, 3	.95	.90	1, 4	1.90	3.61
2, 4	1.30	1.69	2, 5	1.95	3.80
3, 5	1.10	1.21	3, 6	1.40	1.96
4, 6	1.95	3.80	4, 7	1.75	3.06
5, 7	1.35	1.82	5, 1	2.00	4.00
6, 1	2.00	4.00	6, 2	2.45	6.00
7, 2	1.65	2.72	7, 3	.80	.64
Shape sums	10.30	16.14		12.25	23.07

number of unique sums for many-sided polygons means that it is difficult to interpret the sums in terms of shapes, though Bunge has attempted to do this for eight-sided polygons applied to ninety-seven Mexican communes. Thus there remains a considerable amount of experimentation to be undertaken in this branch of quantitative geography in both a theoretical and an applied sense. Obviously, the fact that just one number is produced for each shape by the Boyce-Clark method gives it a distinct advantage in application over the Bunge method even though the former is less precise than the latter.

3

SAMPLING

If the human geographer is to test the hypotheses derived from his theoretical deductions, or to analyze real-world observations in order to postulate some empirically based hypotheses, data are required. The data can be obtained either from government sources (such as census material, health data, assessment information, and so forth), from some supragovernmental organization (the UN, the World Bank), or from private organizations, or it will have to be collected by the researcher himself. If the researcher has to collect the data himself, it is rare that it will be possible to obtain complete coverage, that is, measurements for all the characteristics pertaining to all the population being measured. Furthermore, it is very unlikely that information collected by governmental or other organizations completely enumerates the entire population being considered. The information is therefore a *sample* of the population being analyzed, and a sample is used because to obtain complete coverage would either be too costly or consume too much time. Fortunately, statisticians have developed considerable sophistication in their ability to make statements concerning the mathematical distribution of the population as a whole from samples (Yates, 1949; Cochran, 1953; Cochran, Mosteller, and Tukey, 1954); and the interest by geographers in using these techniques (Garrison, 1959*a* and *b*)

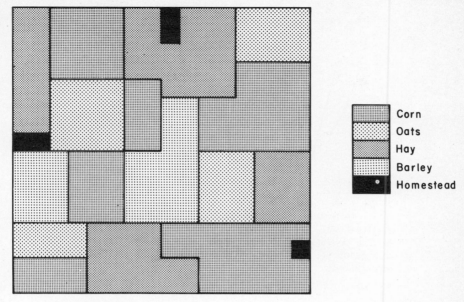

FIGURE 3-1
Crop production in a section of the Midwest (hypothetical).

and determining which is preferable for given spatial situations is attested by the work of Wood (1955), Steiner (1957), Blaut (1959), Berry (1962), Latham (1963), Birch (1964), and Haggett and Board (1964). Furthermore, there has been some consideration (Berry and Baker, 1968) given to the special problems of serial correlation that occur when sampling spatially distributed data (Matérn, 1960).

SOME BASIC CONSIDERATIONS IN SAMPLING

When choosing a sample, the geographer is faced with many basic considerations about which he has some intuitive and, at times, a priori information. These considerations can be referred to as "economic" and "statistical," and both are important. The economic considerations refer to the size of the sample being chosen, and the statistical considerations refer to some problems that are of primary interest to persons interested in areal analysis—aggregation and spatial bias.

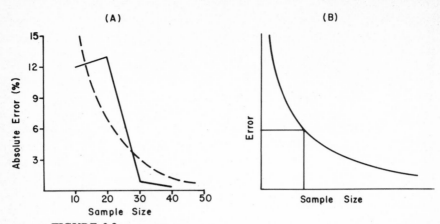

FIGURE 3-2

(*a*) The absolute error incurred when four samples of ten, twenty, thirty, and forty points are taken from Fig. 3-1; (*b*) the relation between sample size and expected error.

The Size of the Sample

A sample is taken from a population so that estimates of the parameters of the population can be calculated. Obviously the researcher wishes to replicate, as closely as possible, the real values of these parameters for the population as a whole, but equally obviously it will be unlikely for him to replicate these values exactly with a sample of the population if that population has a variance greater than zero. Thus the researcher recognizes that any sample will provide estimates of the population parameters subject to some error.

For example, Fig. 3-1 presents a hypothetical agricultural area which contains five different kinds of land use in the form of fields devoted to different crops and the homestead area (farmhouse, barns, vegetable garden, etc.). Estimates of areas devoted to different land uses, whether these land uses are urban or rural, are common problems in human geography (Haggett, 1963). In this example area, 37.9 percent of the land area is in corn, 18.8 percent in oats, 28.1 percent in hay, and 13.3 percent in barley; 1.9 percent is devoted to the various farmsteads. Figure 3-2*a* indicates the absolute error incurred when one sample of each of ten, twenty, thirty, and forty points were dropped randomly on the map in order to determine the proportion of the area devoted to corn. In the first sample, 50 percent of the ten points fell on areas devoted to corn, and thus the absolute error was $50.0 - 37.9 = 12.1$ percent; and in the second sample, 25 percent of the twenty points fell on cornfields, which yielded an absolute error of 12.9 percent. In the third sample of thirty points, the absolute error was 1.3 percent, and in the fourth sample it was less than 1 percent. If this experiment were to be repeated many times for each size of sample and the absolute errors averaged (disregarding signs), the errors would decrease with size of sample in a fashion similar to that indicated by the dashed line in Fig. 3-2a.

The more general shape of this relation is indicated in Fig. 3-2b. Error decreases with sample size but at a decreasing rate, so that doubling the size of the sample does not imply that the error will be halved. Perhaps a good point to use as the determinant of the sample size is at the inflexion of the curve in Fig. 3-2b, for above this point a unit increase in sample size yields a decrease in unit error of unity or greater, but below this point the decrease in unit error is less than unity for an increase in sample size. The problem, however, is that the error-to-size relation varies for the sample design being used, though Haggett (1965, p. 192) suggests that for random samples the "error is proportional to the square root of the number of observations."

The economic implications of the sample size become apparent when cost is taken into account. The larger the sample the greater its cost, but the relation is not direct. Rather, the cost of the sample increases with the size of the sample but at a decreasing rate (Fig. 3-3a); thus the average cost of each sample unit decreases as the size of the sample increases (Fig. 3-3b). This is because the marginal cost of processing each additional observation unit decreases with each increment to the sample size as a result of economies of scale. It is apparent that as these processing costs include not just the cost of collecting data but also the cost of sorting and manipulating the data, which are very much subject to economies of scale through the use of computers, the costs of larger samples are decreasing.

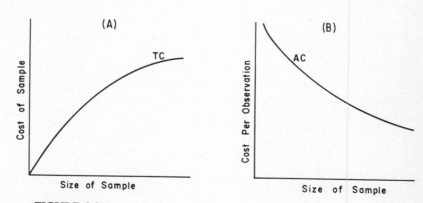

FIGURE 3-3
The relation between size of sample and (a) total cost and (b) average cost per unit of observation.

(A)

I	8	3	4	6	5
2	7	5	3	4	8
5	9	4	8	3	2
6	5	7	I	0	9
8	3	4	6	2	6
6	I	2	8	7	4

(B)

I 8	3 4	6 5
4.5	3.75	5.75
2 7	5 3	4 8
5 9	4 8	3 2
6.25	5.0	3.5
6 5	7 I	0 9
8 3	4 6	2 6
4.5	5.0	4.75
6 I	2 8	7 4

FIGURE 3-4
Problems of aggregation. The numbers in (*a*) indicate the location of a house and in (*b*) the number of people residing within it.

Geostatistical Considerations

The very nature of geographical data—its spatial dispersion—makes the use of statistical techniques in geography extraordinarily difficult. This is particularly true if the data are aggregated or if there are hidden periodicities.

Problems of aggregation It is not at all unusual for the human geographer to be faced with an abundance of information that has been aggregated to some level. By aggregation is meant that the data have been grouped in areas (cells, tracts, etc.) comprising one or more original observations. This type of grouping is found particularly in census data in which the original observations (people, houses, business firms) have been grouped into tracts of some kind in order to protect the identity of the respondents (the "disclosure" rule). For example, data for Canadian cities concerning the socioeconomic characteristics of people and housing are usually published at the census tract level, and these census tracts may contain 4,000 to 10,000 people and 1,000 to 3,000 houses. The summaries therefore pertain to the entire census tract, and are usually in the form of medians, means, or percentages.

These aggregates may conceal more information than they reveal. For example, in Fig. 3-4*a* we have detailed the location of a house and the number of people in each house. It is to be noted that the variation is quite large—in fact the variance is 6.01. Figure 3-4*b* indicates a possible grouping of the data into square cells, each cell containing an equal number of houses, and the number in the center being the average number of people living in each house in each cell. It is to be noted that the averages are quite similar, varying between a low of 3.75 and a high of 6.25, with the variance of these averages being .71. Thus the aggregation of the data has, in this case, concealed quite a large amount of information. On the other hand, if it were possible to group the data into spatially contiguous units in such a way as to minimize the variance within each tract, and to maximize the variance between tracts, then the spatial variation in the data would be preserved.

Thus, if the researcher is to sample housing within each of these tracts in order to study the spatial variation in certain residential characteristics, it would be necessary to replicate not only the average number of persons per house, but also the variation in residential density. In order to do this, not only the average would be required but also some measure of dispersion such as the variance. Then the representativeness of a particular sample could be determined with respect to two parameters rather than one, and in the case of aggregated data these two parameters are vital.

Random sampling   A second point of a geostatistical nature that should be discussed at this juncture concerns bias in sampling. A sample should be as bias-free as possible, and the only way to achieve this is to choose each element in the sample in a random fashion. In other words, each element should have an equal chance of being chosen—no particular element should have a greater chance of being selected than any other. If a sample were not chosen at random, it would be possible for the researcher, purposely or inadvertently, to bias the sample in a particular direction, that is, introduce some systematic error. As we shall observe in the ensuing section, this emphasis on random sampling may well be difficult to accept in geographic situations, but the difficulty can be circumvented by stratifying.

Spatial autocorrelation   A bias-free sample is thus made up of elements that should be independent of each other. That is, there should be no systematic relation between the value of one observation and the value of another. This is one of the characteristics of a sample that random selection attempts to ensure. However, the data that geographers deal with are distributed spatially, and though items may be chosen randomly in space, this does not ensure that the relative location of one observation to another does not affect the items being measured. In effect, there is usually some spatial periodicity or regularity in the data, and thus most geographic data are spatially autocorrelated (Curry, 1966) or serially correlated. A sample may therefore be chosen that quite inadvertently emphasizes, for example, certain peaks in the data, and ignores the troughs. Alternatively, if the parent population exhibits a gradation from one direction

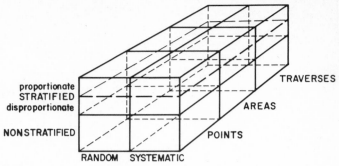

FIGURE 3-5
A three-dimensional classification of sampling strategies.

to another, the sample may be concentrated in one part and almost absent in another. This type of problem can be minimized by stratification, but once again, this type of procedure requires some a priori information concerning the spatial nature of the data, probably through a cursory pilot traverse of some type. Two-stage sampling of this kind can, in fact, be suggested as a necessary precursor to most sample procedures if adequate results are to be ensured.

SAMPLE UNITS AND DESIGN

There are many different types of sample units, measurement, and designs that can be used by the geographer. A sample can consist of points, areas, and traverses; these may be randomly or systematically located; and they may or may not be stratified. The interrelation of the different types and designs is indicated in Fig. 3-5, which suggests that twelve main sampling strategies can be derived from these different combinations. For each of the twelve a different type of measurement can be used, depending on the characteristics to be measured. The ensuing discussion will concentrate on these twelve different strategies, and will also describe the design of a "hybrid" type.

Points

As is evident from Fig. 3-5, point samples can be dropped randomly or systematically. The form of measurement associated with a point sample may be nominal (a characteristic is either present at that point, or it is not), or it may be some measurement pertaining to that location (a land value, or a population density). At the outset it is important to raise, once again, the distinction between continuous and discrete spatial distributions, for the procedure by which

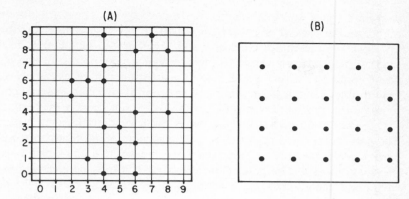

FIGURE 3-6
Point sampling: (*a*) random sample, (*b*) systematic sample.

the sample is selected varies accordingly. For a continuous spatial distribution, points can be located randomly by scaling two orthogonal edges (edges at right angles) of the area to be sampled 0 to 9 or 99; and by treating the edges as coordinates and using pairs of random numbers, points can be located in the "two-space." For example, in Fig. 3-6*a* twenty points have been located with respect to axes calibrated in ten equal intervals by using the following pairs x, y of one-digit random numbers: 6, 8; 4, 3; 4, 9; 4, 6; 8, 8; 8, 4; 4, 7; 3, 1; 3, 6; 6, 2; 5, 1; 2, 6; 4, 0; 1, 8; 5, 2; 6, 4; 6, 0; 7, 9; 2, 5; 5, 3. On the other hand, if the data are discrete, a random sample need not be generated by using coordinates, for each item can be assigned a number and the numbers can be drawn randomly. For example, if a sample of residential units in a given urban area is to be analyzed, a city directory or a utility company listing can be used as a source containing the complete population, and a random sample can be compiled from this listing without immediate recourse to a map.

There are several observations on the random location of points that are pertinent at this stage in the discussion. First, a random pattern usually exhibits elements of clustering; if it did not, it would be dispersed, as was noted in our discussion of nearest-neighbor analysis. Thus, if there is some periodicity or gradation in the data, there is a chance that these clusters may overemphasize one aspect of the spatial distribution. Secondly, although the phrase "random sample" implies that every point has an equal chance of being chosen, this is patently not the case in Fig. 3-6*a*, nor is it in any sample of continuous data unless the "point" is exactly the same size as the mesh on the grid generated by the coordinates. Thus random samples constructed with data distributed continuously over space are only random in so far as each intersection of the coordinates has an equal chance of being chosen. The third observation is mundane but nevertheless very important to the researcher: Random points are difficult to locate in the real world, for they can be situated in awkward, inaccessible locations. Thus a sample design having points located at random when applied to a real-world sampling situation can be extremely expensive. On the other hand, if the points are to be dropped on a map or aerial photograph in a laboratory situation, this observation does not necessarily apply.

Figure 3-6b presents a sample of twenty points located systematically. The pattern can be chosen to suit any particular whim, fancy, or convenience. For example, the area to be sampled may be within a city which is comprised of square blocks. The point pattern might, therefore, be arranged in squares, each point being found in the center or at the edge of a block. The major disadvantage of this method is that each item does not have an equal chance of being chosen, which increases the possibilities of bias, and this is just as true for the discrete distribution as the continuous one. However, the geographer can be assured of complete spatial coverage, for the pattern does not depend upon the vagaries of the random numbers used, and he can place his points in accessible locations and thus reduce costs or increase the sample size for a given outlay. This advantage should not, however, obscure the fact that systematic sampling can lead to severe biases.

Traverses

Traverses are particularly useful for data that are distributed continuously over an area. Commonly, a traverse is a line along which the proportion of the given characteristic(s), or the incidence of the given characteristic(s), is enumerated by field observation. For example, if the data to be estimated concern the amount of a given land use in an area, the length of the line which passes through that particular land use will be calculated, and this amount will be expressed as a proportion of the total length of the line. Thus each traverse is, in effect, one observation for which a measure or a series of measures can be calculated.

Random traverses can be constructed in a number of ways by a number of different methods, but for the sake of brevity the discussion in this section will be limited to two, random lines and random "walks." One method of constructing random lines is to calibrate the perimeter of the area to be sampled into equal lengths, assign a number to each interval, and then use random number tables to obtain pairs of numbers between which a line can be drawn. This procedure has been followed in Fig. 3-7a, in which the perimeter of the square area has been calibrated into 100 equal lengths numbered from 0 to 99 consecutively around the edge. Then, ten pairs of two-digit random numbers have been read from a random-number table (35, 55; 69, 88; 53, 99; 37, 14; 05, 96; 50, 27; 57, 42; 60, 12; 55, 33; 58, 26), and a line has been drawn between

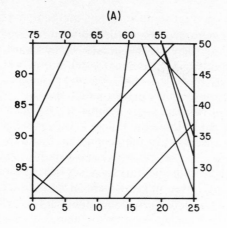

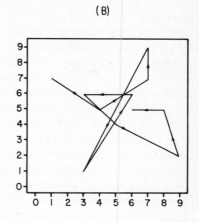

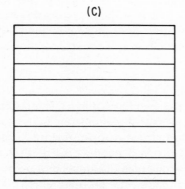

FIGURE 3-7
Sampling with traverses: (*a*) random traverses, (*b*) a random walk, (*c*) systematic parallel traverses.

each pair. It is to be noted that these random traverses exhibit clustering similar to that which occurs with random points, the result of which is that one part of the map is sampled more intensively than another.

An alternative method to the one described above is to sample along the segments of a random walk. This type of sample can be constructed by defining a set of coordinates for the area to be sampled, then progressing from the point defined by one set of coordinates to the point for the next set, and so building a series of randomly located lines. As an example, in Fig. 3-7*b* a random walk of ten segments has been constructed by defining lines between the following eleven pairs of random numbers: 1, 7 → 4, 5 → 7, 7 → 7, 9 → 3, 1 → 6,

$6 \to 3, 6 \to 5, 4 \to 9, 2 \to 8, 5 \to 6, 5$. A disadvantage of this method compared with the random traverse method described previously is that it is more likely to lead to bias because the position of each segment is determined in part by the position of that immediately preceding. On the other hand, a practical advantage is that a random walk is likely to be less costly because it is more continuous—the researcher is not continuously hunting for random lines.

There are as many different ways of constructing a sample of systematic traverses as there are systematic points, and of these the utility of two, parallel and rotated parallel traverses, has been discussed in the geographic literature (Haggett and Board, 1964; Latham, 1964). Parallel traverses consist simply of a number of lines parallel to each other, and rotated parallel traverses include the superimposition of lines at a particular angle over an initial parallel set in order to increase the density of coverage. From Fig. 3-7c it is apparent that ten parallel traverses provide much greater spatial coverage than ten random lines, but they also increase the possibility of bias. For example, the researcher may choose a traverse along parallel township-line roads (in the Midwest) or concession roads (in Southern Ontario), which provide ease of access but may greatly distort the sample owing to the radically different distributional patterns found along rural roads compared with those in less accessible areas.

Quadrats

Quadrats are areas, ideally of the same size, that can be used in a fashion similar to traverses. The characteristic that is to be measured is enumerated completely for the defined area, and the data are used in closed or open form depending upon whether the quadrats vary in size. Thus each quadrat is, in effect one observation, but the basic difference between this type of sample and points or traverses is that the area of the quadrat is a fundamental property which affects the number of observations used. If the area of the quadrat is quite large relative to the entire area comprising the population being sampled, then the number of quadrats needed is very few. On the other hand, if the size of the quadrat is small relative to the area of the population being sampled, then the number of quadrats that would be needed is greater. For example, in Fig. 3-8a and b each quadrat is $\frac{1}{100}$ of the total area, and thus a sample of twenty quadrats provides a 20 percent coverage of the area. A second consideration about the area of the quadrat is that it is, in fact, a particular level of aggregation. The data measured within the quadrat pertain to it as an observation, and this is conventionally treated in nonspatial terms. Thus the spatial variation within the quadrat may well be ignored when the data are aggregated to pertain to the quadrat as a whole, and this can become an important source of bias if the size of the quadrat is large.

Random and systematic samples can be designed in a manner similar to those for points and traverses. If random quadrats are to be used and the size

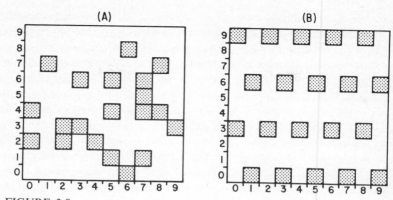

FIGURE 3-8
Sampling with quadrats: (*a*) random quadrats, (*b*) systematic quadrats.

of the quadrat has been determined, the area is gridded into a convenient system, and axes are established and calibrated to provide coordinates. Random numbers can then be used to generate a random distribution of quadrats (Fig. 3-8*a*). Alternatively, a systematic distribution of quadrats will simply follow some design acceptable to the researcher that provides reasonable coverage of the entire area (Fig. 3-8*b*). The advantages and disadvantages of each design in bias and spatial coverage are similar to those discussed for points and traverses.

Quadrat sampling, in one form or another, has been fundamental to the development of human geography. In a sense, any study which includes the analysis of a region (however defined) or a comparison between regions is really a form of quadrat sampling. On the basis of detailed analysis and intellectual insight, regional geographers have attempted to synthesize the characteristics that different areas have in common or that they hold uniquely. The characteristics that they have in common can lead to generalizations and theories concerning spatial patterns, and those that are held uniquely can lead to further analyses (for example, of the cross-cultural type) that are designed to illuminate the processes of areal differentiation. Quadrat sampling is therefore vital in regional analysis.

Stratified Samples

Stratified samples have been alluded to previously as possible solutions for a number of problems that may occur in geographic sampling. One of the most frequent types of problem occurs when an area consists of two or more environments that affect the properties of the characteristic being measured. For example, in a rural area a rich productive farming zone may lie adjacent to a barren unproductive area. Thus population densities, farm output, settlement patterns, cultural characteristics, and so forth, are likely to be affected by these different conditions. The researcher may therefore conclude from some kind of a priori information obtained from a rapid field traverse that he must be sure to obtain an adequate sample in both areas. This can be assured by *stratifying* the sample, that is, by dividing the area, in this case, into two and sampling in each. If the sample is to be proportionate, then the number of points, traverses, or quadrats used in each area will depend upon the proportion of the area in each of the different environments; if one-third of the area is barren, the one-third of the sample will be located in that area and two-thirds in the productive area.

In some situations there may be some compelling reason to go beyond the simple proportionate stratified sample to one that is disproportionate, that is, where one area is sampled more intensively than another. The type of situation in which such a strategy is most compelling is when the spatial variation in the data in one environment is apparently greatly different to that in the other. For example, land values are usually higher in the central business district than elsewhere in a city. But the spatial variation in land values within the central business district is also much greater than anywhere else in a city. Land values are not only much higher for corner lots than midblock lots, they may also be two to three times as great along a fashionable street as on a nonfashionable street bounding a parallel adjacent block. Furthermore, there is a very steep dropoff in land values at the edge of the central business district. Thus, it would be very important to sample more intensively in this zone of greater spatial variation than in the rest of the city where the spatial variation is not as great. How much more intensively is a matter of equal importance; a suggestion might be that the difference in intensity should depend upon the difference in degree of spatial variation between the two areas. Some knowledge of this difference could be obtained by a two-stage sampling process in which traverses radiating from the peak-value intersection provide a rough estimate of the contrast.

Systematic Stratified, Unaligned Sample

One sampling method promoted by Berry (1962) that appears to preserve elements of the randomness prerequisite for unbiased samples and yet also preserves the desire for spatial coverage required by geographers is the *systematic stratified, unaligned sample*. Stratification to assure complete coverage is achieved by gridding the area into a series of equal-size square cells. Within this frame, random points are determined through a novel method designed to minimize the tedium of the repetitive looking-up of random numbers. For the first stratum of cells an x coordinate is chosen randomly, x_1, and this is used for all the cells in the tier. Each y coordinate is then chosen randomly, $y_1, y_2, y_3,$

y_4, y_5, for each cell in the first tier. Thus the locations of the points in the first tier are

$$x_1 y_1 \qquad x_1 y_2 \qquad x_1 y_3 \qquad x_1 y_4 \qquad x_1 y_5$$

In the second tier a new random number for the x coordinates is obtained, but the random numbers used for the y coordinates in the first tier are also used for the y coordinates in the second. Thus the locations of points in the second tier are

$$x_2 y_1 \qquad x_2 y_2 \qquad x_2 y_3 \qquad x_2 y_4 \qquad x_2 y_5$$

Similarly the locations of points in the third tier are

$$x_3 y_1 \qquad x_3 y_2 \qquad x_3 y_3 \qquad x_3 y_4 \qquad x_3 y_5$$

An example of this type of sample design is indicated in Fig. 3-9.

The efficacy of this design has been tested in a number of situations (Berry, 1962; Berry and Baker, 1968) and has been used successfully by Burton (1960). The results of these tests indicate that it gives more accurate estimates of land-use coverage than is achieved from a random or systematic sampling of points. The method is therefore probably useful in that particular type of research situation. However, it must be noted that the points are not really randomly distributed; that aspect of the sample is really an illusion.

TESTING THE ADEQUACY OF SAMPLES

This brief discussion of some of the different types and designs of samples leads one to the question, How do we know that a particular sample is an adequate representation of the population? A purist may answer, You will never know, because whatever is done, there is bound to be some assumption that has been disregarded. That may be true, but if that argument were to be accepted, "human geographers" (and, for that matter, social scientists in general) would be very limited in the kind of empirical enquiry they could undertake. Probably the best answer to the question is to indicate that there are statistical tests that can be used to indicate the adequacy of a sample, and if these tests are used with the minimum number of assumptions being violated and they are interpreted in the educated light of current theoretical and empirical knowlege concerning the problem being investigated, then some statement can be made on the adequacy of the sample.

Hypothesis Testing

Before describing some of the statistical tests that could be used, it is necessary to comment briefly on the nature of hypothesis testing. Although it has been indicated previously that the empirical evaluation of hypotheses provides the

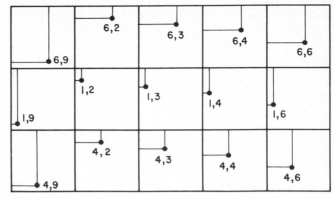

FIGURE 3-9
A systematic stratified, unaligned sample.

building blocks of theory, it is very difficult in geography to have a theory that can be completely proved, because it is difficult to envisage a situation where a theory can be verified under all possible conditions. As a consequence, one does not try to prove that a hypothesis is true; one tries, instead, to reject the general statement that the hypothesis is not true. This general statement is referred to as the *null hypothesis*, and it states that there is no relation or no difference between two or more variables. The *research hypothesis*, on the other hand, states the exact aim of the research, which may well be that there is no relation or no difference between, for example, *A* and *B*; or that *A* is related to *B*; or perhaps, more precisely, that *A* is positively related to *B*, or that *A* is negatively related to *B*.

In the case of sampling, for example, we may wish to test whether a large sample of a given size with a mean $\overline{X}$ is an adequate representation of the population with mean μ from which the sample has been taken. One way of testing this is to examine whether there is any significant difference between the means. Thus, in this case, the null hypothesis H_0 would be the same as the research hypothesis H_1. Stated symbolically these are

$$H_0: \quad \overline{X} = \mu \quad \text{or} \quad \overline{X} - \mu = 0$$

$$H_1: \quad \overline{X} = \mu \quad \text{or} \quad \overline{X} - \mu = 0$$

As the sample is but one of many samples that could be drawn from the population, some difference between $\overline{X}$ and μ would be acceptable. In fact, one of the basic theories in sampling, the *central-limit theorem*, implies that if the population is normally distributed, and if many samples are drawn randomly from that population, the means of these samples (and thus the errors) will also be normally distributed, and the mean and variance of these means will equal the mean and variance of the population. That is, there will be many samples having a small error (difference between the population mean and sample mean), and a very few having quite a large error. The questions that arise, therefore, are whether a difference between a sample mean and the population mean could have occurred by chance alone because the sample is drawn at random, or whether the difference is so great that one would not normally expect such an error to occur even in a random sample. The examination of these questions is feasible if it is possible to assume that the means are distributed normally, for then the mean of the distribution of means should be the population mean (which can be set at zero), and the standard deviation of the distribution of means is the standard error of estimate of the mean. With these two parameters it is possible to calculate the standard score for the difference between a sample mean and the population mean, and this statistic can then be used to state the probability of such a difference occurring.

For example, in Fig. 3-1 corn comprises 37.9 percent of the total area, and a large sample of 100 points dropped randomly over the area produces an estimate that 39.0 percent of the arca is devoted to corn. What is the probability of such a difference in estimated proportions occurring? If it is assumed that this estimated proportion, which is analogous to a mean, forms part of a normal distribution of estimated proportions, then the standard score of that estimate, which is the standard error of estimate of the proportion, can be calculated in a manner similar to that of Eq. (2-2). In this case, the standard deviation of the distribution of all possible large sample estimates of the proportion is the standard deviation of the binomial distribution (Walker and Lev, 1953, p. 30). The standard deviation of the binomial distribution is $\sqrt{PQ/N}$, where P is the proportion of the population that contains that characteristic, and $Q = 1 - P$. Thus

$$Z = \frac{p - P}{\sqrt{PQ/N}} \qquad (3\text{-}1)$$

As N, the total number of observations in the population, is unknown in our example, the standard error of estimate of the proportion will be estimated from $\sqrt{pq/n}$. Thus,

$$Z = \frac{.390 - .379}{\sqrt{\frac{.2354}{100}}} = .7189$$

The table of areas under the normal curve (Table 2-5) indicates that 26 percent of all samples of 100 random points would be expected, in this case, to give estimates of the population proportion within 0 to 1.5 percent of the true population proportion.

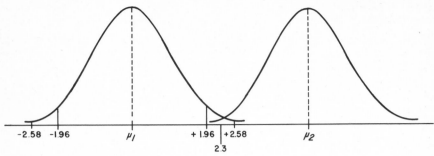

FIGURE 3-10
The distribution of two populations.

Choosing the Confidence Level

With this information it is now possible to determine the amount of error that is to be regarded as significant. In a previous discussion of errors the observation has been made that the researcher has to be willing to make errors. That discussion was couched in terms of Type I and Type II errors, that is, the possibility of rejecting a hypothesis that is in fact true, or accepting a hypothesis that in reality is false. Imagine two populations with the same variance but different proportions of a given characteristic, P_1 and P_2 (Fig. 3-10). From one of these a large sample has been drawn containing proportion p of that characteristic. The researcher is sure that this sample has been drawn from the population with proportion P_1, and as a consequence, he wishes to be very confident of the statement to be made. Thus he wishes to indicate that he is 99 percent sure that the difference between P_1 and p could have occurred by chance alone through the vagaries of random sampling. The standard score for this percentile of confidence level is either $+2.576$ or -2.576, for it is these values which enclose 99 percent of the area under the normal curve, and thus leave .5 percent in each tail. By using Eq. (3-1), the standard score for the difference between p and P_1 is calculated to be 2.3, and the researcher therefore accepts the null hypothesis that there is no difference between the two proportions and that the sample is drawn from the population with proportion P_1.

The researcher's overconfidence has, however, led him to make a Type II error, for the sample has, in fact, been drawn from the population with proportion P_2. If the researcher had been a little less confident, and chosen to indicate that he was 95 percent sure that such a difference could have occurred by chance alone, the standard score for the percentile of confidence level would have been ±1.96, and as 2.3 is greater than 1.96, the null hypothesis would have been rejected. On the other hand, if the sample *had* come from the population with proportion P_1, and a 95 percent confidence level was used, the null hypothesis would have been rejected, and a Type I error would have been made. The confidence level is therefore critical, and the level must be chosen with some clear a priori information. If the theory and previous empirical work is robust, then the researcher may have clear grounds for making a very confident statement. If the theory is weak and the previous empirical work insufficient, or a large number of assumptions are ignored, then the researcher will have to temper his natural confidence. In the previous example in which the z score is estimated to be .718, the null hypothesis would have been accepted at either confidence level.

Tests of Differences between Proportions

Equation (3-1) presents a very useful test that can be applied to a number of situations. There is obviously no real reason to estimate a proportion if the parent proportion is already known. On the other hand, it may be useful to check a broadly based questionnaire interview sheet for bias and adequacy of sample size by obtaining data for one or two variables for which the parameters are known. These can then be used to test the adequacy of the sample. For example, a sample survey of housing and housing characteristics in various parts of an urban area may contain questions that permit the researcher to estimate the proportion of families with two children living in three rooms or less. This information can then be compared with the proportions published in the national census, and some valuable knowledge concerning the adequacy of the sample can be gleaned.

Alternatively, the researcher may wish to compare samples of the same or different sizes to see whether they give estimates of parameters that are not significantly different from each other. In this case the hypothesis would be that the two proportions p_1 and p_2, the former obtained from a sample size of 40, and the other from one of 100, come from two populations that have the same mean. That is

$$H_0: \quad p_1 = P_1 \quad p_2 = P_2 \quad P_1 = P_2$$
$$H_1: \quad p_1 - p_2 = 0$$

They can be tested by using p_1 and p_2 jointly to estimate the standard deviation of P_1 and P_2. Thus

$$p = \frac{N_1 p_1 + N_2 p_2}{N} \tag{3-2}$$

where p is the combined population proportion and $N = N_1 + N_2$. If $p_1 = .375$ and $p_2 = .390$, then

$$p = \frac{40(.375) + 100(.390)}{140} = \frac{15 + 39}{140} = .3857$$

and

$$q = 1 - .3857 = .6143$$

The equation for the standard score of the difference between p_1 and p_2 is

$$z = \frac{p_1 - p_2}{\sqrt{pqN/N_1 N_2}}$$
$$= \frac{-.015}{.091}$$
$$= -.16 \tag{3-3}$$

If we choose a 95 percent confidence level, the critical values are ± 1.96, and as the standard score of the difference lies between these two values, the research hypothesis and the null hypothesis can be accepted. The researcher is 95 percent sure that a difference as large as this can occur as a result of chance error due to the vagaries of random sampling.

  If the sample is stratified, the method outlined above can also be used for obtaining the parameters for the entire sample taken together. For example, if there are two stratifications and the number of observations in each stratum are N_1 and N_2, and the proportion of the area in corn in each stratum is p_1 and p_2, then the estimate of p for the entire sample is as in Eq. (3-2), and the estimate of the standard deviation for the sample is as in the denominator of Eq. (3-3).

Tests of Differences between Means

If a large sample containing N observations with a mean $\overline{X}$ is drawn from a normally distributed population of known mean μ and variance σ, then the hypothesis $H_0: \overline{X} = \mu$ can be tested by calculating z as in Eq. (3-1), with $\sigma/\sqrt{N}$ as the standard error of estimate of the mean, $\sigma_{\overline{x}}$. Thus

$$z = \frac{\overline{X} - \mu}{\sigma_{\overline{x}}} \tag{3-4}$$

If the sample is large and σ is not known, then the standard error of estimate of the mean may be estimated from the standard deviation of the sample and substituted for $\sigma_{\overline{x}}$ in Eq. (3-4) as $s_{\overline{x}} = s/\sqrt{N}$.

  The significance of the difference between two sample means $\overline{X}_1$ and $\overline{X}_2$ can also be tested for large samples if σ_1 and σ_2 are known, and the hypothesis is that both samples are drawn from the same normally distributed population, that is, that $\mu_1 = \mu_2$. The standard score of the difference between the sample means in this case is

$$z = \frac{\overline{X}_1 - \overline{X}_2}{\sqrt{\sigma_1^2/N_1 + \sigma_2^2/N_2}} \tag{3-5}$$

If the samples are large and the variances are not known, then z may be estimated by using the variances of the samples

$$z = \frac{\overline{X}_1 - \overline{X}_2}{\sqrt{s_1^2/N_1 + s_2^2/N_2}} \tag{3-6}$$

If, however, the size of the sample is small, the normal distribution cannot be used, for s is not a good estimate of σ.

Using Small Samples

The reason that s cannot be regarded as a good estimate of σ in small samples is that as the sample size decreases, the likelihood of the sample distribution of means being similar to the parent population distribution decreases. This is because the spread of the distribution increases as the sample size decreases, though the distribution still tends to be normal. Furthermore, a British statistician, who wrote under the pseudonym "Student," noticed that the spread of the distribution of sample means (defined by the standard deviation of the sample means, or the standard error of the mean) increased systematically as the sample size decreased (Student, 1908). Thus the critical limits on the abscissa of the normal curve containing, for example, 95 and 99 percent of the area under the normal curve, which limits are ± 1.96 and ± 2.576, no longer apply for small samples.

Because the spread increases systematically as the sample size decreases, and because this systematic spreading also has a definite theoretical base, it is possible to obtain critical values for any confidence level by using the sample mean, standard deviation, and size if it can be assumed that the parent population is normally distributed. These critical limits have been calculated by using Student's t distribution for small samples, and the critical limits for the 95 and 99 percent confidence level are presented in Table 3-1. As the sample size approaches 30, the critical limits are not far removed from those defined by the normal distribution; in other words, Student's distribution approaches the normal distribution for sample sizes greater than thirty.

Thus, if the hypothesis is that there is no difference between the population mean μ and the sample mean $\overline{X}$, then the standard score of the difference using Student's t distribution is

$$t = \frac{\overline{X} - \mu}{s/\sqrt{N - 1}} \tag{3-7}$$

and the critical value of t at the 95 and 99 percent confidence level can be determined from Table 3-1 with $n = N - 1$, for 1 degree of freedom is lost in the calculation of s in Eq. (3-7).

For testing the significance of the difference between two small sample means from populations where the parameters are unknown, the same equation (3-6) is used. This is, in reality, the statistic for estimating t except that for large samples we have taken advantage of the fact that the t distribution approaches the normal distribution for sample sizes greater than thirty. The degrees of freedom n, if the standard deviations of the parent populations are presumed equal, $\sigma_1 = \sigma_2$, are $N_1 + N_2 - 2$. If the standard deviations of the parent populations cannot be assumed to be equal, n can be estimated from the following formula:

$$n = \frac{(s_1{}^2/N_1 + s_2{}^2/N_2)^2}{(s_1{}^2/N_1)^2[1/(N_1 + 1)] + (s_1{}^2/N_2)^2[1/(N_2 + 1)]} - 2 \qquad (3\text{-}8)$$

For example, the researcher may wish to examine the proposition that the average selling price of homes in large Canadian cities (those with more than 200,000 people in 1965) is significantly different from the average selling price of homes in small Canadian cities (those between 30,000 and 150,000 in 1965). Data have been obtained for the average selling price of homes in 1967 for a

Table 3-1 VALUES OF t CORRESPONDING TO STATED PROBABILITIES IN A TWO-TAILED TEST FOR 95 AND 99 PERCENT CONFIDENCE LEVELS

n	$t_{0.95}$	$t_{0.99}$
1	12.71	63.66
2	4.30	9.93
3	3.18	5.84
4	2.78	4.60
5	2.57	4.03
6	2.45	3.71
7	2.37	3.50
8	2.31	3.36
9	2.26	3.25
10	2.23	3.17
15	2.13	2.95
20	2.09	2.85
30	2.04	2.75
∞	1.96	2.58

Note: The signs are ignored, for the t values may be either positive or negative.

SOURCE: The entries are extracts from a much larger table in Fisher and Yates (1943, table 3).

random selection of five large cities and twelve small cities. The parameters of the sample data are as follows:

$$N_1 = 5 \qquad \overline{X}_1 = \$22,732 \qquad s_1{}^2 = 2,627,641 \qquad s_1 = \$1,621$$

$$N_2 = 12 \qquad \overline{X}_2 = \$17,164 \qquad s_2{}^2 = 12,588,304 \qquad s_2 = \$3,548$$

The null hypothesis is that

$$H_0: \qquad \overline{X}_1 - \overline{X}_2 = 0$$

while the research hypothesis in this example is that there is a significant difference between the two means

$$H_1: \qquad \overline{X}_1 - \overline{X}_2 \neq 0$$

Thus if the null hypothesis is rejected, the research hypotheses can be inferred. The hypothesis is to be tested at the 95 percent confidence level. By substituting the sample data in Eq. (3-6), the value of t is estimated to be 4.45. This value is to be interpreted with $5 + 12 - 2 = 15$ degrees of freedom, for in this case it is a more conservative estimate than that derived from Eq. (3-8). From Table 3-1 it is to be noted that at the 95 percent confidence level with 15 degrees of freedom, the critical limits are ± 2.13. As the computed t value lies beyond these critical limits, the null hypothesis is rejected and the research hypothesis can be inferred.

If the sample is stratified, the mean $\overline{X}_s$ and the variance $s_s{}^2$ for the entire sample have to be estimated for the parameters and sampling intensity of each stratum. Hypothetical data for a random sample of houses, concerning the number of inhabitants in each house, for four census tracts (strata) are presented

Table 3-2 DATA ON A STRATIFIED RANDOM SAMPLE OF HOUSES IN FOUR CENSUS TRACTS, CONCERNING THE NUMBER OF INHABITANTS IN EACH HOUSE (HYPOTHETICAL)

Data	Census tract 1	Census tract 2	Census tract 3	Census tract 4	Total
$\overline{X}$	4.5	5.0	5.2	4.0	
d^2	.5	26.0	50.8	16.0	93.3
n	2	4	5	6	17
s^2	.5	8.67	12.7	3.2	
N	10	16	30	18	74

Note: n = number of houses sampled in each census tract.
N = total number of houses in each census tract.

in Table 3-2. The means and the variances have been calculated for each stratum in the usual way. The mean for the sample as a whole is

$$\overline{X}_s = \frac{\sum\limits_{k=1}^{m} N_k \overline{X}_k}{\sum\limits_{k=1}^{m} N_k} \tag{3-9}$$

where k designates the stratum, there being m strata. The sample data, therefore, estimate $\overline{X}_s$ to be

$$\overline{X}_s = \frac{\sum\limits_{k=1}^{4} N_k \overline{X}_k}{\sum\limits_{k=1}^{m} N_k} = \frac{353}{74} = 4.77$$

The variance of the sample as a whole is given by

$$S_s^2 = \frac{\sum\limits_{k=1}^{m} (\sum d_k^2)}{\sum\limits_{k=1}^{m} n_k - m} \tag{3-10}$$

which for the sample data in Table 3-2 yields

$$S_s^2 = \frac{93.3}{17 - 4} = 7.176$$

It is to be noted that 1 degree of freedom is lost for each stratum. These estimates can then be used to test the significance of the sample or its adequacy by using the methods outlined previously. Other tests for these and different types of sample design are discussed in Cochran (1953), Mills (1955), Walker and Lev (1953), and Delenius (1957).

Two- and One-tailed Tests

The idea of hypothesis testing has been introduced in this chapter primarily as a method for obtaining some knowledge concerning the adequacy of certain sample sizes and designs. The discussion proceeded slightly beyond this objective for an example concerning the selling prices of houses in large and small Canadian cities. In that example the research hypothesis and the null hypothesis were opposed, for the researcher was concerned with testing the proposition that the average selling price of homes in large Canadian cities is different from that in small cities. This proposition could be extended by speculating that as the growth of large Canadian cities in recent years has been much greater than that of small urban areas, the selling prices of homes should not be simply different between the two classes of urban areas but should be greater in the larger cities. The pressure of population increases in large cities through immigration from small towns, rural areas, and abroad has resulted in disproportionate increases in house prices as a result of an excess in demand over supply. The null hypothesis therefore remains

$$H_0: \quad \overline{X}_1 - \overline{X}_2 = 0$$

but the research hypothesis is that the mean selling price of houses in large Canadian cities is significantly greater than that in small Canadian cities

$$H_1: \quad \overline{X}_1 > \overline{X}_2$$

This hypothesis is much different from that discussed previously when there was no preference for which mean was the greater. The first hypothesis therefore involved a two-tailed test of significance, for the researcher was only concerned in whether the computed t value lay within the critical limits defined by the chosen level of significance.

In the second case, however, the researcher is interested in whether $\overline{X}_1$ is significantly greater than $\overline{X}_2$. Thus if $\overline{X}_2$ is greater than $\overline{X}_1$, the null hypothesis is bound to be accepted, and the research hypothesis thereby rejected. The region of acceptance of the research hypothesis is therefore (in this case) when t is positive, and the critical limit depends upon the level of confidence chosen. If the 95 percent confidence level is chosen, the limit will be at that point which divides the area under the curve into two portions, 95 percent to the left, and 5 percent to the right. The difference between this one-tailed situation and the two-tailed test is indicated in Fig. 3-11 for a normal curve. The critical limits for a two-tailed test at the 95 percent confidence level for large samples are ± 1.96, for it is this value which leaves 2.5 percent of the area under the curve in each tail (Fig. 3-11a). Similarly, if the test were at the 99 percent confidence level, the critical limits would be ± 2.58, for this value leaves 0.5 percent of the area under the normal curve in each tail. A one-tailed test would therefore leave 5 percent of the area under the curve in one of the tails, and in the example being discussed this would be the right-hand tail. From Table 2-5 it can be discerned that this value is 1.64 (Fig. 3-11b).

For small samples, a similar procedure is followed, but as discussed previously, there are separate values for each n. These values for the one-tailed test are listed in Table 3-3. For our Canadian house sales example the critical limit at the 95 percent confidence level can be observed to be 1.75, which is considerably less than the computed t value of 4.45. Thus the null hypothesis is rejected, and the research hypothesis that the sales price of homes in large Canadian cities is greater than that in small cities can be inferred. This difference between one- and two-tailed tests becomes extremely important in the ensuing chapter, which is concerned with simple correlation and regression.

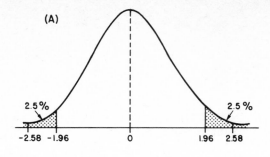

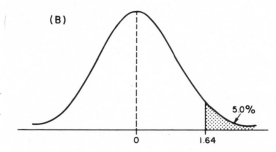

FIGURE 3-11
Two- and one-tailed tests.

Table 3-3 VALUES OF t CORRE-
SPONDING TO STATED
PROBABILITIES IN A
ONE-TAILED TEST FOR
95 AND 99 PERCENT
CONFIDENCE LEVELS

n	$t_{0.95}$	$t_{0.99}$
1	6.31	31.82
2	2.92	6.96
3	2.35	4.54
4	2.13	3.75
5	2.02	3.36
6	1.94	3.14
7	1.89	3.00
8	1.86	2.90
9	1.83	2.82
10	1.81	2.76
15	1.75	2.60
20	1.72	2.53
30	1.70	2.46
∞	1.64	2.33

Note: The signs are ignored, for the t values may be either positive or negative.

SOURCE: The entries are extracts from a much larger table in Fisher and Yates (1943, table 3).

SIMPLE CORRELATION AND REGRESSION

One of the techniques most used by geographers, and other social scientists for that matter, is simple regression and correlation (Robinson et al., 1961; Haggett, 1964; Gould, 1969). These are methods for determining the type and strength of a relation between two variables that are measured in interval or ratio form. All that the techniques provide is information concerning the association; they do not imply that the association actually means anything, for the interpretation of the relation is up to the researcher. Thus if simple regression and correlation techniques suggest the existence of a relation between two variables, this does not, of itself, imply that the relation has any real-world significance. Consequently, the researcher must have some real reason, either derived from theoretical deduction or from some empirically based inductive reasoning, that such a relation does have some real-world implication before he uses the techniques to determine its form and strength.

THE FORM OF A RELATION

Simple regression is a method for determining the existence of a linear, or straight-line, relation between two variables. To illustrate, assume that the researcher wishes to determine the form of the relation between the number of

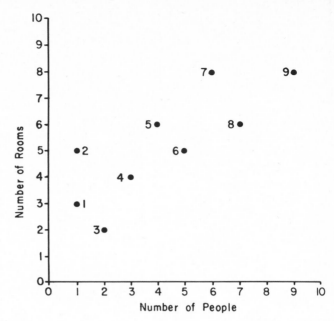

FIGURE 4-1
A scatter diagram of the relation between the number of persons in a house, X, and the number of rooms in a house, Y. Data from Table 4-1.

rooms in a residence and the number of persons living in that residence. The expectation is that there should be a positive relation: the greater the number of persons living in a house, the more space (expressed in number of rooms) there should be in that house. A brief glance at the data listed in Table 4-1 suggests that such a relation is possible, and when the data are plotted on a graph, the scattergram (Fig. 4-1) indicates that the existence of such a relation appears not only possible but probable.

There is, however, quite a wide scatter of points (the houses) over the graph, and so the researcher is interested in determining the average relation indicated by this scatter of points. If it is assumed that the relation is, in fact, a linear one, then the average relation could be indicated by fitting a straight line through the cloud of points. Obviously, many straight lines can be passed through the cloud of points; so what the researcher requires is that line which best fits the scatter. The criterion for determining the best fit is the line which minimizes the sum of the squared deviations of points from the line, that is, the least-squares best fit.

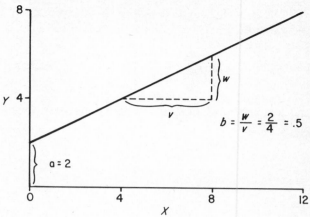

FIGURE 4-2
Graph of $Y = 2 + .5X$.

Once this line has been determined, it is characterized by two parameters, which are usually designated a and b. The parameter a is the intercept of the line with the Y axis (Fig. 4-2). This can obviously be positive, negative, or zero and it indicates the position of the line when X is zero. The second parameter, b, is the *regression coefficient*, and it indicates the slope of the line, that is, the increase (or decrease) in Y that is to be expected with a unit increase (or decrease) in the value of X. For example, in Fig. 4-2, a is 2; thus when X is zero, Y is 2,

Table 4-1   DATA CONCERNING THE RELATION BE-
TWEEN THE NUMBER OF PERSONS LIVING
IN A HOUSE, X, AND THE NUMBER OF ROOMS
IN THE HOUSE, Y, FROM A SAMPLE OF NINE
HOUSES IN A HAMLET (HYPOTHETICAL)

Observation	Number of rooms, Y	Number of persons, X
1	3	1
2	5	1
3	2	2
4	4	3
5	6	4
6	5	5
7	8	6
8	6	7
9	8	9

and b is .5, which suggests that for a unit increase in X there is a .5 increase in the value of Y. Thus, though the researcher may conjecture that Y is some function of X,

$$Y = f(x)$$

the assumption of linearity implies an algebraic function of the form

$$Y = a + bX \qquad\qquad (4\text{-}1)$$

which in our example is

$$Y = 2 + .5X$$

The Normal Equations

Therefore, in order to determine the best-fit line for the scatter of points in Fig. 4-1, it is necessary to determine the parameters a and b of that line. The sample data in Table 4-1 suggest a variety of equations, each one relating to each observation unit. These are

$$3 = a + b(1)$$
$$5 = a + b(1)$$
$$2 = a + b(2)$$
$$4 = a + b(3)$$
$$6 = a + b(4)$$
$$5 = a + b(5)$$
$$8 = a + b(6)$$
$$6 = a + b(7)$$
$$8 = a + b(9)$$

This system of observation equations overdefines the problem, for there are nine equations but only two unknowns, a and b. However, from these nine observation equations, two *normal* equations can be derived with two unknowns, and these can be solved to find the parameters by using the method of simultaneous equations.

The first normal equation is obtained by multiplying each observation equation by the coefficient of a (which is 1), and then adding the equations. Thus

$$\left.\begin{array}{l} 3 = 1a + b(1) \\ 5 = 1a + b(1) \\ 2 = 1a + b(2) \\ 4 = 1a + b(3) \\ 6 = 1a + b(4) \\ 5 = 1a + b(5) \\ 8 = 1a + b(6) \\ 6 = 1a + b(7) \\ 8 = 1a + b(9) \end{array}\right\} \quad \text{multiplies by 1}$$

$$\overline{47 = 9a + b(38)}$$

It is to be noted that this first normal equation can be represented more generally as

$$\sum_{i=1}^{n} Y_i = Na + b \sum_{i=1}^{n} X_i \tag{4-2}$$

where N is the sample size.

The second normal equation is obtained by multiplying each observation equation by the respective coefficient of b and adding the equations. Thus

$$\begin{array}{llr} 3 = & 1a + b(1) & \times\ 1 \\ 5 = & 1a + b(1) & \times\ 1 \\ 4 = & 2a + b(4) & \times\ 2 \\ 12 = & 3a + b(9) & \times\ 3 \\ 24 = & 4a + b(16) & \times\ 4 \\ 25 = & 5a + b(25) & \times\ 5 \\ 48 = & 6a + b(36) & \times\ 6 \\ 42 = & 7a + b(49) & \times\ 7 \\ 72 = & 9a + b(81) & \times\ 9 \end{array}$$

$$\overline{235 = 38a + b(222)}$$

This second normal equation can be represented more generally as

$$\sum_{i=1}^{n} X_i Y_i = a \sum_{i=1}^{n} X_i + b \sum_{i=1}^{n} X_i^2 \tag{4-3}$$

There are now two equations with two unknowns,

$$47 = 9a + b(38)$$

$$235 = 38a + b(222)$$

which, when solved simultaneously, yield an estimate of a as 2.7151 and b as .5938. The best-fit line passing through the scatter of points in Fig. 4-1 is therefore described by the equation

$$Y = 2.7151 + .5938X$$

and the position of this line is indicated in Fig. 4-3. It is to be noted that as the equation provides a parameter b which indicates the change in Y associated with a unit change in X, then Y is usually referred to as the *dependent variable* and X as the *independent variable*. Thus the sample variables should be placed logically according to this dependent-independent implication. As a consequence, throughout the discussion the number of rooms has been designated the dependent variable, and the number of persons the independent variable. The equation therefore describes a hamlet in which a single-person family tends to occupy a little over three rooms, and each unit increase in family size appears to be associated with the addition of a little over half a room. This interpretation does *not suggest causality*, though this may be an implication that the researcher might wish to infer. Such a suggestion is up to the researcher and should be based on theoretical considerations concerning the demand for residential space, as the equation does not of itself imply causality.

Residuals

The best-fit regression line in the housing example has been estimated to be $Y_i = 2.7151 + .5938X_i$, and when this line is superimposed over the actual scatter of points (Fig. 4-3), it is apparent that some of the observations lie almost on the line, such as houses 1 and 9, while others are far removed from the line. The regression line, which is, in a sense, the average trend if an assumption of linearity is accepted, therefore "predicts" observations 1 and 9 quite well, but falls far short of predicting the value of observation 7. This prediction is, of course, with respect to the number of rooms in a house, given the number of persons living in the house; i.e., the equation is the result of regressing Y against X. One very important part of regression analysis is to analyze the variation in accuracy of the prediction for each observation, for these residuals (Thomas, 1968) may well suggest further variables that could be related to the dependent variable.

The residuals for each observation are calculated by determining the predicted value of Y, which is referred to as Y_p, for each value of X, and then subtracting this from the actual value of Y. That is,

$$Y_{res} = Y - Y_p \qquad (4-4)$$

For example, the value for X in observation 5 is 4; so the predicted value of Y for that observation is

$$Y_p = 2.7151 + (.5938)(4) = 5.0903$$

and the residual is

$$Y_{res} = 6 - 5.0903 = .9097$$

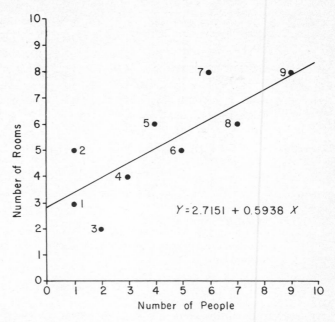

FIGURE 4-3
The best-fit straight-line relation between the number of persons in a house and the number of rooms in a house.

The residuals for each observation are listed in Table 4-2. The regression equation should, therefore, be modified to $Y_i = 2.7151 + .5938X_i + e_i$, where the e_i's are the errors or residuals.

Table 4-2 DATA AND RESIDUALS FOR THE REGRESSION EXAMPLE

Observation	X	Y	Y_p	Y_{res}	Y_{res}^2
1	1	3	3.3089	−.3089	.0954
2	1	5	3.3089	1.6911	2.8598
3	2	2	3.9027	−1.9027	3.6202
4	3	4	4.4965	−.4965	.2465
5	4	6	5.0903	.9097	.8275
6	5	5	5.6841	−.6841	.4679
7	6	8	6.2779	1.7211	2.9621
8	7	6	6.8717	−.8717	.7598
9	9	8	8.0593	−.0593	.0035
Total	38	47		.0013*	11.8427

* This value is not zero, owing to rounding error in calculations.

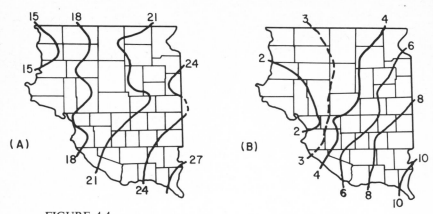

FIGURE 4-4
South Dakota east of the Missouri River: (*a*) distribution of mean annual rainfall, (*b*) distribution of rural farm population density, 1960, in persons per square mile.

An example Both Thünen's and Ricardo's views of economic rent have implications concerning the varying intensity of spatial distributions. The Thunen view implies that the closer a given unit of land is located to the market-place, the more intense is the use of that land. The Ricardian view would be that the more productive the land, the more intense is the use. In this particular example we shall examine the Ricardian view through the regression equation, and the Thunen view through the spatial distribution of the residuals. The area chosen for study is South Dakota east of the Missouri River, and the variables are defined by counties within that region. Intensity of land use is operationally defined as rural farm population density, for it is suggested that the less intense the use of the land, the larger are the farms, the more extensive is the farm operation, and therefore the less is the farm population. The productivity is operationally defined in terms of average annual precipitation, for in this part of the Great Plains plant growth is particularly sensitive to moisture.

The spatial variation of each variable is demonstrated in map form in Fig. 4-4. Figure 4-4*a* shows the spatial distribution of average annual precipitation, where the isohyets are constructed from meteorological stations data in the defined area. The rural farm population density surface is presented in a manner similar to that of the isohyet map of rainfall (Fig. 4-4*b*). The densities are calculated on a county basis; the center of each county is then regarded as an observation point, and isolines of equal density are sketched for the entire area with reference to these points. The two variables are therefore defined with respect to these observation points, the calculated densities are regarded as

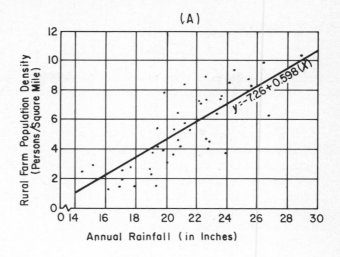

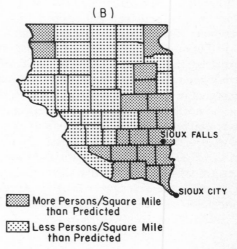

FIGURE 4-5
South Dakota east of the Missouri River: (a) the relation between rainfall and rural farm population densities, (b) map of residuals.

pertaining to the center of the county, and the rainfall is interpolated for these points from the isohyet map.

These data can be used to construct a scatter diagram, with population density as the dependent variable and rainfall as the independent variable, and a line of best fit can be passed through the line of points. This line is described by the equation

$$P_i = -7.26 + .598R_i$$

where P_i = rural farm population density of the ith county

R_i = interpolated average annual precipitation at the center of the ith county

and it indicates the "average" or predicted change in rural farm population densities associated with changes in precipitation (Fig. 4-5a). The line of best fit suggests that in the eastern part of South Dakota, rural farm population densities increase by .598 persons per square mile with each increase of 1 inch of rainfall. The fact that the parameters of the equation should not be applied beyond the defined area of study is well illustrated by the prediction that if the mean rainfall were 10 inches, the rural farm population density would be −1.28 persons per square mile.

However, by using the line of best fit as a predictor for eastern South Dakota only, the difference between the actual rural farm population density and the predicted can be mapped (Fig. 4-5b). The distribution of positive residuals (those counties where the density is greater than expected) and the distribution of negative residuals (those counties where the density is less than expected) in Fig. 4-5b do seem to reveal separate contiguous patterns. Densities are greater than expected in the southeastern part of the area and less than expected in the central and western half, with two counties standing as outliers in the northwest. This general arrangement of negative and positive residuals may well reflect the effect of proximity of counties in the southeast to the market centers of Sioux Falls (the largest city in South Dakota, having a population of about 65,000) and Sioux City, Iowa (approximately 97,000). Thus the line of best fit, which has a positive slope, gives credence to Ricardian notions in this area, while the distribution of the residuals suggests the coexistence of Thunen principles as well. These principles have been examined in microscale by Found (1970).

Testing the Significance of Regression Coefficients

In many cases in human geography, sample data are used to estimate the parameters of the best-fit line. In the housing example discussed previously the data were clearly derived from a sample survey within the hamlet. The South Dakota example could in one sense be regarded as a population, and in another as a sample. In the former case it could be argued that as all the data have been obtained at the stated level of aggregation for the entire defined study area, then the data used constitute the population (Meyer, 1972). On the other hand, it could be argued that South Dakota east of the Missouri river is a sample area of many that could have been used, and thus the data are a sample of this population.

If the data being used to calculate the parameters of a regression line are a sample, then these parameters are estimates of the parameters that would have been derived had the population data been used. Thus, just as the $\overline{X}$ is an estimate of μ, so are a and b estimates of the respective population parameters. Of these two, b, the regression coefficient, is the most interesting because it indicates the effect of X on Y, and in econometrics it can be used to derive elasticity. In the housing example, if b was unity, it would suggest that for every additional person in a family there was an additional room; if b was 2, then each additional person would have two additional rooms. The question that therefore arises is whether b is an adequate estimate of the regression coefficient that would have been obtained had the population data been used. This population regression coefficient is commonly referred to by the symbol β. Thus the null hypothesis would be

$$H_0: \quad b = \beta \quad \text{or} \quad b - \beta = 0$$

Unfortunately β is invariably not known, and so some logical substitute has to be used. This substitute is usually zero; for the aim of the research is to find some relation between two variables, and if b were zero, there would be no relation. The null hypothesis therefore becomes

$$H_0: \quad b = 0 \quad \text{or} \quad b - 0 = 0$$

and the research hypothesis is usually

$$H_1: \quad b \neq 0 \quad \text{or} \quad b - 0 \neq 0$$

Alternatively, the research may be concerned with examining the proposition that the relation is positive, or that it is negative. Thus

$$H_2: \quad b > 0 \quad \text{or} \quad b - 0 > 0$$

or

$$H_3: \quad b < 0 \quad \text{or} \quad b - 0 < 0$$

Parenthetically, it is to be noted that H_1 obviously involves a two-tailed test, and H_2 and H_3 a one-tailed test.

Standard error of estimate of a regression coefficient   In the previous chapter considerable use was made of the theory of errors, which states that sample errors, given enough of them, will distribute themselves normally. If this assumption is accepted, then regression coefficients, given enough of them calculated from samples drawn from the same population, will also distribute themselves normally and the mean of this distribution will be β. Therefore, if the difference between the calculated b and β is expressed in standardized form, the normal distribution for large samples, and the t distribution for small samples, can be used to test whether the regression coefficient is not significantly different from β. The regression coefficient can be expressed in standard-score form in an equation directly similar to Eq. (3-4).

$$z_b = \frac{b - \beta}{\sigma_\beta} \tag{4-5}$$

where z_b is the standard score of the regression coefficient and σ_β is the standard deviation of β. As σ_β is not known, this parameter has to be estimated from the sample data. This estimate is referred to as the "standard error of estimate of the regression coefficient" and is expressed as s_b. Thus

$$z_b = \frac{b - \beta}{s_b} \tag{4-6}$$

The standard error of estimate of the regression coefficient is directly related to the error estimates already perceived in the regression equation. For example, it has been noted previously that if the number of rooms for five persons were to be predicted from the regression equation, the error would be $-.6841$. The sum of these errors is zero, just as the sum of the deviations around the mean is zero. However, the sum of the *squared deviations* indicates the total variation of the errors, and in the housing example this value is 11.8427 (see Table 4-2). The mean of the sum of squared deviations is the error variance, and the square root of the error variance is the standard error of estimate of the regression equation. The calculations are as follows:

$$s_{Y.X} = \sqrt{\frac{\sum\limits_{i=1}^{n} (Y - Yp)_i^2}{N - 2}} = \sqrt{\frac{\sum\limits_{i=1}^{n} (Y_{res})_i^2}{N - 2}}$$

$$= \sqrt{\frac{11.8427}{9 - 2}} = 1.3 \tag{4-7}$$

where $s_{Y.X}$ is the standard error of estimate of the regression equation of Y with respect to X; and N is reduced by the number of parameters, a and b, required to obtain the predicted values, for these are calculated from sample data. This standard error of estimate is quite large, for if it is assumed that the errors are normally distributed, it indicates that 68 percent of the actual values can be predicted with an error of ± 1.3 or less.

As the regression coefficient indicates the change in Y associated with a unit change in X, the standard error of estimate of the regression coefficient, s_b, is calculated with respect to $s_{Y.X}$ and the standard deviation of X, namely s_X, modified by the square root of the sample size. Thus

$$s_b = \frac{s_{Y.X}}{s_X\sqrt{N-1}}$$

(4-8)

Therefore, in the housing example

$$s_b = \frac{1.3}{2.613\sqrt{9-1}} = .1778$$

This value is the standard error of estimate of the regression coefficient, .5938, in the housing example.

Importance of the assumption of normality Substituting the parameters estimated above in Eq. (4-5),

$$z_b = \frac{.5938 - 0}{.1778} = 3.3397$$

It is to be noted that as the sample size is small, the t distribution is to be used rather than the normal distribution, with $t = z_b$ and with the degrees of freedom being $N - 2 = 7$ because 2 degrees of freedom are lost with the estimation of a and b. The null hypothesis states that there is no difference between b and β, that is, that there is no relation between X and Y. Our research hypothesis, on the other hand, is that there is a positive relation between the two variables.

If it can be assumed that the regression coefficients from a large number of samples drawn from this population form a normal distribution with mean β, then the normal distribution for large samples, and the t distribution for small samples, can be used as the model against which to compare z_b. A good test of this assumption is whether the errors are normally distributed, for, as has been indicated above, these errors are used to calculate the standard error of estimate of the regression equation, which is, in turn, used to estimate the standard error of the regression coefficient. The errors will usually be normally distributed if the variables X and Y are normally distributed. Thus, though a straight line can be fit through any scatter of points, if the significance of the regression co- efficient is to be tested, it is wise to embark upon the calculations with variables that are normally distributed. Of course, if population data are used, no test of significance is required and there is no need for normally distributed variables.

As the housing data are a hypothetical sample, the normality assumption is quite important. A quick fractile-diagram check (Fig. 4-6) illustrates that the errors, given the smallness of the sample size, tend to be normally distributed. The hypothesis is to be tested at the 95 percent confidence level, and from Table 3-3 it can be determined that the critical value of t at that level of confidence for a one-tailed test with 7 degrees of freedom is 1.89. As this value is less than 3.34, the researcher may state that he is 95 percent sure that such a difference

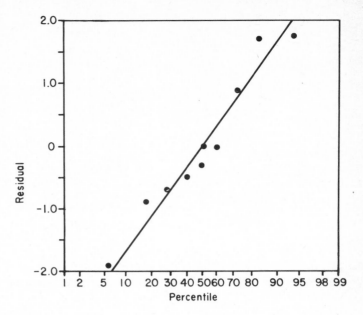

FIGURE 4-6
Fractile diagram of the residuals in Table 4-2.

could not have occurred by chance alone. The null hypothesis is rejected and the research hypothesis that the regression coefficient is significantly greater than zero can be inferred.

Nonlinear Relation

Curvilinear relations of a number of kinds can be expressed in linear form by transforming one or both of the variables. A curvilinear relation that appears often in human geography is the exponential curve (Fig. 4-7a). This curve illustrates quite a simple common phenomenon: the increase, or decrease, at any moment is proportional to the size already attained. An example of the positive form of this curve is compound interest; an example of the negative form is Clark's (1951) model of population density decline in urban areas. The exponential curve appears linear when plotted on a semilogarithmic graph (Fig. 4-7b), where the ordinate is expressed in common logarithms. The relation is expressed algebraically as

$$Y = ab^x \qquad (4\text{-}9)$$

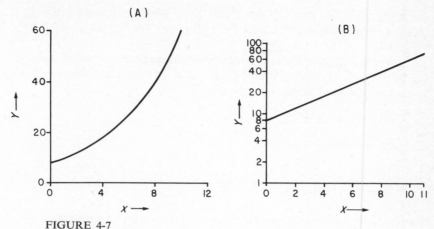

FIGURE 4-7
The exponential curve: (*a*) arithmetic case, (*b*) semilogarithmic case.

or when the slope is negative, as

$$Y = \frac{a}{b^X} \tag{4-10}$$

and in common logarithms as

$$\log (Y) = \log a + (X) \log b$$

or

$$\log (Y) = \log a - (X) \log b$$

where the only variable that is transformed is Y. The exponential curve is frequently written in the form

$$Y = ae^{bX} \tag{4-11}$$

or

$$Y = ae^{-bX} \tag{4-12}$$

where e is the base of the natural logarithms, ln. These equations can be expressed in linear form in natural logarithms as

$$\ln Y = \ln a + bX$$

or

$$\ln Y = \ln a - bX$$

The advantage of using natural logarithms is that the regression coefficient b is the relative *rate* of increase or decrease, that is, the rate of change per unit of Y

per unit of X. The common logarithm form does not give this relative rate of increase, but it can be obtained by multiplying the logarithm of b by 2.3026 ($= \ln 10$).

Another frequently occurring curvilinear expression often derived from the logarithmic normalization of both X and Y is the logarithmic curve. If the curve has a positive slope, the equation is

$$Y = aX^b \tag{4-13}$$

and with a negative slope, it is

$$Y = \frac{a}{X^b} \tag{4-14}$$

These equations are expressed in linear form in common logarithms as

$$\log(Y) = \log a + b \log(X)$$

and

$$\log(Y) = \log a - b \log(X)$$

A transformation into logarithms of both variables will put into linear form any hyperbola. An equation of this form is often used for measuring the ratio of the rate of change in Y to the rate of change in X, the rate of change being indicated by b, which to the economist is a measure of elasticity.

Measurement of distance decay Geography has been referred to as a discipline in distance (Watson, 1955), and nowhere is this more true than in studies of spatial diffusion in cultural geography. Hagerstrand (1967) analyzes the effect of distance in a simulation model concerning the diffusion of an innovation through social contacts in Asby in southern Sweden by calibrating the effect of distance with the use of migration data. He assumes that a person's perception of distance, as far as social contacts are concerned, is reflected in this part of Sweden by the distances over which people migrate. Thus the number of migrating households from Asby is determined in a series of annular rings, and these are then expressed for analytical purposes as the number of migrating households per square kilometer, and plotted on a graph against the midpoint of each band.

The trace of the scatter of points which indicate the relation between distance and migrating density is considered approximately linear when both variables are logarithmically transformed (Fig. 4-8a). The average trend can be calculated as

$$\log(H) = .79657 - 1.585 \log(D)$$

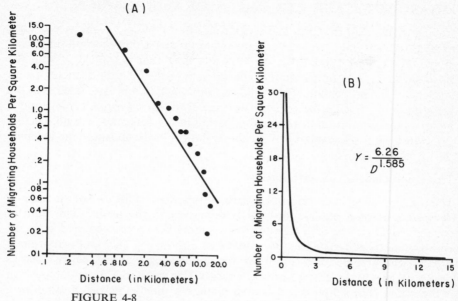

FIGURE 4-8
Distance decay function calculated from Asby, Sweden, local migration data:
(a) logarithmic case, (b) arithmetic case. [*From Hagerstrand* (1953), *p.* 190, *and
Marble and Nystuen* (1963), *p.* 101.]

which in antilogarithm form is

$$H = \frac{6.26}{D^{1.585}}$$

where H = number of migrating households per square kilometer
D = distance of midpoint of each distance band from center of Asby

The graph of the antilogarithmic equation is presented in Fig. 4-8b, which
illustrates that the tendency is for the number of migrating households per
square kilometer to decline rapidly with distance for about 1.5 kilometers, and
to decrease much less rapidly from this distance on. This type of decline with
distance is referred to in human geography as *distance decay*, and the empirical
form of the relation can be used to calibrate *mean information fields* for different
parts of the world (Marble and Nystuen, 1963). It is for this reason that great
care must be taken to choose the correct transformation (Olsson, 1967, p. 51;
Taylor, 1971), and one doubts whether the transformation chosen by
Hagerstrand is the best.

MEASURING THE STRENGTH OF A RELATION

Having determined the form and significance of a relation, it is now necessary to measure its strength. The relation being examined is the association between Y and X, or more specifically, the variation in Y that is associated with the variation in X. A good measure of the strength of the relation is, therefore, an estimate of the proportion of the total variation in Y that is associated with the variation in X. Such a measure is called the *coefficient of determination*, and it indicates the proportion of the total variation in the dependent variable that is associated with, or "explained" by, the variation in the independent variable.

The Coefficient of Determination

The total variation in the dependent variable is defined as the sum of the squared deviations of each observation unit with respect to the mean. This sum of squared deviations is, of course, the quotient that has to be calculated when the variance and standard deviation have to be estimated. This total variation is presented in graphic form (Fig. 4-9a) for the housing example, where a line is drawn parallel to the Y axis from each observation point to a straight line which is the mean. The simplest and crudest method of predicting the Y value for a given X is, of course, to use the mean; so it is appropriate that this is the benchmark against which the strength of the prediction is to be measured. Thus the total variation in Y is defined as

$$\sum_{i=1}^{n} y_i^2 = \sum_{i=1}^{n} (Y_i - \bar{Y})^2 \tag{4-15}$$

where n is the number of observations. In the housing example the total variation is calculated to be 33.56.

As the concern is with calculating the variation in Y that is associated with, or explained by, the variation in X, it is appropriate to divide the total variation into two portions, one that *is* associated with, or explained by, the variation in X, and one that *is not*. Thus it can be postulated that

$$\sum_{i=1}^{n} y_i^2 = \text{explained variation} + \text{unexplained variation} \tag{4-16}$$

As this is a simple equality, it is apparent that if either the explained or the unexplained variation can be determined, then both segments are known. Fortunately, the unexplained variation has already been derived, for in determining the standard error of estimate of the regression equation, the total variation of the errors was calculated. This is defined in Eq. (4-7) as

$$\sum_{i=1}^{n} y_{\text{res}}^2 = \sum_{i=1}^{n} (Y - Y_p)_i^2 \tag{4-17}$$

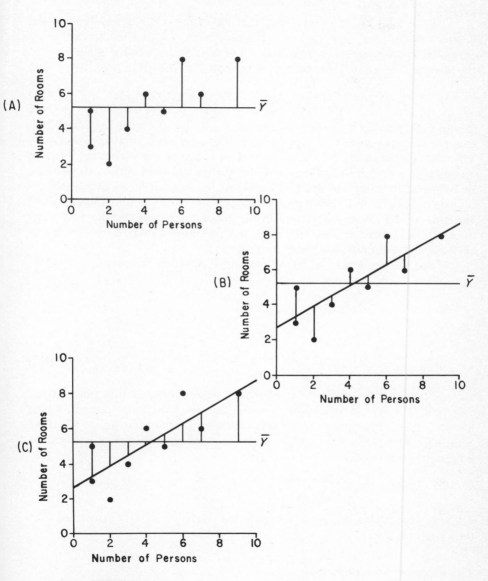

FIGURE 4-9
The components of the total variation of the dependent variable: (a) the total
variation of Y, (b) the unexplained variation, (c) the explained variation.

and for the housing example it has been calculated to be 11.8427, which can be rounded to 11.84. The residuals are presented in graphic form for comparative purposes in Fig. 4-9b.

As the total variation represents the sum of the squared deviations of the *observed* values of Y_i with respect to the mean, the variation accounted for, or explained by, the regression equation is the sum of the squared differences of the *predicted* values of Y for each X_i with respect to the mean (Fig. 4-9c); thus

$$\sum_{i=1}^{n} y_{exp}^2 = \sum_{i=1}^{n} (Y_p - \overline{Y})_i^2 \tag{4-18}$$

It is to be noted that if all the points in the scatter lay along the regression line, then the total explained variation would be the same as the total variation in Y. Thus the coefficient of determination, which indicates the percentage of total variation in Y explained by the regression of Y on X, would in this extreme case be 100 percent. Alternatively, if all the points in the scatter were evenly distributed on either side of the line but very distant from it, the amount of unexplained variation would be very large and in the extreme would equal the total variation. In this extreme case the explained variation would be zero, and the coefficient of determination would be 0 percent.

Thus, the coefficient of determination, r^2, which is defined as

$$r^2 = 100 \frac{\sum y_{exp}^2}{\sum y^2}$$

or

$$r^2 = 100 \frac{\sum y^2 - \sum y_{res}^2}{\sum y^2} \tag{4-19}$$

varies between a lower limit of 0 percent, which indicates that none of the variation in Y is associated with the variation in X, and 100 percent, which indicates that all the variation in Y is replicated by the variation in X. If we substitute the calculated total variation and unexplained variation from the housing example in Eq. (4-19), we obtain

$$r^2 = 100 \frac{33.56 - 11.84}{33.56} = 100 \frac{21.72}{33.56} = 64.7 \text{ percent}$$

Thus it is concluded that 64.7 percent of the variation in Y is associated with the variation in X.

The Correlation Coefficient

Another measure of the strength of the linear association between two variables is the correlation coefficient. While the coefficient of determination indicates the percentage of the variation in Y that is associated with X, the correlation

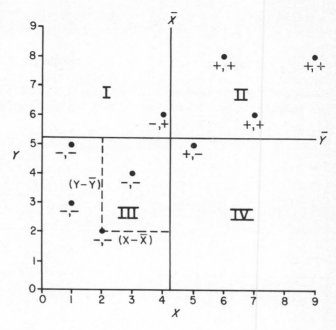

FIGURE 4-10
A scatter diagram of the relation between the number of persons in a house, X, and the number of rooms in a house, Y, to illustrate the construction of the correlation coefficient.

coefficient is an index measure of the degree of linear association between the two variables and as such has been used to measure both the correspondence between isarithmic maps (Robinson, 1962) and the association between crops (Kendall, 1939). As the measure is, in effect, an index of the degree of linearity of the scatter of points, its construction can be explained without regard to the best-fit line.

Consider the scatter of points for the housing data, reproduced in Fig. 4-10. Lines representing the mean of X and Y can be drawn which divide the area of the graph into four quadrants. Each point can be defined not just in terms of its X and Y coordinates, but also in terms of its distribution with respect to its mean. Thus each point can be located in the two-space in terms of its $X_i - \overline{X}$, $Y_i - \overline{Y}$, or more concisely x_i, y_i, where the lower-case letters indicate that deviation scores are being used. It will be recalled that the total *variation* of a single variable can be defined by the sum of the deviations squared [for example, $\sum_{i=1}^{n} (Y_i - \overline{Y})^2$]. Thus, the total *covariation* between two variables is the sum of the cross products of the deviations, that is,

$$\text{Total covariation between } X, Y = \sum_{i=1}^{n} (X_i - \overline{X})(Y_i - \overline{Y})$$

$$= \sum_{i=1}^{n} x_i y_i \tag{4-20}$$

Also, just as the mean of the total variation of a single variable is the *variance*, the mean of the total covariation is defined as the *covariance*.

N	9	ΣX^2	222	ΣY^2	279	ΣXY	235
ΣX	38	$-\dfrac{(\Sigma X)^2}{N}$	-160.44	$-\dfrac{(\Sigma Y)^2}{N}$	-245.44	$-\dfrac{(\Sigma X)(\Sigma Y)}{N}$	-198.4444
ΣY	47	Σx^2	61.56	Σy^2	33.56	Σxy	36.5556
$\overline{X}$	4.2222	$\dfrac{\Sigma x^2}{N}$	$S_x^2 = 6.84$	$\dfrac{\Sigma y^2}{N}$	$S_y^2 = 3.73$		
$\overline{Y}$	5.22222	$\sqrt{\dfrac{\Sigma x^2}{N}}$	$S_x = 2.613$	$\sqrt{\dfrac{\Sigma y^2}{N}}$	$S_y = 1.931$		

$$b = \frac{\Sigma xy}{\Sigma x} = \frac{36.56}{61.56} = 0.5938$$

$$a = \overline{y} - b\overline{x} = 5.2222 - 2.5071 = 2.7151$$

$$r = \frac{\Sigma xy}{N\, s_x s_y} \quad \text{or} \quad \frac{N(\Sigma XY) - (\Sigma X)(\Sigma Y)}{\left[N\Sigma X^2 - (\Sigma X)^2\right]\left[N\Sigma Y^2 - (\Sigma Y)^2\right]}$$

$$= \frac{36.56}{9(2.613)(1.931)} = \frac{36.56}{45.4113} = 0.805$$

$$r^2 = 64.80\%$$

$$S_{yx} = \sqrt{\frac{\Sigma y^2 - b(\Sigma xy)}{N - 2}} = \sqrt{\frac{33.56 - 21.7067}{7}} = \sqrt{\frac{11.8533}{7}} = 1.3$$

FIGURE 4-11
Worksheet for simple linear regression and correlation.

The total covariation between X and Y is an interesting quantity. If the points in the scatter diagram lie in quadrants II and III, then the sum of the cross products of the deviations in both quadrants will be positive (Fig. 4-9) and therefore the total covariation will be *positive* and quite large. On the other hand, if the points in the scatter diagram lie in quadrants I and IV, the total covariation will be quite large but *negative*. But if the points lie fairly evenly in I, II, III, and IV, the negative scores of the covariation in I and IV may cancel out the positive scores in III and II, and the total covariation would be either negative or positive but it would definitely be small. Thus the total covariation between two variables is used as the base of the correlation coefficient.

The total covariation, however, is affected by two factors. The first is the size of the sample; obviously the number of points will affect the covariation quantity. This can be taken into account by dividing the covariation by the sample size, or in other words, by calculating the *covariance*. The second factor concerns the magnitudes of the figures being used, for the data on one axis may be many times larger than the data on the other and thus grossly inflate the covariance. As a consequence, the covariance is divided by the standard deviations of both variables. Thus the correlation coefficient r, sometimes referred to as the "Pearsonian product-moment correlation coefficient," is defined as

$$r = \frac{\sum_{i=1}^{n} (X_i - \overline{X})(Y_i - \overline{Y})}{N s_x s_y} = \frac{\sum_{i=1}^{n} x_i y_i}{N s_x s_y} \tag{4-21}$$

This index varies between -1 and $+1$, with zero indicating no linear association, and -1 and $+1$ indicating perfect negative and perfect positive associations respectively.

The correlation coefficients for the housing example can be calculated by substituting the figures detailed in the worksheet in Fig. 4-11. It is to be noted that this worksheet contains computational shortcuts [as described, for example, in Eq. (2.4)] for obtaining the necessary parameters. As the coefficient of determination is the square (multiplied by 100) of the correlation coefficient, it is not necessary to partition the total variance in Y, namely, $\sum y^2$, into its explained and unexplained components, for it can be derived directly from the correlation coefficient. Thus

$$r = \frac{36.56}{9(2.613)(1.931)} = .805$$

and

$$r^2 = 64.8 \text{ percent}$$

The very small difference in value between the coefficient of determination by the worksheet method and that by the partitioning method is the result of rounding errors in the procedures.

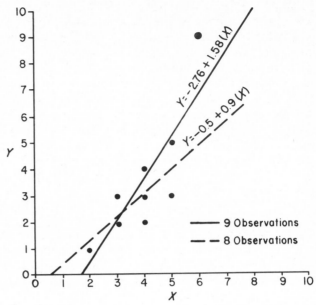

FIGURE 4-12
The effect of adding an extreme value to one variable in a regression and correlation analysis.

Homogeneity of Variance

A quick review of the methods described to find the best-fit line, the coefficient of determination, and the correlation coefficient suggests that the presence of one or two extreme values in a distribution may have a serious effect on the parameters and the coefficients calculated. For example, in Fig. 4-12 we plotted the best-fit lines for two sets of observations, one containing eight observations, and the other nine. The set of nine is different from the set of eight only insofar as the ninth observation is an extreme value for Y, though it is not untowardly extreme for X. The best-fit lines indicate that this one extreme observation for Y has a great effect on the regression line, "pulling" the line toward it regardless of the general trend of the other eight observations. Furthermore, this one extra, extreme value results in a large increase in the coefficient of determination, from 55 percent for the set of eight to 68 percent for the set of nine.

This greater difference in value of the parameters of the regression line, with inflation in the coefficient of determination, is due to the greater homogeneity of variance between the two variables in the set of eight than in the set of nine. The variances of X and Y in the set of eight are .94 and 1.36, and in the set of nine 1.33 and 4.91. In other words, whereas the variance of Y is $1\frac{1}{2}$ times as great as that of X in the set of eight, it is over $3\frac{1}{2}$ times as great as in the set of nine, and this difference is due to the great increase in the variance of Y as a result of the addition of one extreme value. Thus, though it is not necessary for the variances of the variables to be similar, it is necessary for the variance of each variable to be fairly stable with respect to sample size. As the sample size changes, the variances should not differ considerably for each variable, that is, they should be homogeneous or *homoscedastic*. Random samples drawn from normally distributed populations are usually homoscedastic, and that is another very good reason for using variables that are normally distributed.

Spatial Autocorrelation

With the great use of regression and correlation analysis in human geography over the past two decades has come a growing awareness of the problem of spatial autocorrelation (Dacey, 1968). Just as in the analysis of time series data, econometrists have long been aware that each observation of a given variable may not be independent of another observation, so geographers have become aware that each observation in space may not be independent of the other observations. This lack of independence may lead to spurious results, for a basic assumption in regression analysis is that each observation is independent of the others. The spatial autocorrelation problem is more complex, however, than the time series autocorrelation problem. With time series data the auto-correlation is in one direction only, backward in time, though the interval may vary. With data distributed spatially, the autocorrelation can be in any direction, and, furthermore, it can diminish sharply or only gradually with distance.

Consequently, the progress thus far in measuring spatial autocorrelation has been limited despite the extensive work of Moran (1950), Geary (1954), and Whittle (1954). The statistics for spatial autocorrelation developed by Moran and Geary examine the effect on county data of immediately contiguous counties only, and thus ignore the possible effect of those noncontiguous, and Whittle concentrates primarily on an extension of spectral analysis as a possible solution to the problem. Cliff and Ord (1969) have attempted to incorporate the effect of distance in a statistic by permitting the researcher to choose a set of weights that may appropriately measure the degree of contact between counties. This statistic is

$$r_{\mathrm{CO}} = \frac{n \sum\limits_{i=1}^{n} \sum\limits_{j=1}^{n} w_{ij} z_i z_j}{\sum\limits_{i=1}^{n} \sum\limits_{j=1}^{n} w_{ij} \sum\limits_{i=1}^{n} z_i^{2}} \qquad \text{for all } i \neq j \qquad (4\text{-}22)$$

where n = number of observations

$z_i = X_i - \overline{X}$, the deviation score

w_{ij} = the weight, or influence, of point or area i on point or area j

In a comparison of the utility of this statistic against those developed by Moran and Geary on a set of data for Eire, Cliff and Ord used a weighting in which

$$w_{ij} = d_{ij}^{-1} q_i(j)$$

where d_{ij} = distance from center of county i to center of county j

$q_i(j)$ = proportion of length of boundary of i which is in contact with county j

It must be noted, of course, that this is a possible weighting among many that could be used.

Although Cliff and Ord demonstrate the superiority of this statistic over those proposed by Moran and Geary, there are some serious deficiencies. The first is that it may be quite sensitive to the system of weights that are used, and obviously considerable a priori research must be undertaken to support the weights that are eventually chosen. Secondly, r_{co} does not vary within a bounded fixed range as does the Pearson correlation coefficient, though the limits of the statistic may be evaluated for any sets of scores and weights (Cliff and Ord, 1971). The importance of the technique to geographic research, however, may be that it could yield a statistic for measuring the degree of spatial autocorrelation among the errors, or residuals (Cliff and Ord, 1972). The statistic could then be used in a manner similar to the Durbin-Watson (1950, 1951) statistic, for tests of significance of regression and correlation coefficients require not only normality, but independence among the errors (residuals) as well.

The Modifiable-Unit-Area Problem

Another problem of a strictly geographic nature is the modifiable-unit-area problem, which has been referred to in the previous chapter with respect to sampling. In that section it was noted that the means and variances of data may vary according to the level of aggregation of the observation unit. As most observation units in human geography are areas of one kind or another, this is a fundamental source of error, and has repercussions in many of the techniques used. The result of these possible differences in means and variances of data pertaining to areas in correlation and regression analysis is that the coefficients and parameters will usually change as the level of aggregation changes. Thus the parameters and coefficients obtained from correlating data pertaining to census tracts for a given urban area will usually not be the same as those obtained from data pertaining to enumeration areas in that same urban area. The "solution" to this problem presented by Robinson (1956) has been shown by Thomas and Anderson (1965) to be a particular solution rather than a general one, and though they point in the direction of a general solution, one is not available as yet.

The modifiable-unit-area problem is of even greater concern when the results of studies from different areas are to be compared. If the parameters and coefficients from variables correlated at differing levels of aggregation within the same study area vary, then it is not difficult to envisage the horrendous difficulties in comparing statistical studies of interrelations between the same variables in different regions or countries. For example, counties vary in size enormously between the eastern and western parts of the United States, and in Canada counties are so ridiculously shaped with respect to the general distribution of population and economic activity in the country that they are almost impossible to use as observation units in any kind of statistical analysis.

Thus it is very important for the human geographer to recognize these difficulties arising from nonhomoscedasticity, spatial autocorrelation, and modifiable unit areas and to attempt to take them into account in research. As it is impossible, however, to be little more than intuitive about two of the three problems listed, it is important that abject pessimism should not replace intelligent caution. Curry's (1965) admonition, "We still really do not know what we are doing in spatial regressions," should be regarded as a clarion call for further research into the problems of spatial autocorrelation and modifiable unit areas, rather than the ultimate freeze from the icy north. In a partial response to this call, Curry (1972) has developed a method for measuring the correlation between two maps which is not rooted in any form of statistical procedure. Consequently, it can be regarded as a very important first step in the development of quantitative measures for spatially distributed data.

LINKAGE ANALYSIS

Thus far we have been concerned with discussing regression and correlation analysis between two variables. The correlation coefficient, which indicates the degree of linear association between two variables, can also be used to determine the basic structure of relations between a number of variables. Suppose that the correlation coefficient between a number of variables has been calculated, each variable being correlated with every other. The correlation coefficients can be presented in a square symmetrical table (a matrix) with the correlation between each variable and the matrix represented as unity, and an example of the use of this kind of matrix can be found in Davis (1971). This table can then be used to divide the variables into associated groups.

In Table 4-3 are listed the correlation coefficients between twenty-one different socioeconomic-geographic variables measured for each county

Table 4-3 CORRELATION COEFFICIENT MATRIX

	TP	TCPI	LA	TRM	AVF	TVFPS	DN	PCI	% under $3,000	% PI	% 65+
Total population	1.00	*0.99*	0.44	0.35	*0.69*	0.46	−0.33	0.49	−0.48	0.43	0.03
Total civilian production income		1.00	0.46	0.32	0.65	0.47	−0.32	0.49	−0.46	0.38	−0.01
Land area			1.00	*0.61*	0.32	0.53	−0.43	0.46	−0.37	0.27	−0.05
Road mileage				1.00	0.25	0.62	0.04	0.29	−0.27	0.12	−0.07
Av. value per acre farmland					1.00	0.48	−0.58	0.51	−0.47	0.63	0.19
Total value farm prod. sold						1.00	−0.34	0.46	−0.33	0.22	0.08
Degrees north							1.00	−0.60	0.47	−0.49	−0.23
Per capita income								1.00	−0.77	0.57	−0.07
% under $3,000									1.00	−0.72	0.14
% population increase										1.00	0.13
% 65 and over											1.00
% urban											
% rural farm											
Physical location											
% manufacturing											
% agriculture											
% mining and fishing											
% serv., prof., govt.											
Population density											
Road mileage per sq. mile											
% nonwhite											

Note: the "underlined" coefficients are in italics.

Table 4-3 (CONTINUED)

	% U	% RF	PL	% M	% A	% MF	% T	PD	RMD	% N
Total population	0.62	−0.31	−0.22	0.02	−0.36	−0.13	−0.06	0.68	0.10	−0.18
Total civilian production income	0.58	−0.26	−0.20	0.02	−0.32	−0.12	−0.07	0.60	0.03	−0.16
Land area	0.40	−0.28	−0.11	0.01	−0.12	−0.10	−0.18	0.00	−0.45	−0.13
Road mileage	0.35	−0.22	0.16	0.06	−0.27	−0.07	0.00	0.21	0.25	−0.03
Av. value per acre farmland	0.61	−0.35	−0.22	−0.12	−0.26	0.00	−0.04	0.62	0.13	−0.27
Total value farm prod. sold	0.41	−0.22	0.07	−0.05	0.06	−0.05	−0.36	0.21	0.01	−0.09
Degrees north	−0.44	0.37	0.46	0.34	−0.08	−0.04	0.30	−0.20	0.35	0.25
Per capita income	0.62	−0.48	−0.37	0.03	−0.14	−0.15	−0.20	0.35	−0.10	−0.18
% under $3,000	−0.73	0.66	0.34	−0.16	0.44	0.17	−0.02	−0.36	0.06	0.33
% population increase	0.66	−0.53	−0.33	−0.04	−0.41	−0.08	0.08	0.37	−0.06	−0.37
% 65 and over	0.15	−0.09	−0.21	−0.34	0.10	0.09	−0.32	0.23	0.08	−0.26
% urban	1.00	−0.59	−0.25	0.02	−0.47	−0.11	−0.05	0.54	0.06	−0.26
% rural farm		1.00	0.34	−0.17	0.63	−0.16	−0.05	−0.27	0.01	0.16
Physical location			1.00	−0.08	0.24	−0.18	0.24	−0.19	0.22	0.19
% manufacturing				1.00	−0.35	−0.18	−0.15	0.02	−0.02	0.04
% agriculture					1.00	−0.20	−0.42	−0.33	−0.21	0.20
% mining and fishing						1.00	0.08	−0.13	0.05	−0.04
% serv., prof., govt.							1.00	−0.03	0.26	−0.06
Population density								1.00	0.56	−0.19
Road mileage per sq. mile									1.00	0.05
% nonwhite										1.00

(sixty-seven) in the state of Florida in 1961. The first half of the table *only* is presented, as the second half is symmetrical with the first half. A grouping of these variables can be obtained by using a form of *linkage analysis* developed by McQuitty (1957) that provides a technique for determining "typal" structures. A typal structure is one in which every member of a type is more like some other member of that type than it is to any member of any other type.

The method of analysis, as explained by McQuitty, can be outlined as follows:

1 Underline the highest *positive* correlation coefficient in each column of the correlation coefficient matrix (Table 4-3).

2 Select the highest entry in the matrix. In this case the value is .99 and indicates that the first *reciprocal relation* is between Total population and Total civilian production income (TCPI). These, therefore, constitute the first two members of the first type.

3 By reading across the Total population row and the Total civilian production income row of Table 4-3, select those variables that are highest correlated with them (they are underlined). Thus, AVF (Average value per acre of farmland) and PD (Population density) are highest correlated with Total population, and no variable (other than Total population) is highest correlated with TCPI (Total civilian production income). These relations can be called *first relations*.

4 For all first relations, select *second relations*, if they exist, in a manner similar to that described in step 3 above. For rows Average value per acre of farmland and Population density an underlined correlation coefficient will identify those variables that are highest correlated with them. Thus in Table 4-3 it can be seen that RMD (Road mileage density) and Percentage of population aged sixty-five and over (% 65+) are highest correlated with Population density (PD).

5 In an analogous fashion, third- and fourth-order relations can be determined. There are none of these in this first type.

6 Select a second reciprocal relation excluding all those variables classified in the first type, and repeat the above steps until all the variables are grouped into typal relations.

The McQuitty linkage analysis reveals a structure of types which are diagrammatically represented in Fig. 4-13. Although the diagrammatic representation seems to suggest four exclusive groups, it is well to remember that these are only highest relations. Many of the variables are also intercorrelated with others in other typal groups, and so an impression of exclusiveness is misleading.

The first typal group concerns the *impact of numbers of people*. Counties with large numbers of people have a high civilian production income and generally higher population densities, which in turn generate high road mileage

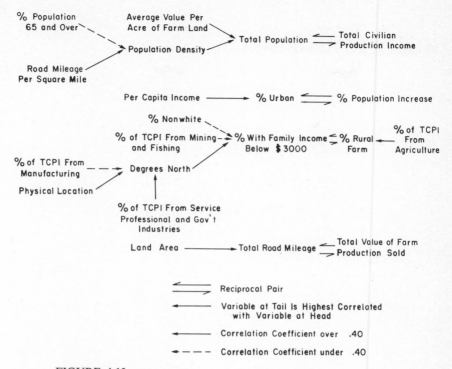

FIGURE 4-13
McQuitty linkage analysis of the association between twenty-one socioeconomic-geographic variables pertaining to the counties of Florida in 1960.

densities and increase the value of land. Also, in Florida, high road mileage densities include large groups of aged persons. The second typal group concerns *urban affluence and growth*. The most urbanized counties had the highest population growth rate between 1940 and 1960, and the highest per capita incomes. The third typal grouping revolves around counties exhibiting *rural deficiency*, and the location of these counties within the state. The fourth typal grouping concerns factors related to the sheer *physical size* of the counties.

Regression and correlation analysis can therefore lead the geographer into some fruitful areas of descriptive and deductive enquiry. In fact, the methods discussed in this chapter developed from the cornerstone of much quantitative analysis that at times appears extremely complex. It is the task of the ensuing chapter to indicate how some more complex techniques are merely extensions of the simple methods and procedures discussed thus far.

5

MULTIPLE REGRESSION

Thus far the discussion has concerned the relation between two variables, and the graph of this relation can be expressed in two dimensions with the variable on the ordinate being termed the dependent variable and the variable on the abscissa being termed the independent variable. Multiple regression concerns the association of two or more independent variables (taken together) with one dependent variable (Mills, 1955, pp. 612–656; Blalock, 1960, pp. 326–359). Therefore, in the case of two independent variables and one dependent variable, the graph is in three dimensions and the line of best fit in a two-dimensional case becomes a surface of best fit in the three-dimensional case. With more than two independent variables, the visual cognition of such a relation becomes impossible because the analysis is dealing with four, five, and so on, dimensions. The mathematics of the situation, therefore, becomes more and more complex and requires the use of more complex algebra. However, it is quite simple to understand what a multiple-regression model indicates, and there are many instances of the use of this type of model in human geography (Thomas, 1960; Taaffe, Morrill, and Gould, 1963; Roberts and Rumage, 1965; Cox, 1968; Laber, 1969; Massam, 1971; Brown, 1971).

THE MODEL

It will be recalled that the simple regression equation discussed in the previous section was presented in the form

$$Y_i = a + bX_i + e_i$$

where Y and X are variables; a is the Y intercept; b the regression coefficient of Y on X, namely, b_{YX}; and e_i the errors. The multiple-regression equation is a simple extension of this simple regression by adding more independent variables.

$$Y_i = a + b_{y1.2,3,\ldots,m}X_{1i} + b_{Y2.1,3,\ldots,m}X_{2i}$$
$$+ b_{Y3.1,2,\ldots,m}X_{3i} + \cdots + b_{Ym.1,2,3,\ldots,m-1}X_{mi} + e_i \qquad (5\text{-}1)$$

where a is the constant, or Y intercept, and the b's are the regression coefficients. In this equation there is one dependent variable and m independent variables. The regression coefficients indicate the unit change in Y associated with a unit change in X, *all other independent variables included in the analysis being held constant*. This is implied by the subscripts associated with each regression coefficient, for $b_{Y2.1,3,\ldots,m}$ means the slope between Y and X_2 with $X_1, X_3, \ldots,$ X_m being held constant. For the sake of simplicity this proliferation of subscripts is usually simplified to be

$$Y = a + b_1X_1 + b_2X_2 + b_3X_3 + \cdots + b_mX_m + e \qquad (5\text{-}2)$$

The independent variables are, as the name suggests, supposed to be independent one of the other, though perfect independence is rarely achieved in human geography. If there is a great deal of intercorrelation between two "independent" variables, then both are in a sense measuring the same thing, and thus the regression coefficients express relations that are held in common by both variables (Riddell, 1970b). The strength of the relation between the dependent and independent variables taken together can be indicated by a multiple regression correlation coefficient R and a multiple coefficient of determination, R^2.

An Example of the Use of a Multiple-Regression Model

Before proceeding to a discussion of how multiple regression coefficients, correlation coefficients, standard errors, and so forth, are calculated, the reader may well be entertained by a short discussion and formulation of a "geographic" example that uses a multiple-regression equation. The example concerns a model that incorporates some factors associated with changes in the areal distribution of manufacturing in the United States between 1929 and 1954. The model is one of a number developed by Fuchs (1962a), who has analyzed changes in the location of manufacturing in the United States in many different ways. One of his chief concerns is to determine those factors associated with gains or losses in manufacturing at the state level of aggregation.

Definition of variables in the model Manufacturing gains or losses can be defined in a number of ways, of which value added and employment are the most commonly used measures. Both terms are self-explanatory: Value added refers to the amount by which a product has increased in value by the process of manufacture, and employment refers to the number of persons working in manufacturing industries. In this section manufacturing growth (or decline) between 1929 and 1954 will be measured by using value-added data for each state in the United States. Fuchs (1962*b*) uses the value-added data to calculate the gain or loss of manufacturing, G_s, in state s in the following manner:

$$G_s = Y_s - H_s$$

and

$$H_s = X_s \frac{Y}{X}$$

where X_s = value in the initial year (1929) of all industries in state s
Y_s = value in the final year (1954) of all industries in state s
X = value in the initial year (1929) of all industries in the United States
Y = value in the final year (1954) of all industries in the United States

Thus H_s is an abstract number representing the value in state s of manufacturing that would exist if the state had grown at the United States rate.

The difference between the actual value Y_s and H_s can then be converted into a percentage gain or loss, or *shift and share* index, by the following:

$$\frac{100(Y_s - H_s)}{Y_s \text{ or } H_s}$$

The larger of the two terms in the numerator is always used in the denominator, and as a consequence, the range is limited from $+100$ to -100 percent. Thus California exhibits a comparative gain in manufacturing of 46.2 percent, which means that manufacturing in California gained 46.2 percent more than it would have if it had grown at the same rate as the United States between 1929 and 1954. By contrast, Nebraska shows a loss in manufacturing of -14.9 percent, which means that the growth of manufacturing in Nebraska is 14.9 percent less than it would have been if it had grown at the same rate as manufacturing in the United States between 1929 and 1954. Fuchs further refines the percentage growth (or decline) index by adjusting it for the influence of the preexisting industrial structure in the state. Industries established during the past thirty years have been high-growth industries (for example, aircraft and electronics), whereas industries established prior to this time have grown comparatively slowly, and some have declined. Therefore in order to take into account the preexisting industrial structure of a state, the percentage change in manufactur-

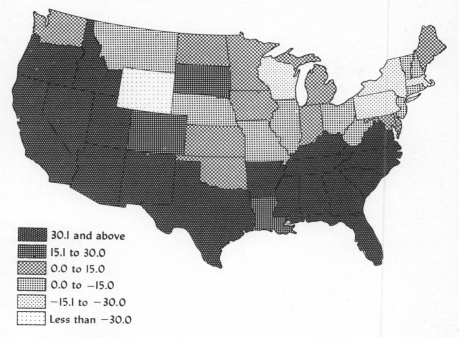

30.1 and above
15.1 to 30.0
0.0 to 15.0
0.0 to −15.0
−15.1 to −30.0
Less than −30.0

FIGURE 5-1
United States: comparative percentage gain or loss in manufacturing (as calculated from value-added data adjusted for historical structure), by state, 1929 to 1954. (*From: Fuchs*, 1962*a, pp.* 64–65.)

ing is adjusted by weighting G'_s. As a result, California exhibits a gain in manufacturing of 38.8 percent instead of 46.2 percent, and Nebraska a comparative loss of 2.5 percent instead of 14.9 percent. These adjusted indices indicate that the greatest comparative increases in manufacturing between 1929 and 1954 were recorded in the Western, Southwestern, and Southern states of the United States, and the greatest losses in southern New England and New York State (Fig. 5-1).

According to Fuchs, changes in the location of manufacturing between 1929 and 1954 may be associated with three main factors. One of these is unionization, for it is often thought that manufacturers seek to avoid the rules and regulations adopted by states where labor unions have been a powerful political force for a lengthy period. This variable can be measured for a convenient period (1939) by calculating the degree of unionization in state s, namely, U_s, as

$$U_s = \frac{L_s}{M_s}$$

where $M_s = \sum_{i=1}^{m} W_{is}R_i$

L_s = actual union membership of state s in 1939

W_{is} = number of workers in the ith industry group in state s, there being m industrial groupings

R_i = national (United States) rate of union membership for the ith industrial group

Therefore, if U_s is positive, the state has a relatively higher degree of unionization than it would have if it conformed to the United States average. The hypothesis is that as the degree of unionization increases in a state, the growth of manufacturing decreases.

The second factor that Fuchs speculates may well be associated with changes in the spatial distribution of manufacturing is climate. This is because the new industries, particularly those dealing with aircraft, favor a mild climate with clear skies where round-the-year outdoor testing is possible. Also, people tend to prefer to live in mild climates, and so any trend by industry in this direction is encouraged by the ready mobility of workers. This variable can be, quantified by defining the climate of state s, C_s, as

$$C_s = \frac{\sum_{i=1}^{12} |T_i - 65°F|_i}{12}$$

where T_i is the mean monthly temperature (in degrees Fahrenheit) for the largest city in state s. Signs are ignored; therefore the hypothesis is that the growth of manufacturing should decrease as the average monthly temperature deviations increase.

Space is the third factor that Fuchs associates with spatial variations in manufacturing growth. The widespread use of the automobile has increased the radius of the plant "laborshed," for workers are now often prepared to commute as much as eighty miles in a day. Thus areas with low population densities, low land costs, and uncongested roads have become relatively important areas for plant location. This variable can be quantified by using population per square mile for each state in 1940, P_s, as an operational definition of the amount of space available. Those states with low population densities are therefore defined as those with large amounts of space available; so the hypothesis is that as population densities of states increase, manufacturing growth decreases.

The multiple-regression analysis of the hypotheses   The hypotheses can be examined jointly in a multiple-regression equation of the form

$$G'_s = a + b_1 U_s + b_2 C_s + b_3 P_s + e_s \tag{5-3}$$

The degree of independence among the independent variables can be examined by calculating the matrix of simple correlation coefficients between all possible combinations of pairs of the three variables. From Table 5-1 it will be noticed that the intercorrelation between the independent variables is negligible, and as a consequence it can be assumed that they are truly independent. It must be noted, however, that such low intercorrelations as these among the independent variables is a rarity in most geographical studies.

The parameters for Eq. (5-3) are estimated by Fuchs to be

$$G'_s = 96.61 - .2343U_s - 3.258C_s - .095P_s$$

The multiple correlation coefficient R, which measures the degree of association between the three independent variables and the dependent variable, has a value of .804. Thus the three independent variables together "explain" (R^2), 64 percent of the variation in the dependent variable. Furthermore, the signs of the regression coefficients are as hypothesized. A high rate of manufacturing growth in a state between 1929 and 1954 *is* associated with a low degree of unionization, a mild climate, and a low population density. However, these should not necessarily be interpreted as causal factors.

The Normal Equations

The methods used to find the parameters and coefficients of the multiple-regression model are analogous to those used for simple regression and correlation. The model for which we need to make these estimates can be stated in abstract form as follows:

$$Y = a + b_1X_1 + b_2X_2 + b_3X_3 \tag{5-4}$$

The first task is to derive the normal equations required for solving the constants in Eq. (5-4). It will be recalled that for the equation

$$Y = a + bX$$

Table 5-1   MATRIX OF SIMPLE COR-
RELATION COEFFICIENTS
FOR THE THREE INDE-
PENDENT VARIABLES,
UNIONIZATION, CLIMATE,
AND   POPULATION
DENSITY

	U_s	C_s	P_s
U_s	1.00	.08	.00
C_s	.08	1.00	.00
P_s	.00	.00	1.00

the normal equations, with subscripts deleted for clarification purposes, are

$$\sum Y = Na + b \sum X \tag{4-2}$$

$$\sum XY = a \sum X + b \sum X^2 \tag{4-3}$$

Therefore, by extension, the normal equations for Eq. (5-4) are

$$\sum Y = Na + b_1 \sum X_1 + b_2 \sum X_2 + b_3 \sum X_3 \tag{5-5}$$

$$\sum X_1 Y = a \sum X_1 + b_1 \sum X_1 X_1 + b_2 \sum X_1 X_2 + b_3 \sum X_1 X_3 \tag{5-6}$$

$$\sum X_2 Y = a \sum X_2 + b_2 \sum X_2 X_1 + b_2 \sum X_2 X_2 + b_3 \sum X_2 X_3 \tag{5-7}$$

$$\sum X_3 Y = a \sum X_3 + b_3 \sum X_3 X_1 + b_2 \sum X_3 X_2 + b_3 \sum X_3 X_3 \tag{5-8}$$

The normal equations can be reduced in number and the a parameter removed by expressing the new data for each variable in terms of *deviations from the mean.* It will be recalled from Chap. 2 that the sum of the deviations from the mean, or the first moment about the mean, is zero. Thus, if the data are in deviation form, Eq. (5-5) reduces to zero, and $a \sum X_1$, $a \sum X_2$, and $a \sum X_3$ also reduce to zero. Therefore, instead of four equations with four unknowns, we now have three equations with three unknowns

$$\sum x_1 y = b_1 \sum x_1 x_1 + b_2 \sum x_1 x_2 + b_3 \sum x_1 x_3 \tag{5-9}$$

$$\sum x_2 y = b_1 \sum x_2 x_1 + b_2 \sum x_2 x_2 + b_3 \sum x_2 x_3 \tag{5-10}$$

$$\sum x_3 y = b_1 \sum x_3 x_1 + b_2 \sum x_3 x_2 + b_3 \sum x_3 x_3 \tag{5-11}$$

with the deviation data being indicated by the lower-case letters for the variables. More important than the reduction in number of the equations and unknowns is the fact that the deviation matrix of the independent variables is square and symmetrical.

Note concerning the form of matrices The term matrix has crept into the discussion in a number of sections previously because it is a useful framework for defining complex concepts (Golant, 1971), but it is in this chapter that our use of *matrix algebra* begins. The minimum basic amount of matrix algebra will be explained at each stage in the discussion where it is deemed necessary, so that the reader comprehends the necessity for it. A matrix is a rectangular array of numbers in rows and columns, which can be expressed in general as follows:

$$\begin{bmatrix} a_{11} & a_{12} & a_{13} & \cdots & a_{1m} \\ a_{21} & a_{22} & a_{23} & \cdots & a_{2m} \\ a_{31} & a_{32} & a_{33} & \cdots & a_{3m} \\ \cdots & \cdots & \cdots & \cdots & \cdots \\ a_{n1} & a_{n2} & a_{n3} & \cdots & a_{nm} \end{bmatrix}$$

Table 5-2 EXPORTS FROM ITALY TO ITS MAJOR TRADING PARTNERS IN 1963, WITH THE PER CAPITA INCOME (IN U.S. DOLLARS) AND TOTAL NATIONAL INCOME (IN BILLIONS OF DOLLARS) FOR EACH TRADING PARTNER, AND THE DISTANCE OF EACH TRADING PARTNER FROM ITALY (IN MILES); ALL DATA LOGARITHMICALLY TRANSFORMED

Country	Exports	Per capita income	Total national income	Distance
1	2.1173	3.4711	3.5320	2.8041
2	3.0689	3.7301	4.0679	3.8417
3	2.5752	4.1567	4.1948	4.0059
4	3.1206	3.9130	3.7686	2.6803
5	3.2627	4.0752	4.0582	2.9415
6	2.6263	3.4735	4.3629	3.7569
7	2.6911	4.2148	4.4774	3.6208
8	2.2405	3.8550	3.7700	3.7016
9	2.2878	3.1565	5.0257	3.7048
10	1.6435	2.7126	2.8887	3.5051
11	2.7193	4.1296	3.8010	2.9768
12	2.3711	4.0198	3.6770	3.3128
13	3.7218	4.1015	4.7813	2.8382
14	2.1106	3.9345	4.1386	2.8751
15	3.9579	4.1136	4.8573	2.8388
16	2.2201	3.3560	3.2217	3.4200
17	2.8096	3.6341	3.5635	2.8235
18	2.4265	3.8021	3.8059	2.6937
19	2.4900	2.8633	4.5263	3.5645
20	2.0755	2.7980	3.7939	3.8267
21	2.3284	3.2140	3.5599	3.5416
22	1.9191	3.3204	3.1593	3.2610
23	2.6232	3.7089	4.6908	3.7878
24	2.5051	3.6828	2.9380	3.1339
25	2.6857	3.3023	2.4065	2.8189
26	2.4683	3.5586	4.1431	3.8028
27	2.3579	3.1232	3.2302	3.0719
28	2.2672	3.9912	4.0692	2.9025
29	1.8513	4.1753	3.5798	4.0607
30	2.4728	4.0714	3.6357	3.0980
31	2.1106	2.9036	3.8974	3.5179
32	2.5315	3.7779	4.2649	2.9112
33	2.4281	3.4180	3.4118	3.0648
34	2.0792	3.2225	2.9385	3.1477
35	2.9201	3.6103	4.1027	2.9263
36	2.1959	2.9624	3.0708	3.3226
37	3.0273	4.2567	4.1377	3.0864
38	3.5335	4.2113	3.9754	2.6474
39	2.3118	3.2665	2.9180	2.5478
40	2.5855	3.3363	3.8170	2.5353
41	2.7973	3.1617	3.6072	3.1209
42	2.7284	3.6650	3.8974	3.7202
43	3.4344	4.1000	4.8312	2.9581
44	3.6798	4.3991	5.6764	3.6315
45	1.9031	3.8782	3.2858	3.7839
46	3.0607	3.9321	5.2838	3.1735
47	2.5821	3.8919	3.8028	3.7160
Mean	2.5939	3.6522	3.8860	3.2558

where there are n rows and m columns. For example, in Table 5-2, there are forty-seven countries with which Italy had some significant trade in 1963, so $n = 47$, and four variables, so $m = 4$. The above matrix can be written in more general form as

$$\underset{n \times m}{\mathbf{A}} = \underset{n \times m}{[a_{ij}]} \qquad \begin{aligned} i &= 1, 2, 3, \ldots, n \\ j &= 1, 2, 3, \ldots, m \end{aligned}$$

where n and m are integers indicating the number of rows and columns, and the a_{ij}'s stand for real numbers. Thus, the *order*, or *dimension*, of a matrix is an order pair of integers, n, m, where the first number is the number of rows and the second number is the number of columns. Parenthetically, we may add that an *element* of a matrix is any particular a_{ij}, a *zero matrix* is a matrix in which every element is zero, and a *square matrix* is a matrix in which $n = m$.

A *vector* is a special case of a matrix, and there are two kinds of vectors. A *row vector* is an array of numbers written in one row, or a $1 \times m$ matrix.

$$\underset{1 \times 4}{[6 \quad 8 \quad 34 \quad 36]}$$

and a *column vector* is an array of numbers written in one column, or an $n \times 1$ matrix

$$\underset{3 \times 1}{\begin{bmatrix} 36 \\ 22 \\ 35 \end{bmatrix}}$$

A *scalar* is a 1×1 matrix, or a single number,

$$\underset{1 \times 1}{\mathbf{A}} = [36]$$

It is so called because in transformations of numbers scales can be changed by multiplying by a single number.

The transpose of a matrix $\mathbf{A}$ is a matrix $\mathbf{A}^T$ in which the rows and columns of $\mathbf{A}$ are interchanged. For example, if

$$\mathbf{X} = \underset{2 \times 3}{\begin{bmatrix} x_{11} & x_{12} & x_{13} \\ x_{21} & x_{22} & x_{23} \end{bmatrix}} \qquad \text{then} \qquad \mathbf{X}^T = \underset{3 \times 2}{\begin{bmatrix} x_{11} & x_{21} \\ x_{12} & x_{22} \\ x_{13} & x_{23} \end{bmatrix}}$$

and if

$$\mathbf{A} = \underset{1 \times 3}{[a_1 \quad a_2 \quad a_3]} \qquad \text{then} \qquad \mathbf{A}^T = \underset{3 \times 1}{\begin{bmatrix} a_1 \\ a_2 \\ a_3 \end{bmatrix}}$$

Or in general terms, if

$$\underset{n \times m}{\mathbf{M}} = [m_{ij}] \qquad \text{then} \qquad \underset{m \times n}{\mathbf{M}^T} = [M_{ji}]$$

Finally, in this note concerning the form of matrices, we shall define the *equality of matrices*. Two matrices are equal if they are of the same order and if each entry in one matrix is equal to the corresponding element in the second. Thus

$$\begin{bmatrix} 4 & 3 \\ 2 & 1 \end{bmatrix} = \begin{bmatrix} 4 & 3 \\ 2 & 1 \end{bmatrix} = \begin{bmatrix} 2+2 & \frac{6}{2} \\ \frac{8}{4} & 9-8 \end{bmatrix}$$

but

$$[0 \quad 0] \neq [0]$$

Thus $M \neq M^T$ except in the special case where $n = m$ and each element a_{ij} is equal to each element a_{ji}. In this special case the matrix is defined as a *square symmetrical matrix*.

Note concerning some matrix operations Most operations in matrix algebra are as simple as the definitions of the form of matrices outlined above. For example, if $A = a_{ij}$ and $B = b_{ij}$ and they have the same order, then $A + B$ is also a matrix, and is obtained by adding corresponding elements. Thus

$$\begin{bmatrix} 2 & 4 \\ 3 & 7 \\ 6 & 1 \end{bmatrix} + \begin{bmatrix} 4 & 5 \\ 2 & 0 \\ 6 & 7 \end{bmatrix} = \begin{bmatrix} 6 & 9 \\ 5 & 7 \\ 12 & 8 \end{bmatrix}$$

Subtraction follows the same element-by-element procedure. The basic restriction is, therefore, that matrices are *conformable* for addition and subtraction only if they are of the same order. Matrices can, as a consequence, be manipulated in a fashion similar to that in conventional algebra. For example, we wish to solve for the matrix X

$$X + B = A$$
$$X + B - B = A - B$$

but as $B - B$ is a zero matrix, then

$$X + 0 = A - B$$

and

$$X = A - B$$

Matrix multiplication is a little more complex than addition and subtraction. An ordered pair of matrices is conformable for multiplication only if the number of columns in the first matrix is equal to the number of rows in the second. Thus $\underset{2 \times 4 \quad 4 \times 3}{A \cdot B}$ is conformable for multiplication whereas $\underset{4 \times 3 \quad 2 \times 4}{B \cdot A}$ is *not* conformable for multiplication. The multiplication procedure is carried out by cross multiplying and summing each row vector of the first matrix of an ordered pair with each column vector of the second. For example,

$$\begin{bmatrix} 1 & 2 & 4 & 6 \\ 3 & 8 & 7 & 2 \end{bmatrix}_{2 \times 4} \cdot \begin{bmatrix} 5 & 9 & 7 \\ 6 & 7 & 5 \\ 2 & 8 & 2 \\ 1 & 3 & 4 \end{bmatrix}_{4 \times 3}$$

$$= \begin{bmatrix} (1 \times 5) + (2 \times 6) + (4 \times 2) + (6 \times 1) \\ (3 \times 5) + (8 \times 6) + (7 \times 2) + (2 \times 1) \end{bmatrix}$$

$$\begin{matrix} (1 \times 9) + (2 \times 7) + (4 \times 8) + (6 \times 3) \\ (3 \times 9) + (8 \times 7) + (7 \times 8) + (2 \times 3) \end{matrix}$$

$$\begin{matrix} (1 \times 7) + (2 \times 5) + (4 \times 2) + (6 \times 4) \\ (3 \times 7) + (8 \times 5) + (7 \times 2) + (2 \times 4) \end{matrix}_{2 \times 3}$$

$$= \begin{bmatrix} 5 + 12 + 8 + 6 & 9 + 14 + 32 + 18 & 7 + 10 + 8 + 24 \\ 15 + 48 + 14 + 2 & 27 + 56 + 56 + 6 & 21 + 40 + 14 + 8 \end{bmatrix}$$

$$= \begin{bmatrix} 31 & 73 & 49 \\ 79 & 145 & 83 \end{bmatrix}$$

or in general terms,

$$\begin{bmatrix} a_{11} & a_{12} & a_{13} & a_{14} \\ a_{21} & a_{22} & a_{23} & a_{24} \end{bmatrix} \cdot \begin{bmatrix} b_{11} & b_{12} & b_{13} \\ b_{21} & b_{22} & b_{23} \\ b_{31} & b_{32} & b_{33} \\ b_{41} & b_{42} & b_{43} \end{bmatrix}$$

$$= \begin{bmatrix} a_{11}b_{11} + a_{12}b_{21} + a_{13}b_{31} + a_{14}b_{41} \\ a_{21}b_{11} + a_{22}b_{21} + a_{23}b_{31} + a_{24}b_{41} \end{bmatrix}$$

$$\begin{matrix} a_{11}b_{12} + a_{12}b_{22} + a_{13}b_{32} + a_{14}b_{42} \\ a_{21}b_{12} + a_{22}b_{22} + a_{23}b_{32} + a_{24}b_{42} \end{matrix}$$

$$\begin{matrix} a_{11}b_{13} + a_{12}b_{23} + a_{13}b_{33} + a_{14}b_{43} \\ a_{21}b_{13} + a_{22}b_{23} + a_{23}b_{33} + a_{24}b_{43} \end{matrix}$$

Thus the product of $\mathbf{A} \cdot \mathbf{B}$ is a matrix $\mathbf{C}$ of order 2×3. Likewise, $\underset{n \times m}{\mathbf{M}} \cdot \underset{m \times p}{\mathbf{H}} = \underset{n \times p}{\mathbf{Y}}$. If $\mathbf{M}$ and $\mathbf{H}$ are vectors, $\mathbf{M} \cdot \mathbf{H}$, then the product $\mathbf{Y}$ is a scalar. If $\underset{1 \times 4}{\mathbf{M}}$ is a vector and $\underset{4 \times 1}{\mathbf{H}}$ a matrix, $\underset{1 \times 4}{\mathbf{M}} \cdot \underset{4 \times 2}{\mathbf{H}}$, then the product $\mathbf{Y}$ is a vector of order 1×2. But if $\mathbf{M}$ is a scalar and $\mathbf{H}$ a matrix, the product $\mathbf{Y}$ is the matrix $\mathbf{H}$ with each element multiplied by $\mathbf{M}$.

Inverse of a matrix   Finding the inverse of a matrix is one of the most important operations in matrix algebra. In this section we shall indicate the importance of the inverse, and then show why the concept is vital to an understanding of multiple-regression procedures. First, it is necessary to define an *identity matrix*. An identity matrix of order $n \times m$ is a square matrix I where

$$I = [e_{ij}]$$

and $e_{ij} = 1$ for all $i = j$, and zero for all $i \neq j$. In other words, an identity matrix is a square matrix consisting of unities for the elements on the diagonal and zeros for the elements off the diagonal. For example,

$$I = \begin{bmatrix} 1 & 0 & 0 & 0 \\ 0 & 1 & 0 & 0 \\ 0 & 0 & 1 & 0 \\ 0 & 0 & 0 & 1 \end{bmatrix}$$

If I is multiplied by a matrix A, the product is the matrix A.

$$\begin{bmatrix} 1 & 0 & 0 \\ 0 & 1 & 0 \\ 0 & 0 & 1 \end{bmatrix} \cdot \begin{bmatrix} a_{11} & a_{21} \\ a_{12} & a_{22} \\ a_{13} & a_{23} \end{bmatrix} = \begin{bmatrix} 1a_{11} + 0a_{12} + 0a_{13} & 1a_{21} + 0a_{22} + 0a_{23} \\ 0a_{11} + 1a_{12} + 0a_{13} & 0a_{21} + 1a_{22} + 0a_{23} \\ 0a_{11} + 0a_{12} + 1a_{13} & 0a_{21} + 0a_{22} + 1a_{23} \end{bmatrix}$$

If A were a square matrix, then it could be shown that $IA = AI = A$; for when an indentity matrix I is multiplied by a square matrix A of the same order as I, the order of multiplication does not matter. If the product of two matrices $A \cdot C = I$, then C is described as the *inverse* of A. The inverse of A is usually represented symbolically as A^{-1}; thus $A \cdot A^{-1} = I$.

Finding the Regression Coefficients of a Multiple-Regression Equation

At this juncture it is possible to indicate the relevancy of the matrix algebra definitions and operations described. The system of equations represented in Eqs. (5-9) to (5-11) can be presented in matrix algebra form as follows:

$$\underset{3 \times 1}{\begin{bmatrix} x_1 y \\ x_2 y \\ x_3 y \end{bmatrix}} = \underset{3 \times 3}{\begin{bmatrix} x_1 x_1 & x_1 x_2 & x_1 x_3 \\ x_2 x_1 & x_2 x_2 & x_2 x_3 \\ x_3 x_1 & x_3 x_2 & x_3 x_3 \end{bmatrix}} \cdot \underset{3 \times 1}{\begin{bmatrix} b_1 \\ b_2 \\ b_3 \end{bmatrix}}$$

or in more general form as

$$\underset{m \times 1}{G} = \underset{m \times m}{A} \cdot \underset{m \times 1}{B} \tag{5-12}$$

The square symmetric matrix A can be obtained by isolating the data for the *independent variables*, calculating the deviation scores for each variable to form a data matrix D, and premultiplying this matrix by its transpose. Thus, if there are n observations and m independent variables, the matrix A is $\underset{m \times m}{A} =$

$\mathbf{D}^T \cdot \mathbf{D}$. It is to be noted that the diagonals of the matrix $\mathbf{A}$ are the sum of
$$\underset{m \times n}{} \underset{n \times m}{}$$
squared deviations from the mean for each variable, that is, the total variation, and the elements off the diagonal indicate the total covariation between the independent variables. Thus if $\mathbf{A}$ is multiplied by the scalar $1/N - 1$ (N being the number of observations), the variances and covariances are obtained. It is for this reason that $\mathbf{A}$ is frequently referred to as a *variance-covariance* matrix. The matrix $\mathbf{G}$, which is the cross product of the deviation scores for the *dependent variable* with each independent variable, can be represented in matrix algebra form as $\underset{m \times 1}{\mathbf{G}} = \underset{m \times n}{\mathbf{D}^T} \cdot \underset{n \times 1}{\mathbf{Y}}$, where $\mathbf{G}$ is a vector indicating the covariation between the dependent and independent variables. These operations may seem difficult if undertaken manually, but in a computer they can be handled easily.

The task is, therefore, to solve for the one unknown matrix $\mathbf{B}$ in Eq. (5-12). The steps in the solution are as follows:

$$\underset{m \times 1}{\mathbf{G}} = \underset{m \times m}{\mathbf{A}} \cdot \underset{m \times 1}{\mathbf{B}}$$

so by premultiplying each side of the equation by the inverse of $\mathbf{A}$, we obtain

$$\underset{m \times m}{\mathbf{A}^{-1}} \cdot \underset{m \times 1}{\mathbf{G}} = \underset{m \times m}{\mathbf{A}^{-1}} \cdot \underset{m \times m}{\mathbf{A}} \cdot \underset{m \times 1}{\mathbf{B}}$$

and as $\mathbf{A}^{-1}\mathbf{A} = \mathbf{I}$,

$$\underset{m \times m}{\mathbf{A}^{-1}} \cdot \underset{m \times 1}{\mathbf{G}} = \underset{m \times m}{\mathbf{I}} \cdot \underset{m \times 1}{\mathbf{B}}$$

$$\underset{m \times m}{\mathbf{A}^{-1}} \cdot \underset{m \times 1}{\mathbf{G}} = \underset{m \times 1}{\mathbf{B}} \tag{5-13}$$

because the product of an identity matrix and a matrix is the matrix. Thus the matrix $\mathbf{B}$ can be found if it is possible to find the inverse of $\mathbf{A}$.

Finding the inverse of a matrix   There are many methods that can be used to find the inverse of a matrix (Hohn, 1964). Among these the most popular is the method of determinants, for it is the most accurate and easily programmable for computers. However, as this method requires a greater understanding of matrix algebra than that presumed possessed by the reader, we shall use a method which involves no greater use of mathematics. This method is known as synthetic elimination, for it uses the iterative replacement of each element of a matrix by the appropriate element of an identity matrix, with the methods used to achieve this being applied to an accompanying identity matrix of the same order.

Suppose we have a 3×3 square symmetric matrix $\mathbf{W}$. This can be written alongside an identity matrix

$$
\begin{array}{l}
\text{Row 1} \\
\text{Row 2} \\
\text{Row 3}
\end{array}
\left[
\begin{array}{ccc|ccc}
a & b & c & 1 & 0 & 0 \\
b & d & e & 0 & 1 & 0 \\
c & e & f & 0 & 0 & 1
\end{array}
\right]
$$

The *first step* is the transformation of the first column to 1, 0, and 0, with the operations performed on the matrix also being performed on the accompanying identity matrix. Thus if we (1) multiply row 1 by $1/a$, this reduces a to unity and creates row 4 below; (2) multiply row 4 by $-b$ and add the result to row 2, this reduces b to zero; and (3) multiply row 4 by $-c$ and add to row 3, this reduces c to zero. These operations yield

$$
\begin{array}{l}
\text{Row 4} \\
\\
\text{Row 5} \\
\\
\text{Row 6}
\end{array}
\left[
\begin{array}{ccc|ccc}
1 & \dfrac{b}{a} & \dfrac{c}{a} & \dfrac{1}{a} & 0 & 0 \\
0 & d + \dfrac{b}{a} - b & e + \dfrac{c}{a} - b & 0 + \dfrac{1}{a} - b & 1 & 0 \\
0 & e + \dfrac{b}{a} - c & f + \dfrac{c}{a} - c & 0 + \dfrac{1}{a} - c & 0 & 1
\end{array}
\right]
$$

which can be expressed more conveniently as

$$
\begin{array}{l}
\text{Row 4} \\
\text{Row 5} \\
\text{Row 6}
\end{array}
\left[
\begin{array}{ccc|ccc}
1 & g & h & m & 0 & 0 \\
0 & i & j & n & 1 & 0 \\
0 & k & q & p & 0 & 1
\end{array}
\right]
$$

The *second step* is the transformation of column 2 to 0, 1, and 0. This may be achieved by (1) multiplying row 5 by $1/i$, which reduces i to unity and creates row 8 below; (2) multiplying row 8 by $-\dot{g}$ and adding the row to row 4, which reduces g to zero; and (3) multiplying row 8 by $-k$ and adding the row to row 6, which reduces k to zero. These operations yield

$$
\begin{array}{l}
\text{Row 7} \\
\\
\text{Row 8} \\
\\
\text{Row 9}
\end{array}
\left[
\begin{array}{ccc|ccc}
1 & 0 & h + \dfrac{j}{i} - g & m + \dfrac{n}{i} - g & 0 + \dfrac{1}{i} - g & 0 \\
0 & 1 & \dfrac{j}{i} & \dfrac{n}{i} & \dfrac{1}{i} & 0 \\
0 & 0 & q + \dfrac{j}{i} - k & p + \dfrac{n}{i} - k & 0 + \dfrac{1}{i} - k & 1
\end{array}
\right]
$$

which can be expressed more conveniently as

$$
\begin{array}{l}
\text{Row 7} \\
\text{Row 8} \\
\text{Row 9}
\end{array}
\left[
\begin{array}{ccc|ccc}
1 & 0 & r & u & v & 0 \\
0 & 1 & s & w & x & 0 \\
0 & 0 & t & y & z & 1
\end{array}
\right]
$$

The *third step* is the transformation of column 3 to 0, 0, and 1. This can be achieved by (1) multiplying row 9 by $1/t$, which reduces t to unity and creates row 12 below; (2) multiplying row 12 by $-r$ and adding the row to row 7, which reduces r to zero; and (3) multiplying row 12 by $-s$ and adding the row to row 8, which reduces s to zero. These operations yield

$$
\begin{array}{c}
\text{Row 10} \\[20pt]
\text{Row 11} \\[20pt]
\text{Row 12}
\end{array}
\left[
\begin{array}{ccc|ccc}
1 & 0 & 0 & u + \dfrac{y}{t} - r & v + \dfrac{z}{t} - r & 0 + \dfrac{1}{t} - r \\[12pt]
0 & 1 & 0 & w + \dfrac{y}{t} - s & x + \dfrac{z}{t} - s & 0 + \dfrac{1}{t} - s \\[12pt]
0 & 0 & 1 & \dfrac{y}{t} & \dfrac{z}{t} & \dfrac{1}{t}
\end{array}
\right]
$$

The matrix on the right-hand side is now the inverse of **W**, and as **W** is a square symmetric matrix, the inverse is also a square symmetric matrix. Thus a good check of the accuracy of the calculations is the symmetry of the elements.

For an example we shall invert a 3×3 matrix of very small numbers.

$$
\begin{array}{c}
\text{Row 1} \\
\text{Row 2} \\
\text{Row 3}
\end{array}
\left[
\begin{array}{ccc|ccc}
2 & -2 & 4 & 1 & 0 & 0 \\
-2 & 3 & 2 & 0 & 1 & 0 \\
4 & 2 & -1 & 0 & 0 & 1
\end{array}
\right]
$$

The first step is to multiply row 1 by $\frac{1}{2}$ to give row 4. Then multiply row 4 by 2 and add the row to row 2, and multiply row 4 by -4 and add to row 3. The result is

$$
\begin{array}{c}
\text{Row 4} \\
\text{Row 5} \\
\text{Row 6}
\end{array}
\left[
\begin{array}{ccc|ccc}
1 & -1 & 2 & \frac{1}{2} & 0 & 0 \\
0 & 1 & 6 & 1 & 1 & 0 \\
0 & 6 & -9 & -2 & 0 & 1
\end{array}
\right]
$$

The second step is to multiply row 5 by 1 to give row 8. Then multiply row 8 by 1 and add to row 4 to give row 7; and multiply row 8 by -6 and add to row 6 to give row 9. The result is

$$
\begin{array}{c}
\text{Row 7} \\
\text{Row 8} \\
\text{Row 9}
\end{array}
\left[
\begin{array}{ccc|ccc}
1 & 0 & 8 & \frac{3}{2} & 1 & 0 \\
0 & 1 & 6 & 1 & 1 & 0 \\
0 & 0 & -45 & -8 & -6 & 1
\end{array}
\right]
$$

The third step is to multiply row 9 by $-\frac{1}{45}$ to give row 12. Then multiply row 12 by -8 and add to row 7 to give row 10, and multiply row 12 by -6 and add to row 8 to give row 11. These operations result in

$$
\begin{array}{c}
\text{Row 10} \\
\text{Row 11} \\
\text{Row 12}
\end{array}
\left[
\begin{array}{ccc|ccc}
1 & 0 & 0 & \frac{7}{90} & -\frac{3}{45} & \frac{8}{45} \\[4pt]
0 & 1 & 0 & -\frac{3}{45} & \frac{9}{45} & \frac{6}{45} \\[4pt]
0 & 0 & 1 & \frac{8}{45} & \frac{6}{45} & -\frac{1}{45}
\end{array}
\right]
$$

and the inverse is symmetrical. It is to be noted that with larger numbers and larger matrices the calculations result in elements with many significant figures.

Thus the researcher should be careful to use computer programs in double precision, and should be careful to balance the data around the decimals to avoid loss of accuracy in overflows.

AN APPLICATION

This section is concerned with applying the methods and procedures detailed in the previous section to a set of data, and extending the discussion further by deriving the multiple correlation coefficient and testing the significance of the regression coefficients. The example concerns the development of a geographic model of international trade (Yeates, 1969), and here the research problem is to find some geographic factors that may explain the spatial variation in the volume of exports from Italy in 1963 (Fig. 5-2). One measure of particular importance as far as the magnitude of flows is concerned is the purchasing power of the countries that are buying goods from Italy. Other things being equal, it would be expected that those countries with the greatest total purchasing power would also be the most important trading partners. The purchasing power of a country can be measured in a number of ways; in this analysis, total national income (TNI) is used as an indicator of the disposable income available to a country.

This factor has to be counterbalanced, however, by a second, for some countries have a large purchasing power as units, but a low purchasing power with respect to the number of people involved, who are, in effect, the consumers. A good example of this is India, which has one of the largest TNIs in the world, but one of the lowest per capita incomes. Per capita income (PCI) must therefore be included as a second variable, for when other variables are held constant, Italy's exports should be greatest to the richest countries (as measured by PCI). Thus TNI and PCI are measures of purchasing characteristics of the trading partners.

The third variable concerns the relative location of these trading partners to Italy, for as the distance between Italy and a country increases, so should the transport costs which are usually reflected in the price of the goods sold. Although there has been some discussion of the way in which this "economic distance" should be measured (Beckerman, 1956), it appears that a convenient measure is the distance along the arc of a great circle connecting the capitals of the trading partners to the capital of Italy. Thus as the distance between Italy and its trading partners increases, the volume of exports to them should decrease, other things being equal.

The dependent variable is, therefore, the total volume of exports from Italy to a trading partner (in millions of U.S. dollars); and the dependent variables are the TNI of the countries concerned (in billions of U.S. dollars),

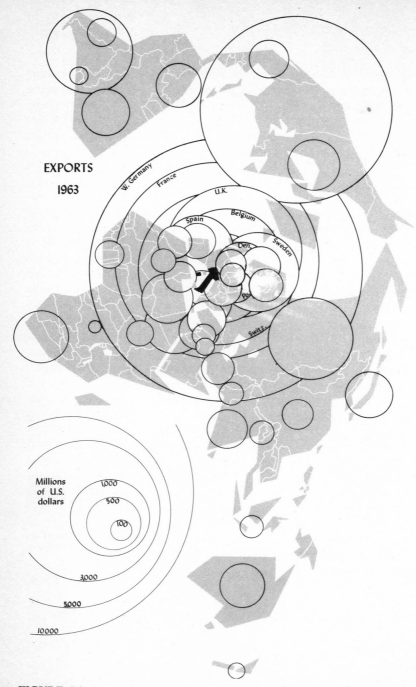

EXPORTS
1963

W. Germany
France
U.K.
Belgium
Spain
Den.
Sweden
Port.
Switz.

Millions
of U.S.
dollars

1,000
500
100
3,000
5,000
10000

FIGURE 5-2
Italy: exports, 1963. (*Data from* United Nations, *Yearbook of International Trade Statistics 1965*.)

the PCI of the countries concerned (in U.S. dollars), and the distance (in miles) along the arc of a great circle connecting Rome to the capital of each trading partner. As there were forty-seven countries importing significant quantities of goods from Italy in 1963, n equals 47. The raw data for each variable are positively skewed and have been logarithmically transformed to approximate normality, and the transformed data are listed in Table 5-2.

The Variance-Covariance Matrix

The model is, therefore, that log exports$_{Ii}$ = log a + b_1 log (PCI)$_i$ + b_2 log (TNI)$_i$ − b_3 log (distance)$_{Ii}$, where the subscripts refer to Italy I and its ith trading partner. The first step is the calculation of the matrix of deviations from the logarithmically transformed data in Table 5-2. To do this, the mean for each variable has to be calculated, and these are listed in Table 5-2. The deviation matrix $\mathbf{D}$ is of the same order, 47 × 4, as the raw data matrix. If this matrix is premultiplied by its transpose $\underset{4\times47\ \ 47\times4}{\mathbf{D}^T \cdot \mathbf{D}}$, a 4 × 4 symmetrical matrix is obtained which consists of elements of both the $\mathbf{A}$ matrix (inner products of the independent variables) and $\mathbf{G}$ vector (cross products of each independent variable with the dependent variable). These are indicated in Table 5-3, where the $\mathbf{A}$ matrix is enclosed by square brackets, and the $\mathbf{G}$ vector is the first row or the first column.

The matrix $\mathbf{D}^T\mathbf{D}$ can be used for many calculations; among them are the calculations of the variances and standard deviations for each variable, and the covariances can be used to calculate the simple correlation coefficients of each variable with every other. The product of $\mathbf{D}^T\mathbf{D}$ and the scalar $1/(47 − 1)$ is the variance-covariance matrix. The elements on the diagonal of the variance-covariance matrix are the variances of each variable, and, of course, the square roots of these are the standard deviations. The standard deviations are indicated

Table 5-3 MATRIX OF SQUARES AND CROSS PRODUCTS OF DEVIATIONS ABOUT THE MEAN $\mathbf{D}^T\mathbf{D}$: ITALY, 1963, TRADE DATA

	Exports	PCI	TNI	Distance
Exports	12.0717 (.51)	5.8747	9.4410	−3.1732
PCI	5.8747	9.0660 (.44)	6.3199	−.8349
TNI	9.4410	6.3199	20.5559 (.67)	2.1679
Distance	−3.1732	−.8349	2.1679	8.3274 (.43)

in parentheses in Table 5-3. Correlation coefficients are required as a test for the independence of the independent variables, for they should not be associated with each other. It will be recalled that the simple correlation coefficient can be estimated from

$$r_{yx} = \frac{\sum xy}{N s_x s_y}$$

The correlation between PCI and TNI is, therefore,

$$r = \frac{6.3199}{47(.44)(.67)} = .46$$

The correlation coefficient matrix for the independent variables is listed in Table 5-4, and the only noticeable correlation indicates that 21 percent of the variation in the PCI of countries is associated with variations in TNI. This variation in common can therefore be regarded as a relatively minor violation of the assumption.

The Calculation of the Parameters and Coefficients

The various steps in obtaining the inverse of A are detailed in Table 5-5. It is to be noted that the inverse in this case is symmetrical to five (corrected) significant figures, though occasionally in other instances slight asymmetry may occur in the fifth significant figure because of rounding errors. The inverse can then be used to calculate the regression coefficients as follows:

$$\underset{3 \times 3}{A^{-1}} \cdot \underset{3 \times 1}{G} = \underset{3 \times 1}{B} \tag{5-13}$$

$$\begin{bmatrix} .1461 & -.0478 & .0271 \\ -.0478 & .0656 & -.0219 \\ .0271 & -.0219 & .1285 \end{bmatrix} \cdot \begin{bmatrix} 5.8747 \\ 9.4410 \\ -3.1732 \end{bmatrix} = \begin{bmatrix} .3213 \\ .4085 \\ -.4552 \end{bmatrix}$$

Table 5-4   MATRIX OF SIMPLE CORRELATION COEFFICIENTS BETWEEN EACH VARIABLE IN THE ITALY, 1963, EXPORT MODEL; CORRELATION CO-EFFICIENT MATRIX FOR INDEPENDENT VARIABLES IS ENCLOSED BY SQUARE BRACKETS

	Exports	PCI	TNI	Distance
Exports	1.00	.56	.60	-.32
PCI	.56	1.00	.46	-.10
TNI	.60	.46	1.00	.16
Distance	-.32	-.10	.16	1.00

Thus the multiple regression coefficients have been calculated, and at the outset, it is interesting to note that the signs of the coefficients behave as predicted.

Having calculated the multiple regression coefficients, it is now possible to estimate the constant a. Recall the normal equation

$$Y = Na + b_1X_1 + b_2X_2 + b_3X_3 \qquad (5\text{-}5)$$

If Eq. (5-5) is divided by N, we obtain

$$\overline{Y} = a + b_1\overline{X}_1 + b_2\overline{X}_2 + b_3\overline{X}_3$$

and therefore,

$$a = \overline{Y} - b_1\overline{X}_1 - b_2\overline{X}_2 - b_3\overline{X}_3 \qquad (5\text{-}14)$$

Substituting the calculated means and estimated regression coefficients in Eq. (5-14), we obtain

$$
\begin{aligned}
a &= 2.5939 - (.3213)(3.6522) - (.4085)(3.8860) - (-.4552)(3.2558) \\
&= 1.3152
\end{aligned}
$$

The multiple regression equation with respect to the export of goods from Italy to its significant trading partners is, therefore,

$$
\begin{aligned}
\log \text{exports}_{Ii} \\
= 1.3152 &+ .3213 \log (\text{PCI})_i + .4085 \log (\text{TNI})_i \\
&- .4552 \log (\text{distance})_{Ii}
\end{aligned}
$$

In antilogarithmic form this equation can be written

$$\text{Exports}_{Ii} = 20.68 \, \frac{(\text{PCI})_i^{.3213}(\text{TNI})_i^{.4085}}{\text{distance}_{Ii}^{.4552}} \qquad (5\text{-}15)$$

Table 5-5   THE INVERSION OF THE MATRIX A, USING THE DIAGONAL METHOD

A			A^{-1}		
9.06576	6.31990	−.83485	1.0	.0	.0
6.31990	20.55591	2.16789	.0	1.0	.0
−.83485	2.16789	8.32742	.0	.0	1.0
1.0	.69710	−.09209	.11030	.0	.0
.0	16.15029	2.74987	−.69710	1.0	.0
.0	2.74987	8.25054	.09209	.0	1.0
1.0	.0	−.21078	.14039	−.04316	.0
.0	1.0	.17027	−.04316	.06192	.0
.0	.0	7.78233	.21078	−.17027	1.0
1.0	.0	.0	.14610	−.04778	.02708
.0	1.0	.0	−.04778	.06564	−.02188
.0	.0	1.0	.02708	−.02188	.12850

taking care to remember, of course, the different units and levels of measurement needed for the various variables. It will be noted that the empirical model in Eq. (5-15) resembles a generalized model of flows between one place and many other places (Olsson, 1965a, p. 45), and this concept will be discussed in greater detail in the next chapter.

The multiple regression coefficients can also be used to calculate the coefficient of multiple determination R^2. The coefficient of multiple determination indicates the proportion of the total variance in the dependent variable that is associated with (or explained by) the three independent variables. This is, of course, the ratio between the explained and the total variations, and one way of obtaining the explained variation is to calculate the residuals and from these to derive the unexplained variation, as discussed in Chap. 4. An alternative procedure is to estimate the explained variation directly from the product of the transpose of vector **B** multiplied by vector **G**, which is a scalar

$$\text{Explained variation} = \underset{1 \times m}{\mathbf{B}^T} \underset{m \times 1}{\mathbf{G}} \tag{5-16}$$

Substituting the data from the Italy export trade example in Eq. (5-16)

$$\text{Explained variation} = [.3213 \quad .4085 \quad -.4552] \begin{bmatrix} 5.8747 \\ 9.4410 \\ -3.1732 \end{bmatrix}$$

$$= 7.1885$$

Thus,

$$R^2 = \frac{7.1885}{12.0717} \times 100 = 59.55 \text{ percent}$$

This figure indicates that nearly 60 percent of the spatial variation in Italy's export trade is associated with factors pertaining to the economic wealth of its trading partners and distance. The multiple coefficient of correlation R is, therefore, .77.

The value of R^2 is, however, influenced by the relation between the number of observations and the number of constants, $a, b_1, b_2, \ldots$. If the number of constants equals the number of observations, R^2 will have a value of 1. When the number of observations is not large, it is advisable to apply a correction for this bias (Mills, 1955, pp. 626–627).

$$\text{Corrected } R^2 = 1 - (1 - R^2) \frac{N-1}{N-M} \tag{5-17}$$

where N is the number of observations, and M the number of constants. Applying this correction factor yields

$$\text{Corrected } R^2 = 1 - \left[(1 - .5955)\frac{47 - 1}{47 - 4}\right]$$

$$= .5673$$

Thus the corrected R is .75.

Testing the Significance of the Multiple Regression Coefficients

It will be recalled that our hypotheses are that, other things being equal, the volume of exports from Italy to its trading partners is greater to the wealthier countries (as measured by TNI and PCI) and less to those farthest away. Thus, whereas the null hypotheses are that

$$H_0: \quad \begin{aligned} b_1 &= \beta_1 & \beta_1 &= 0 \\ b_2 &= \beta_2 & \beta_2 &= 0 \\ b_3 &= \beta_3 & \beta_3 &= 0 \end{aligned}$$

the research hypotheses are that

$$H_1: \quad \begin{aligned} b_1 &> 0 \\ b_2 &> 0 \\ b_3 &< 0 \end{aligned}$$

all which require one-tailed tests. It could be argued that no tests of significance are required, for all Italy's chief trading partners have been included, and that therefore, the regression coefficients are the population coefficients. On the other hand, it could also be argued that the data pertain to 1963 only, and that this is, in effect, a sample year. In this particular case the latter argument will be accepted, and the hypotheses will be tested at the 95 percent confidence level.

The procedure and assumptions are similar to those already explained in Chap. 4 for testing the significance of simple regression coefficients. The first step is to calculate the error variance of the regression equation, which, it will be recalled, is the mean unexplained variation. Thus

$$s^2_{Y.X_{1,2,\dots,n}} = \frac{\text{total unexplained variation}}{N - M} \tag{5-18}$$

where N and M have been defined previously. Substituting in the Italy trade example,

$$s^2_{Y.X_{1,2,3}} = \frac{12.0717 - 7.1889}{47 - 4} = .1136$$

The standard error of estimate, $s_{Y.X_{1,2,3}}$, is, therefore, .337.

The error variance can be used to estimate the standard error of each regression coefficient (s_{b_j}) as follows:

$$s_{b_j} = \sqrt{s^2_{Y.X_{1,2,3,\ldots,n}}c_{ij}}$$
(5-19)

where $i = j$ for each ith regression coefficient, and c_{ij} is the appropriate element on the diagonal of the inverse. For b_1, b_2, and b_3 the standard errors of estimate are

$$s_{b_1} = \sqrt{.1136(.1461)} = .1288 \quad \text{where } \beta_1 = 0$$

$$s_{b_2} = \sqrt{.1136(.0656)} = .0863 \quad \text{where } \beta_2 = 0$$

$$s_{b_3} = \sqrt{.1136(.1285)} = .1208 \quad \text{where } \beta_3 = 0$$

The standard errors of estimate of the regression coefficients are then used in exactly the same way as has been described in Chap. 4 to calculate the values of t.

$$t_1 = \frac{b_1 - \beta_1}{s_{b_1}} = \frac{.3213}{.1288} = 2.495$$

$$t_2 = \frac{b_2 - \beta_2}{s_{b_2}} = \frac{.4085}{.0863} = 4.733$$

$$t_3 = \frac{b_3 - \beta_3}{s_{b_3}} = \frac{-.4552}{.1208} = -3.768$$

The analysis involves a one-tailed test at the 95 percent confidence level with $N - (M + 1)$ degrees of freedom, for 1 degree of freedom is lost for each constant that has been estimated, and 1 degree of freedom is lost in the calculation of the standard error of estimate of the regression coefficients. From Table 3-3 it can be determined that the critical value of t for t_1 and t_2 is 1.64, and for t_3 is -1.64. As each value exceeds its respective critical value, the null hypothesis is rejected and the research hypothesis can be inferred at the 95 percent confidence level.

The Relative Importance of Each Variable

In many cases, the researcher is concerned with determining the relative importance of the different variables. A number of strategies can be used to answer this question, the most common being "stepwise" multiple regression, the calculation of partial correlations, and the standardizing of the regression coefficients. A stepwise multiple regression is really a search procedure, for the technique enters each variable, one at a time, into the regression equation in the order of its contribution to the total variance, the greatest contributor being entered first. Thus, out of any number of independent variables, the stepwise technique "searches out" the greatest contributors to the total variance and effectively rank-orders them. This is a useful technique for selecting the "best" regression equation (Draper and Smith, 1966, chap. 6), but it is only acceptable when a variety of models are theoretically tenable for a particular problem.

Partial correlations indicate the intercorrelation of any one independent variable with the dependent variable, with all the other independent variables held constant. Zero-order correlation coefficients indicate the simple correlation between two variables, for example r_{YX}, and these have been discussed previously. First-order correlation between two variables with a third held constant, for example $r_{YX_1.X_2}$, means the correlation between Y and X_1 with X_2 held constant. Second-order correlation coefficients indicate the correlation between two variables with two others held constant; for example, $r_{YX_2.X_1,X_3}$ indicates the partial correlation between Y and X_2 with X_1 and X_3 held constant. Each successive order requires the computation of the partials of the next lowest order (Mills, 1955, pp. 631–643), and as a consequence it is rather a laborious procedure to follow when an easier alternative strategy is at hand.

A reasonably easy method for comparing the relative importance of the different variables is to use standardized regression coefficients, stb_j. Regression coefficients can be regarded as weights, but normally they do not indicate the relative importance of independent variables with respect to the dependent variable because each is expressed in different types of measures and different magnitudes of numbers. For example, in the present situation CPI is expressed in U.S. dollars, TNI in billions of U.S. dollars, and distance in miles. The relative importance of each of the independent variables can, however, be estimated by "standardizing" the data, that is, presenting each item of the data as a standard score, a procedure which has been explained in Chap. 2. If the data are not already standardized, the regression coefficients themselves can be standardized by multiplying each coefficient by the ratio between the standard deviation of the variable to which the regression coefficient pertains and the standard deviation of the dependent variable.

$$stb_j = b_j \frac{s_j}{s_y} \qquad (5\text{-}20)$$

Substituting in Eq. (5-20),

$$stb_1 = .3213 \frac{.44}{.51} = .2772$$
$$stb_2 = .4085 \frac{.67}{.51} = .5366$$
$$stb_3 = -.4552 \frac{.43}{.51} = -.3838$$

Thus it would appear that the volume of exports from Italy to a trading partner is related primarily to the sheer size of the country concerned as measured by its TNI, secondarily to the distance of that country from Italy, and thirdly to the per capita wealth of the trading partner. It is to be noted that this ordering of standardized regression coefficients (with the effect of the other variables held constant) is *not* reflected by the zero-order simple correction coefficients between the dependent and independent variables, which are listed in Table 5-4.

If the same standardization procedure is applied to the regression coefficients in Fuchs' model concerning industrial location discussed earlier in this chapter, the results are

$$G'_s = -.336U_s - .500C_s - .502P_s$$

As the standardized regression coefficients present the change in standard score of G'_s with a unit standard score change in one independent variable, the other two being held constant, it is apparent that unionization is the least important of the three independent variables. Climate and space considerations appear to be 40 percent more important than unionization.

The multiple-regression model is, therefore, quite easy to understand and has many uses in human geography. In fact, it is probably the most used quantitative technique in the whole of the social sciences and, therefore, occupies a central position in any exposition of the use of quantitative techniques in geographic research. In the ensuing chapter the discussion will focus upon a number of ways in which the application of the multiple-regression model may be extended and applied to the analysis of surfaces and regions. In this spatial context it will be necessary to discuss analysis of variance and its application in testing the significance of the explanatory contribution of independent variables.

6

SURFACES AND REGIONS
AND THE ANALYSIS OF VARIANCE

Perhaps one of the oldest and most easily understood definitions of geography is whereas "History is about chaps, Geography is about maps." McNee (1967) places this definition in perspective when he comments that map lore is, perhaps, the oldest of geographical values. Maps have more than an aesthetic value, however, for they are tools of research and a means of communication. Hence, it is not surprising that a considerable proportion of the total quantitative effort in geography has been directed toward providing a more rigorous framework for map analysis and map comparison than the traditional methods of subjective visual inspection and interpretation. The application of simple regression and correlation to map comparison has been described previously, and in this chapter we are concerned with extending this further with a discussion of the use of multiple-regression techniques in the determination of the form of surfaces, the correlation between surfaces, and the existence of regions. Also, an additional test of significance, known as "analysis of variance," is introduced as a method for estimating the significance of a particular surface or region.

All data that are distributed areally in two-dimensional space describe a surface. Thus the geographer is interested not only in the value of each item of the data, but in the location of the point to which those data refer relative to all other points on the map (Neft, 1966, p. 127). In fact, if the relative location of a point on a map to all other points is a primary concern of analysis, such as in marketing geography and industrial location analysis, it is advisable that the data used reflect not only the absolute value at a point but its value relative to its location vis-à-vis all other points. A useful method that can be used to incorporate relative location is the potential model which is derived from the gravity model.

GRAVITY AND POTENTIAL MODELS

The gravity model has its roots in the "least effort" principles of Zipf (1949) and the social physics concept of Stewart (1942). The origins of the Zipf approach is in the work of Ravenstein (1885, 1889), who observed, from an analysis of migration data, that a population center attracted migrants from other centers in direct proportion to the population of the sending center, and inversely proportional to the distance between the sending center and the receiving center. This principle can be represented as

$$M_R = \frac{P_S}{D_{RS}} \tag{6-1}$$

where M_R = number of migrants at the receiving center
$\quad\quad P_S$ = population of the sending center
$\quad\quad D_{RS}$ = distance between the receiving and sending centers

Zipf hypothesizes that Ravenstein's migration principle is but a corollary of a more general statement that the expected interaction I between any two settlements A and B is directly proportional to the product of the populations of A and B, and inversely proportional to the shortest work distance between the two places. Thus

$$I_{AB} = \frac{P_A P_B}{D_{AB}} \tag{6-2}$$

Zipf examines this general statement for data relating to the movement of goods, the flow of bus, railway, and airline passengers, and the number of telephone calls between pairs of cities in the United States, and concludes that there is a close relation between expected and actual interaction.

   In the early 1940s, Stewart (1942) developed a set of models for use in demography which are analogous to laws in Newtonian physics (Wilson, 1969, p. 231). These physical laws pertain to masses, and as a consequence, the demographic analogs derived from them pertain only to groups or masses. The first analog is derived from Newton's law of gravitational force,

$$F_{ij} = G \frac{P_i P_j}{d_{ij}^2} \tag{6-3}$$

where F_{ij} is the demographic force between i and j, and G is a constant corresponding to the gravitational constant. The second analog is derived from Newton's law of gravitational energy and is called "demographic energy."

$$E_{ij} = G \frac{P_i P_j}{d_{ij}} \tag{6-4}$$

where E_{ij} is the demographic energy between i and j. It is to be noted that the demographic force and the demographic energy equations differ only in the exponent of the distance measure.

Thus, it can be observed that, in general terms, the gravity model postulates that the interaction between two masses is proportional to the product of the size of the two masses and inversely proportional to the space over which the interaction must take place. If it is assumed that the masses are urban areas, and the size of the mass is measured by the population of the urban node, then the general statement is that "interaction between two centers of population varies directly with some function of the population size of the two centers and inversely with some function of the distance between them" (Carrothers, 1956, p. 94)

$$I_{ij} = \frac{f_1(P_i, P_j)}{f_2(D_{ij})} \tag{6-5}$$

This equation we shall call the "general gravity model." If interaction is to be expressed with respect to one mass A and a number of other masses, then the equation can be rewritten

$$I_{Aj} = \frac{f_3(P_j)}{f_4(D_{Aj})} \tag{6-6}$$

There have been numerous empirical attempts to determine the various "functions" of population and distance, and most of these define the function as an exponent of some magnitude. For example, Eq. (6-6) could be rewritten

$$I_{Aj} = \frac{P_j^{\alpha}}{D_{Aj}^{\Delta}} \tag{6-7}$$

where α and Δ are exponents. Iklé (1954) tested the above equation for a variety of data concerning airline and automobile traffic in the United States. By hypothesizing that the exponent P was unity, he was able to solve for Δ, and calculated values varying from .689 to 2.57. Swedish studies on migration have resulted in values of Δ varying from .4 to 3.0 (Hannerberg et al., 1957). The method used by Iklé can be extended to estimate the functions for both the population and distance variables by taking the logarithms of all the variables and then calculating the constants by multiple-regression techniques.

If common logarithms are used, Eq. (6-7) can be expressed as

$$\log I_{Aj} = \log w + \alpha \log P_j - \Delta \log D_{Aj} \tag{6-8}$$

which in antilogarithmic form is

$$I_{Aj} = p \frac{P_j^{\alpha}}{D_{Aj}^{\Delta}}$$

where p is the antilog of w. Mackay (1958) has used an equation of this form to estimate empirically the effect (or strength) of a provincial boundary in Canada on interaction between cities. In the case of interaction between Montreal and other cities in Quebec and Ontario, as measured by telephone calls for a ten-day period in 1956, the equation is

$$T_{Mj} = 1.8 \frac{P_j^{1.4}}{D_{Mj}^{.9}}$$

where the subscript j refers to any one of the seventeen largest cities in Quebec and ten largest cities in Ontario. In effect, the influence of the provincial boundary is determined from the fact that the interaction of Montreal with cities in Quebec is always greater than expected, but with the cities in Ontario it is less than expected. A number of researchers have examined the use of the gravity model with different kinds of data. Smith (1963), using the logarithmically transformed model of Eq. (6-5), determined a variety of distance exponents for airline travel within the fragmented state of Hawaii, which is interpreted as indicating that the friction of distance varies between the different islands. Taaffe (1962), in his studies of airline traffic in the United States, suggests an exponent of 2 for the distance variable in 1940 and 1 for the distance variable in 1950. The temporal element is exceedingly fascinating, for it is intuitively appealing to relate a decline in the distance exponent through time to changing technology.

The Concept of Potential

Up to this point the discussion has been concerned with the expected interaction between pairs of places. The model can be extended to estimate the interaction between a single place i and all other places, there being n places, by the simple summation

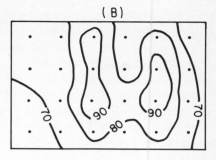

(A)					
25 •1	5 •2	50 •3	5 •4	25 •5	5 •6
5 •7	5 •8	25 •9	5 •10	50 •11	5 •12
5 •13	5 •14	50 •15	5 •16	50 •17	5 •18
5 •19	5 •20	25 •21	5 •22	25 •23	5 •24

FIGURE 6-1
Population potential: (a) data for the population-potential model, population of towns in larger numbers; (b) population-potential surface with isolines at intervals of 10 percent below the point of highest population potential.

$$\frac{P_i P_1}{d_{i1}{}^b} + \frac{P_i P_2}{d_{i2}{}^b} + \frac{P_i P_3}{d_{i3}{}^b} + \cdots + \frac{P_i P_n}{d_{in}{}^b} = \sum_{j=1}^{n} \frac{P_i P_j}{d_{ij}{}^b} \tag{6-9}$$

As P_i is common throughout the whole summation, Eq. (6-9) can be reduced to

$$\sum_{j=1}^{n} \frac{P_j}{d_{ij}{}^b} = V_i \tag{6-10}$$

This division now yields the flow between the ith place and all other places on a per capita basis of the ith place, and has been designated the potential at i. As a consequence, if the potential V at each of the i places is to be calculated, the quantity V_i has to be computed n times.

For example, assume the existence of twenty-four towns, distributed as illustrated in Fig. 6-1a. The population of each town (in thousands) is indicated by the larger numbers in Fig. 6-1a, and the problem is to determine the theoretical flow of persons between each place in the bounded area on a per capita basis, that is, the flow potential at each point. The potential model is to be used as a dynamic representation of reality, and empirical analysis has indicated that, in this bounded area, travel costs are linearly related to distance. Thus, the exponent b is unity. The potential for town 1 is, therefore,

$$\frac{P_2}{d_{1,2}} + \frac{P_3}{d_{1,3}} + \frac{P_4}{d_{1,4}} + \cdots + \frac{P_{24}}{d_{1,24}} + \frac{P_1}{.5d_{1,2}} = V_1 \tag{6-11}$$

The last term is introduced into the equation as a convention in order to try to take into account the effect of the mass of town 1 on itself, for though the center of the town (from which the measures are taken) is a point, the population is distributed over an area.

The potential map resulting from these calculations for each place with every other place (and itself) is presented in Fig. 6-1b with isopotential lines expressed in percentages of the highest potential. On examination, this map illustrates quite clearly the effect of location as it is subsumed by distance in the potential model (as well as the effect of the boundary). The highest potentials are, appropriately enough, encircling the towns of largest population, but one intermediate-sized town (number 9) receives a positive *intervening opportunity effect*, for it is located within the region of highest potential because of its location between two large towns (numbers 3 and 15). Conversely, at the lower end of the scale, the smallest towns have the lowest potentials, except for towns 4 and 10, which have the largest and intermediate-sized towns on all sides.

An application of the concept of potential   Tegsjö and Oberg (1966) have applied the concept of the potential model to a problem concerning egg-price formation in Sweden. Economists have developed an elegant set of postulates concerning the theory of prices which is nonspatial; and the geography of price, which concerns the understanding of the determinants of the spatial distribution of prices, is related to that theory of prices only in the sense that it can be hypothesized that the spatial distribution of prices is related to the spatial distribution of demand and supply. Thus, the contention in the Tegsjö-Oberg model is that the spatial distribution of egg prices P is related to the spatial distribution of demand D and supply S. This can be expressed in a multivariable model for n locations within a country as

$$P_i = S_i, D_i$$

where i is $1, 2, 3, \ldots, n$. As a geographic analysis of price focuses upon location, it is apparent that relative accessibility is of paramount importance in such a study, and as has been demonstrated, relative location may be operationally defined by a potential model. The data used in the analysis are at the county level of aggregation, though the computed potential values and the prices refer to points. These points are positioned at the population median of a county, so that urban centers become the locus of the county in many situations (such as Stockholm, Gothenburg, and Malmo).

According to Tegsjö and Oberg, the demand at a particular point can be expressed by a population-potential model of the following kind:

$$D_i = \sum_{j=1}^{n} \frac{P_j}{d_{ij}} + \frac{P_i}{d_{ii}}$$

This equation is, of course, substantially similar to Eq. (6-10). The symbol d_{ij} refers to economic distance, which is derived in this analysis by taking the straight-line (air line) distance between each reference point and multiplying it by 1.35. The result is considered to give a reasonable approximation of road or railway distances between counties in Sweden. The term P_i/d_{ii} gives weight to the population of the county itself, and therefore serves a function similar to that of $P_i/.5d_{ii}$ in Eq. (6-11). The distance d_{ii} is calculated by finding the radius of a circle which, when placed over the median population point, will encompass half of the county's population. This distance is then multiplied by 1.35 to give d_{ii}. The isolined population-potential map can therefore be considered a demand-potential map if it is assumed that income per capita is distributed similarly among counties in Sweden. The demand-potential map (Fig. 6-2a) shows the distribution of demand relative to the area of greatest demand (which is Stockholm). Thus the highest relative demand is in primarily the Stockholm area and secondarily the Gothenburg area, whereas the lowest demand potential lies in the far north and the offshore islands.

Egg supply potential can be expressed in a model similar to that developed for demand

$$S_i = \sum_{j=1} \frac{S_j}{d_{ij}} + \frac{S_i}{d_{ii}}$$

In the above equation both d_{ij} and d_{ii} are a surrogate for economic distance and are the same numbers as those used previously. The supply S refers to the number of eggs produced in a particular county, for sale in that county and all other counties. This figure takes into account imports, for imports are assigned to the county in which the port of egg entry is located. As a consequence, external egg prices, which affect the inflow of eggs, influence in a realistic way the supply potentials. The egg-supply-potential map for 1963 (Fig. 6-2b) is markedly different from the egg-demand-potential map (which is assumed to represent the demand situation in 1963). The highest point of egg supply potential is in the southwestern part of the country, with egg supply potential diminishing to the east and north.

The dependent surface, which is the map of egg prices (Fig. 6-2c), is notably different from both the demand-potential and supply-potential maps. The interrelation between this surface and the demand and supply surface is expressed in multiple-regression format as

$$P_i = a + b_1 D_i - b_2 S_i$$

where the signs of the coefficients suggest that prices should tend to be highest in areas of greatest aggregate demand and lowest in areas of greatest accessibility to supply. The solution of this equation yields the following parameters:

$$P_i = 574.4 + .1421 D_i - .1974 S_i$$

The signs of the regression coefficients conform exactly to the situation that one would expect, and the multiple correlation coefficient of .68 indicates that 46 percent of the variation of the dependent variable is associated with variations in the two independent variables if a linear relation is hypothesized.

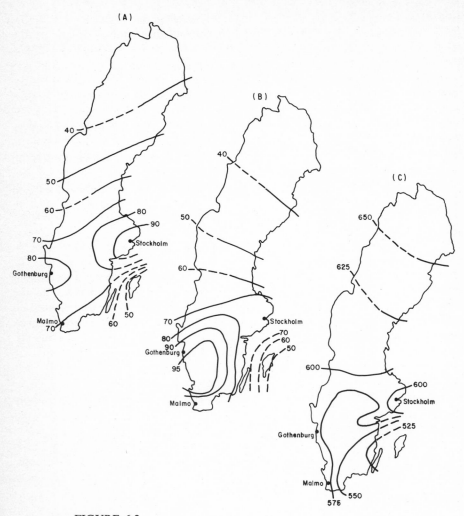

FIGURE 6-2
Sweden: potential maps concerning the distribution of (*a*) egg demand and
(*b*) egg supply, and (*c*) the spatial distribution of egg prices.

Some Comments concerning Gravity and Potential Models

Gravity and potential models have been much used and, many would contend,
much abused by human geographers over the past two decades. A fundamental
criticism is that the gravity model and potential surface of interaction appear to
be empirical regularities that lack the basis of a persuasive theoretical rationale

(Morrill and Earickson, 1969, pp. 262–263). A quick perusal of the major reviews in the literature (Olsson, 1965*a*; Warntz, 1965; Isard et al., 1960, pp. 493–568) would tend to support this criticism, for though the model appears over and over again, it is hardly ever derived initially from realistic theoretical premises. That is not to say that the empirically developed model is not persuasive in the context in which it has been developed. For example, Johnston (1970), in an examination of migration in New Zealand, indicates that the gravity model clearly incorporates the major elements of migration theory, which are the superior attractions for potential migrants of large urban centers, and the diminutive effect of transport costs on migration which are subsumed within the distance variable. While this may be regarded as an ex post facto argument that applies to a particular class of problems, it is persuasive though it does not explain why the model should have such wide geographic generality.

It is this wide generality that is on the one hand so disturbing to geographers, yet on the other so interesting. Probably the most persuasive rationale has been provided by Wilson (1971, 1970), who suggests that the whole family of gravity and potential models can be derived from entropy-maximizing principles, and thus it is not surprising that the model should reappear over and over again as the product of empirical analyses of flows of goods, people, services, ideas, or anything between places. Therefore, though the model has been used primarily for descriptive purposes it may be used also for prescriptive purposes (Morrill and Kelley, 1970) if the entropy-maximizing principle is accepted.

ANALYSIS OF VARIANCE

The discussion in the previous section and the three preceding chapters may have raised a number of questions concerning the difference in variation between samples, and the significance of the contribution of additional independent variables to the explained variation in a multiple-regression model. In the former context, for example, tests of the significance of differences between samples have been limited to cases where only two samples involve two means, two proportions, and two variances. Thus if there are many samples and the researcher wishes to test whether they could have all been drawn from the same normally distributed population, the tests for the significance of differences between proportions or means will be clumsy procedures. A test that will, however, indicate whether several sets of observations could be drawn from the same normally distributed population is available, and this is known as "analysis of variance" (Blalock, 1960, pp. 242–272; Moroney, 1965, pp. 371–457). This procedure can be used also for testing the significance of the contribution of independent variables to the explanation of the variation in the dependent variable, and, as will be demonstrated in the last two sections of this chapter, it is extremely useful in the analysis of surfaces and regions.

Table 6-1 DATA, MEANS, AND STANDARD DEVI-
ATIONS FOR A TWO-SAMPLE CASE OF A
ONE-WAY ANALYSIS OF VARIANCE

| Activity | Threshold value | |
	1940	1964
Filling station	338	492
Food store	342	498
Auto repair shop	352	768
Restaurant	420	592
Hardware store	489	634
Auto dealer	509	840
Tavern	514	806
Animal feed store	579	841
Undertaker	586	1,183
Farm implement dealer	589	815
Construction materials	635	691
Feed mill	635	693
Appliance dealer	636	786
Auto parts dealer	636	813
Drugstore	645	878
Fuel oil dealer	679	1,077
Confectionery	724	1,012
Lumberyard	725	963
Meat market	728	843
Paint and glass store	734	1,144
Sheet metal shop	741	854
Plumbing and heating shop	743	735
Bank	762	906
Family apparel store	778	1,117
Jewelry store	788	1,628
Men's clothing store	802	1,216
Furniture store	837	889
Hotel	843	1,318
Bakery	845	1,206
Electric repair shop	854	1,175
Printing shop	886	1,073
Dry goods store	888	1,234
Dairy products store	892	1,265
Florist	910	1,116
General store	926	742
Shoe store	1,033	1,074
Variety store	1,091	976
Dry cleaner	1,250	1,205
Women's apparel shop	1,277	1,450
Mean	734.5	962.8
Standard deviation	218.2	256.9

SOURCE: Brunn (1968, p. 204).

One-Way Analysis of Variance

Basically, analysis of variance is concerned with comparing two different estimates of variation which together can be used to calculate the variance of the assumed normally distributed parent population from which the samples have been drawn. To explain this, a very simple example will be used, consisting of two samples of threshold values of the same array of business types in north-western Ohio in 1940 and 1964 (Brunn, 1968, p. 204). The null hypothesis is that the two samples could have been drawn from the same population and that the variance estimates for each sample are no different from the variance estimates for the population. The research hypothesis is that the two samples are significantly different, and this is based on the notion that the wealth and opportunities of the population have so changed in the area over a period of twenty-four years that, in terms of marketing conditions, this is not really the same area. Of course, normally this hypothesis would be examined by using the test for the significance of differences between two means, but for this first example of analysis of variance a two-sample case is most appropriate.

The data for this two-sample case (1940 = H; 1964 = M) are listed in Table 6-1 along with the means $\overline{X}_H$ and $\overline{X}_M$ and standard deviations S_H and S_M for each variable. The first step is to obtain an estimate of the variance of the population from which the two samples are supposedly drawn. This can be obtained by calculating a mean GM (for "grand mean") for all the observations in both samples, $N = N_H + N_M$, and then calculating the mean of the sum of squared deviations from this grand mean:

$$\text{Population variance} = \frac{\sum\limits_{i=1}^{n} (X_i - GM)^2}{N - 1}$$

$$= \frac{\sum\limits_{i=1}^{78} (X_i - 848.62)^2}{78 - 1}$$

$$= \frac{5,332,944.46}{77}$$

$$= 69,259.02 \tag{6-12}$$

It is to be noticed that 1 degree of freedom is lost for a parameter already estimated, GM, in calculating the variance. The second step is to obtain an estimate of the pooled variance of both samples. This is, in effect, the variance of both samples based upon their individual means, and is, appropriately, referred to as the total "within" sample variance:

Within sample variance

$$= \frac{\sum\limits_{h=1}^{H} (X_h - \bar{X}_H)^2 + \sum\limits_{m=1}^{M} (X_m - \bar{X}_M)^2}{(H-1) + (M-1)}$$

$$= \frac{\sum\limits_{h=1}^{39} (X_h - 734.46)^2 + \sum\limits_{m=1}^{39} (X_m - 962.8)^2}{(39-1) + (39-1)}$$

$$= \frac{4,244,365.46}{76} = 55,846.91 \qquad (6\text{-}13)$$

In this second step it is to be noticed that 2 degrees of freedom are lost, 1 for each mean calculated in each sample.

Now, if the two samples were drawn from the same population, the pooled variance of both samples would be almost the same as the population variance, because the respective sample variance would not be significantly different from the population variance. The threshold data, however, indicate quite a large difference, and the question to be resolved is whether this difference is greater than would be expected from normal sampling error. The "error" due to the two samples can, in effect, be calculated from the sums of squares already estimated because the *surrogate population* sum of squared deviations based on the combined information of both samples is 5,332,944.46, and the within sample sum of squared deviations is 4,244,365.46. The error in sum of squared deviations due to the two samples is, therefore,

$$5,332,944.46 - 4,244,365.46 = 1,088,579.00$$

This error is to be distributed between the two samples to estimate the "between" sample variance, with the degrees of freedom being determined by the number *not* already consumed in the previous calculations. As the total degrees of freedom available are 77, and 76 were consumed in the calculation of the within sample variance, only 1 degree of freedom is left to estimate the between sample variance. Therefore,

Between variance

$$= \frac{\text{total sum of squares} - \text{within sample sum of squares}}{(N-1) - (H+M-2)}$$

$$= \frac{1,088,579.00}{77 - 76} = 1,088,579.00 \qquad (6\text{-}14)$$

The ratio between the between sample variance and the within sample variance can then be calculated and is referred to as the statistic F.

$$F = \frac{\text{between sample variance}}{\text{within sample variance}}$$

$$= \frac{1,088,579.00}{55,846.91} = 19.49 \tag{6-15}$$

An analysis-of-variance table for the calculation of F is presented as Table 6-2. Obviously, the larger the F statistic, the greater the difference between the estimated population variance and the pooled within sample variance, depending upon the degrees of freedom available. The question that therefore arises is what values of F for various combinations of degrees of freedom indicate significant differences in variances at particular confidence levels?

Whereas the t distribution is used to test the significance of the difference between *means* of samples that are assumed drawn from a normally distributed population, the F distribution is used to test whether the *variances* of two samples could have been drawn from the same normally distributed population. Also, whereas the t statistic is calculated on the basis of the *difference* between the means, the F statistic is calculated as the ratio of the variances, with the larger variance placed as the numerator, and the smaller variance the denominator. Thus $F = s_1^2/s_2^2$, where $s_1^2 > s_2^2$, and it involves, consequently, a one-tailed test. Just as the distribution of t varies according to the size of the samples concerned, so does the distribution of F; but whereas the distribution of t tends to get flatter and wider as the sample decreases, the distribution of F tends to get flatter and wider according to the relative magnitudes of the sample sizes (which determine the degrees of freedom) of both the numerator and denominator.

Snedecor has computed tables of critical values of the F ratio for a large number of combinations of degrees of freedom. An extract from these tables of the critical values (one-tailed) of F at the 95 percent confidence level are

Table 6-2 ONE-WAY ANALYSIS OF VARIANCE FOR THRESHOLD EXAMPLE

Source of variation	Sum of squares of deviations	Degrees of freedom	Estimated variance (mean sum of squares)	Variance ratio F
Between years	1,088,579.00	1	1,088,579.00	
				19.49
Within years	4,244,365.46	76	55,846.91	
Total	5,332,944.46	77		

presented in Table 6-3. More detailed tables at various confidence levels can be found in Snedecor (1946, pp. 222–225) and Arkin and Colton (1962). If the hypothesis with respect to the threshold data is to be tested at the 95 percent confidence level, the critical limit for 1 and 76 degrees of freedom, which can be interpolated from Table 6-3, is about 4.0, and as this is considerably less than 19.49 (Table 6-2), the null hypothesis is rejected and the research hypothesis can be inferred.

Two-Way Analysis of Variance

At this juncture the discussion of analysis of variance can be extended to situations involving more than two variables and more than a unidirectional evaluation. Consider the data in Table 6-4. These are average rates of schizophrenia (in persons per thousand) in subareas in the city of Chicago for the

Table 6-3   CRITICAL VALUES OF F AT THE 95 PERCENT CONFIDENCE LEVEL FOR VARIOUS COMBINATIONS OF DEGREES OF FREEDOM

		Number of degrees of freedom in the greater variance estimate									
		1	2	3	4	5	10	20	40	75	∞
Number of degrees of freedom in the lesser variance estimate	1	161	200	216	225	230	242	248	251	253	254
	2	18.5	19	19.2	19.2	19.3	19.4	19.4	19.5	19.5	19.5
	3	10.1	9.6	9.3	9.1	9.0	8.8	8.7	8.6	8.6	8.5
	4	7.7	6.9	6.6	6.4	6.3	6.0	5.8	5.7	5.7	5.6
	5	6.6	5.8	5.4	5.2	5.0	4.7	4.6	4.5	4.4	4.4
	10	5.0	4.1	3.7	3.5	3.3	3.0	2.8	2.7	2.6	2.5
	20	4.3	3.5	3.1	2.9	2.7	2.3	2.1	2.0	1.9	1.8
	40	4.1	3.2	2.8	2.6	2.5	2.1	1.8	1.7	1.6	1.5
	75	4.0	3.1	2.7	2.5	2.3	2.0	1.7	1.5	1.5	1.3
	∞	3.8	3.0	2.6	2.4	2.2	1.8	1.6	1.4	1.3	1.0

SOURCE: Snedecor (1946, pp. 222–225).

Table 6-4   AVERAGE RATES OF SCHIZOPHRENIA, 1922 TO 1934, FOR SELECTED SECTORS AND RINGS IN THE CITY OF CHICAGO

Ring, miles	Sector			
	North	Northwest	Southwest	South
1–3	47.8	60.1	41.4	84.1
3–5	32.6	34.8	40.5	46.9
5–7	25.0	23.5	34.3	32.6
7–9	17.9	22.5	23.3	21.1
9–11	15.8	18.2	20.0	25.4

SOURCE: Data adapted from Faris and Dunham (1939), with the west sector excluded.

years 1922 to 1934. The subareas are classified by their location in specific geographic sectors of the city, and with reference to their location vis-à-vis the center of the central business district (defined as the intersection of State Street and Madison Avenue). It is to be noted that the average rates of schizophrenia decrease with distance from the center of the city in each sector, and that, furthermore, the rates seem to be higher in some sectors than others. The research problem is, therefore, to decide whether there is a significant difference in variation in rates of schizophrenia between sectors, and whether there is also a significant difference between rings.

If this problem is approached with a one-way analysis of variance, then the "effect" of the spatial division of the data into sectors and rings is examined separately. By following the same procedure outlined previously in the one-way analysis of variance of the threshold data, it can be determined that the F statistic for the sector effect is .61 (Table 6-5), and at the 95 percent confidence level, this is considerably less than the critical limit of F with 3 and 16 degrees of freedom, which is 3.24. Thus the null hypothesis is accepted, and the conclusion will be that there is no significant difference in schizophrenia rates between different geographic sectors in Chicago. A different conclusion is reached for the ring effect if a one-way analysis of variance is performed across the rows. The total variation and total degrees of freedom are, of course, the same as for the sector effect, but this time the variation between the rings is so large and that within the rings so small (Table 6-6) that the null hypothesis is rejected and the research hypothesis inferred at the 95 percent confidence level. The conclusion could be, therefore, that there is a significant difference in schizophrenia rates between different rings in the city of Chicago, and as has been determined from an inspection of the data in Table 6-6, these rates tend to decrease with distance from the center of the city.

Unfortunately, these conclusions are somewhat suspect because the two geographic variables, sectors and rings, affect the data in each subarea jointly, and not separately as has been assumed in the previous paragraph. In clinical terms, each element of data for each subarea is affected by two "treatments,"

Table 6-5   ONE-WAY ANALYSIS OF VARIANCE FOR SCHIZO-PHRENIA EXAMPLE: SECTORS

Source of variation	Sum of squares of deviations	Degrees of freedom	Estimated variance	F
Between sectors	550.93	3	183.64	
				.61
Within sectors	4,805.81	16	300.36	
Total	5,356.74	19		

and so a more correct procedure would be to analyze these two independent treatments jointly, for a subtle sector effect may be overwhelmed by the more dominant ring effect. The model, therefore, is that

$$\text{Total variation} = \text{between sector variation}$$
$$+ \text{ between ring variation} + \text{ within sector and ring variation}$$

As three of the sources of variation, and their associated degrees of freedom, needed in the equation have already been calculated (Tables 6-5 and 6-6), it is a simple matter to determine the within-sector-and-ring variation. These sources of variation and their associated degrees of freedom and variances are listed in Table 6-7.

The within-sector-and-ring source of variation, or "interaction term" or "residual error" as it is sometimes called, is calculated to be 790.86 for 12 degrees of freedom, and the variance is $\frac{790.86}{12} = 65.91$. This variance forms the denominator of the variance ratios that are used to determine the significance of the two effects jointly. The F statistic for the sector effect is $\frac{183.64}{65.91} = 2.79$, and as this is less than 3.45, which is the critical limit of F with 3 and 12 degrees of freedom at the 95 percent confidence level, the null hypothesis is accepted. On the other hand, the F statistic for the ring effect is 15.22, and this is greater than 3.26, which is the critical limit of F with 4 and 12 degrees of freedom at the

Table 6-6   ONE-WAY ANALYSIS OF VARIANCE FOR SCHIZO-PHRENIA EXAMPLE: RINGS

Source of variation	Sum of squares of deviations	Degrees of freedom	Estimated variance	F
Between rings	4,014.95	4	1,003.74	
				11.22
Within rings	1,341.79	15	89.44	
Total	5,356.74	19		

Table 6-7   TWO-WAY ANALYSIS OF VARIANCE FOR SCHIZOPHRENIA EXAMPLE

Source of variation	Sum of squares of deviations	Degrees of freedom	Estimated variance	F
Between sectors	550.93	3	183.64	2.79
Between rings	4,014.95	4	1,003.44	15.22
Within sectors and rings	790.86	12	65.91	
Total	5,356.74	19		

95 percent confidence level. Thus the two-way analysis of variance suggests that of the two independent sources of variation, the zonal or ring effect is significant, whereas the sectoral effect is not. It is to be noted that if the between-ring variation had been larger and the between-sector effect had remained the same, it could have been possible for the sector effect to be significant, because the interaction variance would have been smaller.

The two-way analysis-of-variance design may be extended by including three, four, or more different sources of variation. The procedures used in the solution of such a multiple analysis are analogous to those already detailed, with the sources of variation and degrees of freedom disaggregated in a "nesting" manner. Generally, the more complex analyses of variance have been used very little in human geography. Most designs have a one-way approach, such as those of Knos (1962) in his analysis of the variation in land values among different uses, and Mayfield (1967) in his investigation of the existence of a hierarchy of central places in northern India. A two-way approach has been used by Murdie (1969) to establish whether certain socioeconomic dimensions pertaining to the population of Toronto were distributed sectorally or zonally in 1951 and 1961. A multiple-analysis-of-variance model has been used by Haggett (1964) in his study of factors affecting the distribution of forest cover in southeast Brazil, by Boyce (1965) in an investigation of certain hypotheses affecting urban trip volumes, and by Moellering and Tobler (1972) in their examination of scale effects in hierarchical geographical data structures.

THE USE OF NOMINAL VARIABLES IN THE ANALYSIS OF REGIONS

Nominal variables can be of great use in geographic research (Knos, 1962; Yeates, 1965), and in this section the concern will be to discuss and illustrate their use in the context of estimating the importance of regional subdivision. A nominal variable is one in which a set of observations are allocated the score 0 or 1 depending upon whether or not an observation has a particular defined attribute (Draper and Smith, 1966). In this particular geographic example the attribute will be a particular region; therefore an observation will score 1 if it lies in a particular region, and 0 if it does not.

Suppose the existence of an area U and the desire to examine the relation of three independent variables F, D, and M to one dependent variable Y. The assumption is that these variables are linearly related, and so the general linear model is postulated,

$$Y_i = h + k_1 F_i + k_2 D_i + k_3 M_i + e_i \qquad (6\text{-}16)$$

where the sample size is n ($i = 1, 2, 3, \ldots, n$). The sample points are distributed randomly throughout U, and the evaluation of Eq. (6-16) will yield a multiple coefficient of determination, R^2, which indicates the proportion of the variation in the dependent variable associated with the three independent variables. The researcher is, however, aware that U can be divided into three mutually exclusive subsets (called "regions"). These regions may well account for some of the variation in the dependent variable, for they may indicate three different political areas, three different regions in physical geography, or three different cultural areas in human occupance of the land.

These three regions R_1, R_2, and R_3 can be introduced into the linear equation (6-16) by the use of nominal variables in the following manner: (1) all observations in the sample that fall into region 1 are delimited by assigning them the value 1 for variable R_1, and zero for variables R_2 and R_3; (2) all observations that fall into region 2 are delimited by assigning them the value 1 for variable R_2, and 0 for variables R_1 and R_3; (3) all observations that lie in region 3 are now defined, for those that fall in regions 1 and 2 have been delimited. Variable R_3 can, therefore, be eliminated without excluding it from the analysis. Furthermore, if one of the nominal ("dummy") variables were not excluded, the solution would be indeterminate (Suits, 1957), for the **A** matrix (inner-product matrix) would be a singular matrix.

The linear equation (6-16) can now be enlarged to include the regional concept as follows:

$$Y_i = p + q_1F_i + q_2D_i + q_3M_i + q_4R_{1i} + q_5R_{2i} + e_i \qquad (6\text{-}17)$$

This equation, in effect, reveals only the differences in the constant between regions. If a sample observation lies in region 1, then $R_{1i} = 1$ and the constant for that region becomes $p + q_4R_{1i}$; q_5 is eliminated from the equation as $R_{2i} = 0$. Alternatively, if a sample observation falls in region 2, $R_{2i} = 1$ and the constant becomes $p + q_5R_{2i}$; and this time q_4 is eliminated from the equation as $R_{1i} = 0$. Finally, if a sample observation lies in region 3, both R_{1i} and R_{2i} are zero, and q_4 and q_5 are eliminated from the equation, and the constant is p.

Variations in the regression coefficients between regions can be included by cross-multiplying the nominal variables with each independent variable to form interaction variables. In this way Eq. (6-17) is enlarged to become

$$Y_i = a + b_1F_i + b_2D_i + b_3M_i + b_4R_{1i} + b_5R_{2i} + b_6F_iR_{1i}$$
$$+ b_7F_iR_{2i} + b_8D_iR_{1i} + b_9D_iR_{2i} + b_{10}M_iR_{1i}$$
$$+ b_{11}M_iR_{2i} + e$$

which by gathering terms can be clarified to be

$$Y_i = a + b_4R_{1i} + b_5R_{2i} + F_i(b_1 + b_6R_{1i} + b_7R_{2i})$$
$$+ D_i(b_2 + b_8R_{1i} + b_9R_{2i})$$
$$+ M_i(b_3 + b_{10}R_{1i} + b_{11}R_{2i}) + e \qquad (6\text{-}18)$$

Equation (6-18) represents a composite equation for the three regions, and by substituting 1 and 0 in the appropriate places it can be determined that for those observations lying in region 1,

$$Y_i = a + b_4 R_{1i} + (b_1 + b_6 R_{1i})F_i + (b_2 + b_8 R_{1i})D_i$$
$$+ (b_3 + b_{10}R_{1i})M_i$$

for those observations lying in region 2,

$$Y_i = a + b_5 R_{2i} + (b_1 + b_7 R_{2i})F_i + (b_2 + b_9 R_{2i})D_i$$
$$+ (b_3 + b_{11}R_{2i})M_i$$

and for those observations lying in region 3,

$$Y_i = a + b_1 F_i + b_2 D_i + b_3 M_i$$

The constant a and regression coefficients therefore represent adjustments to the base equation, which indicates the parameters for region 3. It is to be noted that in this disaggregation of the composite equation it is not directly possible to disaggregate the error term; and that if the number of original independent variables is three or more, the addition of each extra region will result in a proliferation of variables in the regression equation which can consume the available degrees of freedom with great rapidity. It is wise to keep the number of independent variables and regions to a minimum, and to use reasonably large samples.

Thus, if it is desired to estimate the importance of regional subdivision with respect to the variables being considered, it can be suggested that such divisions are tenable only if there is a significant increase in explanation for Eq. (6-18) over that for Eq. (6-16). In other words, is the R^2 derived from Eq. (6-18) significantly greater than that from Eq. (6-16)? The fact that it should be greater is known from the discussion of the effect that an increase in the number of regression coefficients on the multiple coefficients had on the multiple coefficient of determination, in the preceding chapter. The significance of this difference can be tested with an analysis-of-variance model, as is described by a specific example in the ensuing section.

The Existence of Two Regions in a Land-Value Surface

Our example consists of a land-value surface in the northernmost part of Chicago in an area adjacent to Lake Michigan known as Rogers Park. The land-value surface being examined has a concave tilt with respect to the lake shore, that is, the land values tend to decrease with distance away from the lake but at a decreasing rate (Yeates and Garner, 1971, p. 259). A random sample of seventy-five land values in the Rogers Park district has been taken from

Olcott's Land Values Blue Book of Chicago, 1961, which refers to the situation in 1960. The data are in the form of average dollar values per front foot of blocks for a constant depth, and they are based on quotations from local real estate dealers. The land values have been logarithmically transformed to achieve normality and at the same time to represent a concave surface by one that approximates linearity. Thus the general model can be expressed in simple regression form as

$$\log (LV)_i = \log a + D_i (\log b) + e$$

where $(LV)_i$ = front-foot land value at ith location in 1961, in hundreds of dollars

D_i = distance of the ith sample point from the lake, in hundreds of feet

The hypothesis is that this land-value surface is not simply one surface influenced by one spatial force (a desire to locate close to the lake for various reasons) but a surface influenced by two different forces which result in two different regions of land values. One region is an area zoned residential, which is, in fact, the bulk of the district (Fig. 6-3), in which there is a desire for a location close to the lakeshore, expressed by an increase in land values toward the lake. A second region is an area zoned business and commercial, in which land values do not decrease away from the lakeshore but behave in accordance with other behavioral considerations such as a desire for a location central to local market areas, and so forth. Thus, there is a theoretical rationale for these two regions, and the question arises whether the division of the area into two regions (residential and business-commercial) is justified by the empirical data.

The data are presented in Table 6-8. The reference numbers refer to the random sample of points located on Fig. 6-3. For each point the logarithm of the land value (in hundreds of dollars) is listed as the dependent variable Y (decimal point excluded and rounded to three figures), and the distance of that observation (in hundreds of feet) is listed as an independent variable X_1. The variable X_2 is a nominal, or dummy, variable, and the score for an observation is recorded as unity if that point lies in an area zoned business or commercial, and zero if it does not. The variable X_3 is the interaction variable and consists in multiplying X_1 by X_2 for each observation. The means and standard deviations for each of these variables are also listed in Table 6-8, and it is to be noted that even though the means are different, the standard deviations (rounded) for X_1 and X_3 are almost the same.

The first equation is for the general model in simple regression form $Y = a + bX_1$, and is calculated to be $Y = 502 - 2.105X_1$. As the total variation of the dependent variable is 1,095,127, and the explained variation 247,858; the multiple R^2 is 22.6 percent. An analysis-of-variance design can be

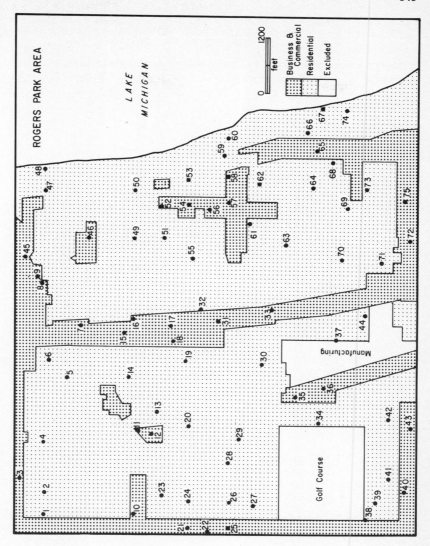

FIGURE 6-3
Zoning in Rogers Park, Chicago, 1960, and the distribution of the random sample.

Table 6-8   DATA FOR NOMINAL VARIABLE EXAMPLE, ROGERS PARK, CHICAGO, 1960

Reference no.	Y	X_1	X_2	$X_1X_2 = X_3$
1	322	77	0	0
2	312	72	0	0
3	477	69	1	69
4	322	62	0	0
5	222	48	0	0
6	301	42	0	0
7	301	36	1	36
8	352	26	1	26
9	352	25	1	25
10	255	79	1	79
11	477	60	1	60
12	439	62	1	62
13	322	57	0	0
14	267	49	0	0
15	477	38	1	38
16	602	36	1	36
17	544	39	1	39
18	176	42	1	42
19	322	47	0	0
20	477	61	0	0
21	477	84	1	84
22	699	86	1	86
23	301	75	0	0
24	243	78	0	0
25	477	85	1	85
26	342	80	0	0
27	371	81	0	0
28	278	71	0	0
29	371	66	0	0
30	322	54	0	0
31	602	40	1	40
32	398	36	0	0
33	352	42	1	42
34	279	70	0	0
35	399	64	1	64
36	439	63	1	63
37	267	53	0	0
38	301	94	0	0
39	301	90	0	0
40	397	89	1	89
41	301	85	0	0
42	301	72	0	0
43	301	75	1	75
44	278	49	0	0
45	477	20	1	20
46	602	17	1	17
47	602	06	0	0
48	740	01	0	0
49	512	18	0	0

Table 6-8   (*Continued*)

Reference no.	Y	X_1	X_2	$X_1X_2 = X_3$
50	512	07	0	0
51	512	19	0	0
52	352	12	1	12
53	544	08	0	0
54	397	13	1	13
55	439	25	0	0
56	397	16	1	16
57	439	17	1	17
58	399	11	1	11
59	602	06	0	0
60	602	03	0	0
61	477	22	0	0
62	512	15	0	0
63	415	30	0	0
64	477	18	0	0
65	301	11	1	11
66	602	06	0	0
67	602	02	0	0
68	512	14	0	0
69	380	24	0	0
70	380	35	0	0
71	398	38	0	0
72	301	34	1	34
73	371	21	0	0
74	602	03	0	0
75	301	26	1	26
Mean	417	43	.4	18
s	122	27	.5	27

used to test whether this degree of explanation is significantly different from zero, for the problem can be stated analogously as whether the variance explained by the regression equation is significantly greater than the variance left unexplained among the observations. The details of the table are indicated in Table 6-9. The total degrees of freedom are $75 - 1$ because 1 degree of freedom is lost in the estimation of $\overline{Y}$ which is used to calculate the total variation. Even though the total error variation, or the sum of the squared residuals (847,269), is calculated with respect to all the observations, 2 degrees of freedom are lost because two estimated parameters a and b are used to calculate the predicted value of each Y_i; therefore the error variance is $847,269/(75 - 2) = 11,606$. Finally, as 74 degrees of freedom are available, and 73 have been allocated to the unexplained variation, this leaves 1 degree of freedom for the explained variation. The ratio of the variances, or F statistic, is 21.36, and this is much greater than the critical value of F for 1 and 73 degrees of freedom at the 95 percent confidence level, which is 3.98. Thus the null hypothesis is rejected, and the research hypothesis that the regression equation explains a significant portion of the total variation is accepted at the chosen level of confidence.

Testing the significance of the inclusion of the nominal and interaction variables   The multiple regression equation for the model to evaluate the importance of the division of the area into two regions by zoning is $Y = h + k_1X_1 + k_2X_2 + k_3X_3$, and the parameters are calculated to be $Y = 560 - 3.64X_1 - 173X_2 + 4.36X_3$. The t values for the regression coefficients are -7.54, -4.17, and 5.34 respectively, which indicate that all the coefficients are significantly greater than zero for a two-tailed test at the 95 percent confidence level. The multiple correlation coefficient is 45.1 percent, and the question arises

Table 6-9   ANALYSIS OF VARIANCE FOR REGRESSION

Source of variation	Sum of squares	Degrees of freedom	Mean sum of squares	F
Explained by regression	247,858	1	247,858	
				21.36
Unexplained by regression	847,269	73	11,606	
Total variation	1,095,127	74		

Table 6-10   ANALYSIS OF VARIANCE FOR DETERMINING THE SIGNIFICANCE OF THE INCORPORATION OF ADDITIONAL INDEPENDENT VARIABLES

Source of variation	Cumulative sum of squares	Additional sum of squares	Degrees of freedom	Mean sum of squares	F
Explanation without regions	247,858	247,858	1	247,858	
					21.36
Unexplained without regions		847,269	73	11,606	
Explanation with regions	493,840	245,982	2	122,991	
					14.52
Unexplained with regions		601,287	71	8,469	
Total variation		1,095,127	74		

whether this division into two regions, which has been represented by the addition of two extra variables, has resulted in a significant increase in explanation. The calculations for testing this are detailed in Table 6-10.

The last two rows, designated "... with regions," detail the explained and unexplained variations as 493,840 and 601,287, which, of course, sum to the total variation, which is the same as that in Table 6-9. The additional sum of squares contributed to the overall explanation by the nominal variable and interaction variable is 493,840 − 247,858 = 245,982. This has to be allocated to the two variables providing this additional sum of squares; so the degrees of freedom are 2 and the mean sum of squares is 122,991. The unexplained variation is 1,095,127 − 493,840 = 601,287, and as explained previously, although the total error variation is calculated with respect to all the observations, 4 degrees of freedom are lost because four estimated parameters h, k_1, k_2, and k_3 are used to calculate the predicted value of each Y_i. Thus the error variance is 601,287/(75 − 4) = 8,469. The ratio of the variances, or F statistic, is 14.52, and as the critical value of F with 2 and 71 degrees of freedom at the 95 percent confidence level is 3.13, it can be inferred that this division of the area into two land-value regions is appropriate on theoretical grounds and significant in terms of the variation in the data.

Finally, it is to be noted that the individual subregion regressions can be calculated from the estimated parameters. For the residential region, where the nominal variable score for each of the forty-five observations is 0, the equation is $Y = 560 − 3.64X_1$; and for the business-commercial-zoned region, where the nominal variable score for each of the thirty observations is 1, the equation is $Y = (560 − 173 = 387) + (−3.64 + 4.36 = .72)X_1$. These parameters are the same as those that would be achieved if separate simple regressions were calculated on the basis of subsets of forty-five and thirty observations. There is, however, no direct method for partitioning the error between the two subregions or for calculating the coefficient of determination for each subset.

TREND SURFACE ANALYSIS

Analysis of variance and multiple-regression models are also used in trend surface analysis, which includes a number of techniques. These techniques are used to separate broad, regional or systematic patterns of variation in mapped data from local, random or nonsystematic variations. Once this separation is achieved, processes or causes are then ascribed to the various trends that have been discerned (Chorley and Haggett, 1965). Thus the aim of the model can be presented symbolically as

$$T(m, n) = R(m, n) + e(m, n)$$

where (m, n) represents the coordinates of a two-dimensional field (for example, m may be a north-south coordinate and n an east-west coordinate); T is the mapped variable; R is the systematic trend; and e is the random, or non-systematic, component.

Approaches to Trend Surface Analysis

This separation can be approached from two main directions, and care should be taken to select the type of model most appropriate for a given situation (Norcliffe, 1969). If the coordinates are determined from a rectangular grid such that the grid intervals are uniform in each direction (they do not have to be uniform in both directions), and if there is some definite reason for assuming that the map patterns take some recurring form (such as a wave type of cyclical pattern), then a Fourier model may be most applicable. Models of this type have been discussed in the geographic literature by Cassetti (1966a), Harbrough and Preston (1968), and Tobler (1969). The advantage of a Fourier model for analyzing surfaces in which a periodicity is apparent is that the periodicity is described succinctly by groups of harmonics. The disadvantage of using the model, even though it may be succinct and powerful, is that human geography finds few instances where a periodicity can be assumed, compared with physical geography and geology where the data are more likely to have a cyclical or oscillatory pattern (Miller and Kahn, 1962, pp. 390–439).

If the data are available in a regular grid pattern but there is no definite observable (or theoretical) reason for assuming a particular periodicity, the systematic and nonsystematic components may be separated by the use of orthogonal polynomials, which are tabulated (DeLury, 1950). The most frequent situation, however, is that the data are not available from some sort of regular rectangular grid design. In this situation the trends can be separated by using nonorthogonal polynomials, and as this form of model has been used the most frequently in human geography, it will be the focus of the ensuing discussion (Haggett, 1968; McDonald, 1968; and Cerny, 1971). In fact, the frequency and ease of its use has lead Tobler (1969, p. 236) to comment that there "appears to be a temptation to apply this model rather indiscriminately to all sorts of geographical situations."

In trend surface analysis with nonorthogonal polynomials, the systematic trend is estimated by a least-squares matrix solution of the following general linear model

$$T(m_i, n_i) = (a + b_1 m_i + b_2 n_i + b_3 m_i^2 + b_4 m_i n_i$$
$$+ b_5 n_i^2 + \cdots) + e(m_i, n_i) \qquad (6\text{-}19)$$

where the polynomial expansion on the right-hand side of the equation will yield $R(m, n)$, or the systematic component, and $T(m_i, n_i) - R(m_i, n_i) = e(m_i, n_i)$

which represents the residuals, or nonsystematic source of variation. Each inflexion in the surface requires an additional expansion, and so complex surfaces require exceedingly large equations. For example, a first-order polynomial in three dimensions is represented generally by $T = a + b_1m + b_2n + e$, which is to be compared with a first-order polynomial in two dimensions, $Y = a + bX + e$. A second-order polynomial in two dimensions is described by $Y = a + b_1X + b_2X^2 + e$, which gives a parabola; but a second-order polynomial in three dimensions is represented generally by $T = a + b_1m + b_2n + b_3m^2 + b_4mn + b_5n^2 + e$. Second-order polynomials in two dimensions have been used by Newling (1969) to describe population densities and change within North American cities. Finally, a third-order polynomial in two dimensions is $Y = a + b_1X + b_2X^2 + b_3X^3 + e$, whereas a third-order polynomial in three dimensions is represented generally by

$$Y = a + b_1m + b_2n + b_3m^2 + b_4mn + b_5n^2 + b_6m^3 + b_7m^2n + b_8mn^2 + b_9n^3$$

Thus if complex surfaces are to be described by power polynomials, the researcher has to be very careful of the total degrees of freedom available and the possible effect of multicollinearity. The expansions of the polynomials for surfaces of orders 1 through 6 are listed in Table 6-11, and examples of the types of surfaces that may be represented by polynomials of orders 1 to 3 are indicated by isoline maps in Fig. 6-4.

The Uses of Trend Surface Analysis

There are many uses of trend surface analysis, the most common being for structured map description. Chorley and Haggett (1965) suggest that this approach is particularly useful in both teaching and research, for it takes advantage of the ordered disaggregation of the surface to provide a logical analytical

Table 6-11   THE SURFACE PYRAMID FOR SURFACES OF ORDERS 1 TO 6

Surface order, cumulative	Variables						
1	m	n					
2	m^2	mn	n^2				
3	m^3	m^2n	mn^2	n^3			
4	m^4	m^3n	m^2n^2	mn^3	n^4		
5	m^5	m^4n	m^3n^2	m^2n^3	mn^4	n^5	
6	m^6	m^5n	m^4n^2	m^3n^3	m^2n^4	mn^5	n^6

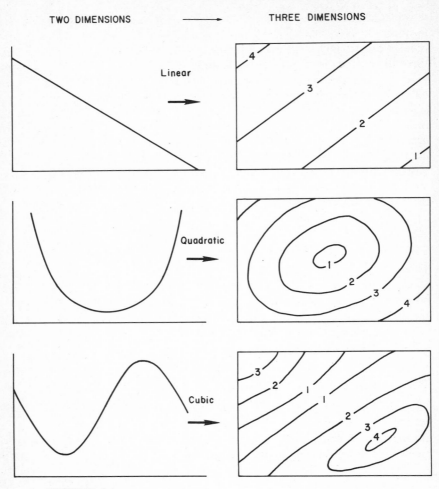

FIGURE 6-4
Examples of some types of two-dimensional trends and three-dimensional trend surfaces: (a) linear, (b) quadratic, and (c) cubic.

sequence. This type of structured description can then lead into the formulation of hypotheses concerning the spatial forces that may affect the configuration of the surface. These hypotheses may be couched in terms of inferences or known process-response models, and can be examined within the framework of a multiple-regression model. A further trend surface analysis of the residuals (Robinson and Fairbairn, 1969) may yield additional insights into the factors influencing the basic pattern. Thus the structural descriptive approach can also be used as part of a model-building process.

Trend surface analysis can also be used for estimating the data for missing observations, or for checking the accuracy of given observations in which some large error may be possible. This estimation can be achieved for observations through the procedures of interpolation and extrapolation, and should be used only if the standard error of estimate is very small. Extrapolation beyond a study area requires an enormous number of assumptions concerning the distribution of the data in an unknown locale, and so extreme caution is advised in this form of estimation. By analogy, the model may be used to provide a missing surface in a known series. For example, if the population distribution for 1930, 1940, 1960, and 1970 is known, trend surface models may be used to interpolate the 1950 surface. Or the 1980 surface could be projected from the 1960 and 1970 surface information. Tobler (1969) has provided impressive evidence for the utility of the double Fourier series model (as a form of spectral analysis) for this type of surface-finding situation. Parenthetically, Rayner (1967) has also suggested that Fourier analysis is a useful tool for examining the degree of correlation between surfaces if the two patterns exhibit a degree of periodicity.

The Significance of a Trend

One of the problems of trend surface analysis with power polynomials lies in establishing the significance of the trend that has been calculated. To illustrate this problem, and to demonstrate some of the procedures that are possible, use will be made of a random sample of the dates of founding of twenty settlements in a portion of New England in the seventeenth century to develop a series of diachronic trend surface models. The dates of founding of these settlements (Fig. 6-5a) have been obtained from Leach (1966, p. 34), and the trend-surface procedure is to be used to investigate the "smoothness" and regularity of the settlement of the area, which, in general, is known to have proceeded from the coast inland. Given that this settlement was affected by many additional factors other than the fact that the settlers came across the Atlantic, such as the variability of access routes along the river valleys, time delays in making treaties with local Indians, the configuration of the coastline itself, and so forth, it is interesting to determine the degree to which a general settlement spread is evident, and the rate of this spread.

The original surface is, then, described by the dates of the founding of the twenty randomly chosen settlements. Trend surfaces for this data have been calculated by using nonorthogonal polynomials of orders 1 to 3. The linear trend surface (Fig. 6-5b), which explains 34.6 percent of the variation in the original pattern, describes a general pattern of settlement development proceeding

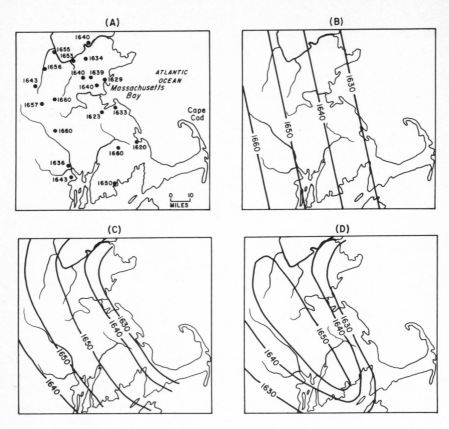

FIGURE 6-5
The spread of settlements in a portion of New England in the seventeenth century: (a) the distribution of the random sample of twenty settlements, (b) the linear surface, (c) the quadratic surface, and (d) the cubic surface.

from east to west. Thus, a little over one-third of the variation in the founding of settlements may be described by the simple phrase, "The settlement of this portion of New England was from east to west," and the average annual rate of penetration of settlements inland was 1.8 miles per year. The quadratic surface (Fig. 6-5c), which explains 58.7 percent of the variation in the original surface, replicates much of the basic trend suggested by the linear surface, though it differs in one important respect. It is basically a ridge, showing that settlement proceeded from east to west, but the ridge "peaks" to the east of the Pawtucket River, and more recent settlements are found in the south around the major entry point of Narragansett Bay. This ridge is further exemplified by the cubic surface (Fig. 6-5d), which explains 62 percent of the variation in the original surface and reemphasizes the importance of the Narragansett Bay entry as well as the east coast around Massachusetts Bay.

The important question that arises, of course, concerns which surfaces explain significant proportions of the variation in the original surface. The method frequently used to test the statistical significance of a surface is to compare the mean sum of squares attributable to the fitted surface with the mean residual sum of squares, and to use the variance ratio, or F statistic (Norcliffe, 1969, p. 346). As an example, a table used for calculating the F ratio for the quadratic surface is presented in Table 6-12. The total degrees of freedom are 19, and these are partitioned among the explained and unexplained sources of variation in exactly the same manner as described in the previous section. The F ratio is 3.98, and as this is greater than the critical limit of F with 5 and 14 degrees of freedom at the 95 percent confidence level, which is 2.96, the surface is accepted as explaining a significantly greater proportion than that which would be achieved by chance alone.

The problem, however, with this form of the analysis-of-variance test is that it does not indicate whether the quadratic surface adds a significant degree of explanation to that given by the linear surface. A method for obtaining an indication of whether the explanation is greater than that which would be achieved by chance alone with the inclusion of extra variables has been detailed for nominal variables and regions in the preceding section. This method is applied to trend surface analysis by Krumbein and Graybill (1965), and the application to the New England series of diachronic trend models is detailed in Table 6-13. The linear surface tests as being significant at the 95 percent confidence level, but the additional sums of squares for the quadratic and cubic surfaces do not add any greater explanation than might have been achieved by chance alone with the additional variables. Thus, it can be concluded that the best model is the linear trend surface, which indicates a general east-west

Table 6-12 ANALYSIS OF VARIANCE OF THE NEW ENGLAND QUADRATIC SURFACE

Source of variation	Sums of squares	Degrees of freedom	Mean sums of squares	F
Explained by model	1,712.10	5	342.42	
Unexplained	1,204.85	14	86.06	3.98
Total variation	2,916.95	19		

regional trend. A map of residuals from this surface would suggest the local variations.

Geographic interpretation of the significance tests   The recurring intuitive nagging problems of spatial autocorrelation, and multicollinearity among "independent" variables that are obviously not independent, has raised several doubts concerning the use of power polynomials in trend surface analysis. Although the F test appears to be the most commonly used measure of the reliability of a fitted trend surface, Chayes and Suzuki (1963) cast some doubt on assuming the existence of a surface when the contribution of that surface to the sum of squares is small. Furthermore, Howarth (1967), using data derived from sixty sets of randomly generated data points, suggests that for low-order surfaces (1 to 3) there are occasions when the F test may be misleading, though the evidence upon which this assertion is based is somewhat flimsy (Norcliffe, 1969).

To gain some insight into the possible effect of these recurring nagging problems on the F ratio, an experiment on simulated data with the type of test detailed in Table 6-13 has been conducted. Two hundred sets of data, each consisting of twenty, forty-five, sixty, and seventy-five observations, and one thousand sets of data containing thirty observations have been generated. The increase in sample size implies an increase in sample intensity. For each set, the values of Y are chosen randomly, and the m and n coordinates are also chosen at random. Thus, on taking into account the level of significance, the null hypoth-

Table 6-13   ANALYSIS OF VARIANCE OF NEW ENGLAND DIACHRONIC SURFACES

Source of variation	Cumulative sums of squares	Additional sums of squares	Degrees of freedom	Mean sums of squares	F
Explained by linear	1,008.98	1,008.98	2	504.49	
					4.49
Unexplained		1,907.97	17	112.23	
Explained by quadratic	1,712.10	703.12	3	234.37	
					2.72
Unexplained		1,204.85	14	86.06	
Explained by cubic	1,808.46	96.36	4	24.09	
					.22
Unexplained		1,108.49	10	110.85	
Total variation		2,916.95	19		

esis should always be accepted; there should be no instance in which the linear surface is regarded as significant, and there should be no instance in which an additional surface contributes a significant increase in the sums of squares for any set.

The details of the results of this series of experiments are presented in Table 6-14. If the 95 percent confidence level is used, then there may be as many as 5 cases in 100 in which a Type II error is made (accepting a hypothesis which is, in fact, false). If the 99 percent confidence level is used, then there may be 1 case in 100 in which a Type II error is made. Table 6-14 shows for each sample size, for each order of surface, and for each level of significance, the percentage number of occasions in which a Type II error is made. Those cases in which more than the *expected number* of Type II errors occurs are in italics. The conclusion is that the F test detailed in Table 6-13 is, on the whole, quite satisfactory for data distributed randomly in space. The Type II errors that do occur above the expected frequency take place for surfaces greater than the cubic, and for the largest sample size. Thus the advice would be: When using power polynomials stay away from surfaces of higher order than the cubic, and be careful of "forcing" a result with a large sample, for a surface that tests as significant may, very occasionally, really be a phantom!

Table 6-14   RESULTS OF SIMULATED EXPERIMENT CONCERNING THE SIGNIFICANCE OF A TREND SURFACE: THE PERCENTAGE FREQUENCY OF OCCURRENCE OF A TYPE II ERROR

Order of surface	Confidence level, %	Expected frequency	Number of observations				
			20	30*	45	60	75
Linear	99	1	1	1	1	0.5	*2*
	95	5	4	4	3.5	3.5	*5.5*
Quadratic	99	1	0	*1.8*	*1.5*	0	0.5
	95	5	4.5	4.9	3	*6*	4.5
Cubic	99	1	0.5	0.5	0	1	1
	95	5	2.5	*5.5*	4.5	4.5	*6*
Quartic	99	1	*1.5*	0.9	1	0.5	0
	95	5	*6.5*	*5.6*	4	4.5	*6*
Quintic	99	1		0.8	*0.5*	0	*1.5*
	95	5		4.1	*5.5*	4	*6.5*
Sextic	99	1		*1.5*	1	*1.5*	*1.5*
	95	5		4.5	*5.5*	4	*7*

* Based on 1,000 sets of randomly generated data; all the rest are based on 200 sets of data.

Note: Computations in double precision. Computer program prepared by Mr. T. G. Nicholson. Computations on an IBM 360-50 at Queen's University, Kingston, Canada.

7

TIME AND DIFFUSION

In the previous chapter, methods for describing and analyzing the distribution of phenomena over space have been presented and discussed. These patterns occur over space in time, and a very important aspect of human geography concerns the way in which these patterns have dispersed over the landscape. Investigations concerned with the spread of phenomena over space through time are referred to as *diffusion studies*, which, as Brown (1968*b*) suggests, involve relocation and expansion. There are many techniques and models that have been used by human geographers concerned with the diffusion of phenomena over space, and many of these have been discussed in different contexts in previous chapters. For example, Riddell (1970*a*) uses trend surface analysis to examine the diffusion of "modernization" trends in Sierra Leone, Hagerstrand (1953) uses simple curve fitting to define a distance decay function which is then used to construct a mean information field to model the diffusion of a farm subsidy program in Sweden, and gravity and interaction models have been used by Porter (1964) for analyzing migration in the upper Midwest of the United States. These, and many others (Brown, 1968*b*), have contributed to the development of diffusion as a flourishing area of interest in human geography, an area which lies firmly within the tradition if not the spirit of Sauer (1952).

In this chapter the discussion will focus upon two models and one technique that have not been covered previously and that are among those being used with increasing frequency by geographers in diffusion studies (Brown, 1968a). As with most models and techniques discussed in this volume, the use of the techniques is by no means limited to diffusion studies and so examples are used and references cited that indicate other contexts in which the models may be utilized (Wilson, 1968). The two models, the "logistic-curve model" and the "Markov chain model," have specific theoretical implications, and these are discussed in the context of change through time as well as spatial diffusion. The technique, known as "simulation," is used in many situations in the social sciences (Orcutt, 1961) and will be explained with respect to Hagerstrand's pioneering work.

LOGISTIC CURVE MODELS

A logistic curve is S-shaped and doubly asymptotic (Fig. 7-1). It resembles an exponential growth curve below the inflection point, and the reverse image of an exponential curve above that point. The equation for the logistic function is

$$Y = \frac{L}{1 + ae^{-bX}} \tag{7-1}$$

where Y = dependent variable

X = independent variable (usually some unit of time such as years)

L = parameter (greater than zero) limiting the maximum value of Y which is approached asymptotically as X increases

b = value greater than zero but less than unity that indicates rate at which Y increases with X

a = parameter (greater than zero) which determines value of Y when X is zero

e = base of the natural logarithms, ln

There are a number of methods that can be used for estimating the parameters of the logistic function (Day, 1963), the most accurate of which are based upon some assumed knowledge of the value of L. This limiting value can be obtained empirically by graphic methods, or it can be measured on some theoretical or logical basis. In the ensuing discussion, two methods will be used for estimating the parameters a and b; both methods assume some a priori knowledge of L and

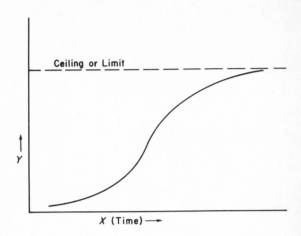

FIGURE 7-1
A logistic curve.

use a transformation of the dependent variable to derive a simple regression equation. These methods are discussed in the contexts of population projection analysis and of the diffusion of the acceptance of hybrid corn in the United States.

A Logistic Curve Projection for the Population of England and Wales

One of the earliest and best-known uses of the logistic function was in the development of models to predict the future growth of population in the world and specific countries. Although the use of the logistic curve appears to have lost popularity in recent years (Isard, 1960, p. 15), some underlying implications of the assumptions and one method of calculation can be illustrated most easily in this context. There are three basic considerations with respect to the growth of the population of the world. One is the amount of space available for habitation and production of food, and this, in the macro sense, is fixed. A second is the technology available, which determines the productivity of land and therefore the output of food per acre. A third is the standard of living that the population of the world is willing to accept, and presumably the minimum level lies a little above mere subsistence. If the technology available is held constant, the population of the world can go on expanding until some maximum level is reached, and beyond that point the surplus either will not be produced or will die off through starvation.

It is postulated that the behavior pattern of people in this type of situation will be analogous to that of flies in a bottle. If flies are enclosed in a bottle (limited space) with a given amount of food, the flies will reproduce until some maximum, at which point the rate of growth of the fly population will cease. Furthermore, the rate of growth is itself related to the maximum value; for the growth rate is exponential in the beginning, but then it decreases at a decreasing rate, approaching the ceiling (or maximum limit) asymptotically. This situation is depicted by the logistic curve in Fig. 7-1. Thus, if it is assumed that the population of the world will grow under analogous restrictive conditions in a manner similar to flies in a bottle, then the population curve for the world, and hence for individual countries, will resemble the growth curve for flies in a bottle (Yule, 1925). Therefore, it is postulated that the logistic model should describe well the historical population data, and can be used for projection purposes.

In this situation, Eq. (7-1) can be rewritten as

$$P_t = \frac{L}{1 + P_0 e^{-bt}} \tag{7-2}$$

where P_t = population at time period t

$\qquad L$ = some estimated maximum population

$\qquad P_0$ = population at an arbitrary starting point in time

$\qquad t$ = time, or some index of time

$\qquad b$ = rate at which population increases in time

The disadvantages of using a function of this kind for fitting a curve to population data and then succumbing to the temptation to predict are only too obvious from the assumptions. For example, the logistic for the population of England and Wales based on decennial data from 1801 to 1911 is presented as calculated by Yule (1925, p. 21) in Fig. 7-2. The estimated figures for the population of England and Wales in 1751 and 1939 and the actual census figures for 1921, 1951, and 1961 are also presented for comparative purposes. In the first place it is interesting to note that the curve fitted to the data used (1801 to 1911) is an extremely good fit. This indicates that in the 110 years preceding 1910 the population of England and Wales (a bounded area) expanded in a geometrical progression that could be considered one part of a logistic growth curve. Secondly, the comparative data for other time periods indicate the great risks in predicting even with a model which has such an apparently good fit. World War I (1914 to 1918), the influenza epidemic that followed it, unemployment in the 1920s, the economic depression of the 1930s, and World War II (1939 to 1945)—all exerted a tremendous impact on birth and death rates.

What, then, would be the shape of the curve if representative data from

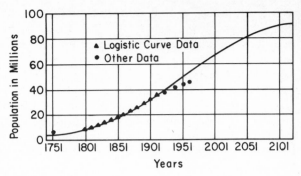

FIGURE 7-2
A logistic curve fitted to the population of England and Wales, 1801 to 1911. (*After Yule*, 1925, *p.* 21.)

1751 to 1961 were used? In order to simplify the presentation of the calculating procedure, five representative years have been chosen, which are, with their associated populations, 1751, 7.3 million; 1801, 8.9 million; 1851, 17.9 million; 1911, 36.1 million; 1961, 46.1 million. The postulated maximum limit is estimated to be 60 million, a figure which would raise the density of 790 persons per square mile in 1961 to 1,028 persons per square mile—a figure far in excess of the current situation in Japan (a little over 700 persons per square mile), a country in which national population control has been encouraged for some years.

Model The basic model can be transformed into a simple regression equation as follows:

$$P_t = \frac{L}{1 + P_0 e^{-bt}} \tag{7-2}$$

and

$$\frac{L}{P_t} = 1 + P_0 e^{-bt}$$

$$\ln\left(\frac{L}{P_t} - 1\right) = \ln P_0 - bt \tag{7-3}$$

Thus, all that is required is the calculation of $\ln\left[(L/P_t) - 1\right]$, and then the worksheet outlined in Fig. 4-11 can be used to estimate the parameters $\ln P_0$ and b. The antilogarithm of $\ln P_0$, with b, will then yield an estimate of the parameters in Eq. (7-2). The step-by-step details in the estimation of the dependent variable are listed in Table 7-1, steps which are, of course, very easy to program.

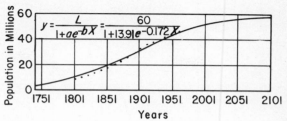

FIGURE 7-3
A logistic curve fitted to the population of England and Wales, 1751 to 1961.

The results of regressing $\ln\left[(L/P_t) - 1\right]$ against an index of time yields an equation with the parameters

$$\ln\left(\frac{L}{P_t} - 1\right) = 2.531 - .167t$$

and so, therefore, P_0 is 12.5, and b is .167. It is interesting to note that these parameters are very similar to those that would be achieved if all the data (1751 and 1801 to 1951) were used (Fig. 7-3). The consequences of using two sets of data from periods of entirely different character and a lower value of L are seen quite clearly in Fig. 7-3, for the curve is flatter than that calculated by Yule (Fig. 7-2), and by no means a good fit, except for the latest data available. This is interesting because it suggests that the population growth curve may well conform to another logistic which at present is difficult to estimate from the limited data available.

A Logistic Curve Analysis of the Spread of Hybrid Corn in the United States

A second, well-known use of the logistic curve with a different kind of transformation of the dependent variable is Griliches' (1957) analysis of the diffusion of hybrid corn in the United States. Hybrid corn was not "invented" in the

Table 7-1 CALCULATION OF THE DEPENDENT VECTOR FOR EQ. (7-3)

Date	Date index	P_t	$\dfrac{60}{P_t}$	$\dfrac{60}{P_t} - 1$	$\ln\dfrac{60}{P_t} - 1$
1751	1	6.3	9.52	8.52	2.142
1801	6	8.9	6.74	5.74	1.747
1851	11	17.9	3.35	2.35	.854
1911	17	36.1	1.66	.66	−.416
1961	22	46.1	1.30	.30	−1.204

(A)

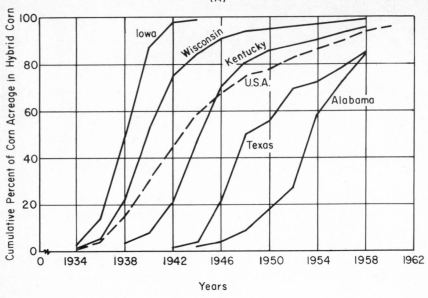

(B)

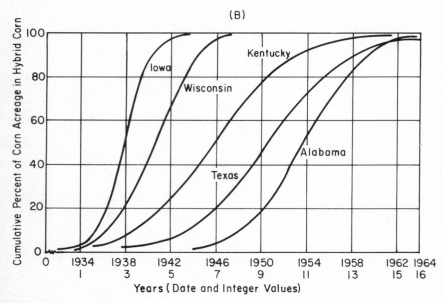

FIGURE 7-4
The adoption of hybrid corn in the United States and five selected states:
(a) ogive curves, (b) logistic curves. (*Data from Agricultural Statistics, U.S.
Department of Agriculture, 1961.*)

same way that the electric lamp or the movie camera was invented. Rather, hybrid corn is the result of the invention of a method of breeding corn for specific localities. Thus a hybrid corn developed for central Iowa is not the same as that developed for northern Alabama. In each case, independent series of crossbreedings and interpollinations with different strains but using the same agrobotanical process resulted in a hybrid corn most suitable for that particular location. The development of the method of breeding hybrid corn is the chief factor underlying the great increase in corn yields per acre in the United States since the 1930s, for some of the hybrids have proved to be much superior to the original varieties used.

Time dimension   Central to the problem concerning the analysis of the spread of the use of hybrid corn is that different states adopted the invention at different times and had different rates of acceptance. This is illustrated in Fig. 7-4a, which presents cumulative percentile diagrams (ogive curves) for five selected states at two-year intervals. The upper limit in each case is 100 percent, which indicates that at this point all the corn acreage in a state is planted in hybrid corn. The diagram illustrates that Iowa, one of the largest producers of corn in the corn belt, was the first of the five states to accept hybrid corn, followed by Wisconsin, Kentucky, Texas, and Alabama. Three of the five states exceeded the United States average in 1958, with the cornlands of Iowa and Wisconsin over 75 percent in hybrid corn before the cornlands of the United States as a whole were 45 percent in hybrid corn.

Table 7-2 presents percentile years, derived from Fig. 7-4a, when at least 10, 50 (the median), and 90 percent of the corn area of each of the five states was planted with hybrid corn. The 10th percentile value is chosen because at this point there would be a significant area of the corn landscape in hybrid corn at an early stage of acceptance. The variation in the year at which this 10th percentile value was attained is related by Griliches (1957, p. 507) to supply

Table 7-2   YEARS IN WHICH 10, 50, AND 90 PERCENT OF THE CORN ACREAGE OF A STATE WAS PLANTED IN HYBRID CORN

State	10%	50%	90%
Iowa	1936	1939	1941
Wisconsin	1937	1940	1946
Kentucky	1941	1945	1954
Texas	1945	1948	1960
Alabama	1949	1954	1960
United States	1938	1943	1956

factors. As the hybrid corn had to be bred independently for each given environment, some areas had hybrid corn seed available before others. This varying
availability was caused, according to Griliches, by the seed producers, who
developed hybrid corn for the principal corn areas first, for it was in these areas
that they could sell the most seed and thereby earn the greatest profits. After
10 percent of the corn area of a state is in hybrid corn, it can be assumed that
enough seed is being produced so that the time difference between 10, 50, and
90 percent area acceptance is related to the varying rates of acceptance within the
individual states rather than the unavailability of the appropriate hybrid corn
seed.

Rate of acceptance and the logistic curve   In order to calculate the average
rate of acceptance within each state, Griliches fits the cumulated percentile
curves to the logistic function. The use of the logistic function for this purpose
has both a sound empirical and a sound theoretical base. Empirically, the curves
presented in Fig. 7-4*a* do resemble the shape of the logistic, particularly that for
Iowa. Theoretically, Casetti (1969) has shown that if it is postulated that
(1) potential users of an innovation become adopters following direct personal
contact with previous adopters, (2) potential users have different levels of
resistance to the idea of accepting a new innovation, and (3) this resistance to
change can be overcome by repeated tellings, then the shape of the curve summarizing the adoption of the innovation will be logistic. The maximum acceptance of the innovation, L, affects the slope of the curve, and Griliches adopts
different ceilings for each state; for example, in Iowa the ceiling was 100 percent,
and in Alabama 80 percent. However, by 1958, two years beyond the time limit
of Griliches' study, 84 percent of the corn acreage in Alabama was already in
hybrid corn, and the trend was for this proportion to increase. In this analysis
the ceilings L have been set at 100 percent, because almost every corn producer
in the United States now uses hybrid corn, and therefore the whole of the corn
acreage in each state should be regarded as potential for hybrid corn.

    Griliches adapts the logistic for his study of the diffusion of an innovation
by adopting Berkson's (1953) transformation of the logistic, which lets

$$a = e^{-\alpha}$$

Therefore, Eq. (7-1) becomes

$$H = \frac{L}{1 + e^{-\alpha}e^{-bt}} \tag{7-4}$$

where H = proportion of corn acreage in a state in hybrid corn

    t = time, integer values

    L = ceiling, or maximum value, of H, here 100 percent, or 1.00

    b = rate-of-acceptance coefficient

    α = constant

Equation (7-4) can be transformed into a simple regression equation as follows:

$$L = H + He^{-(\alpha + bt)}$$

$$\frac{H}{L - H} = e^{\alpha + bt}$$

$$\ln \frac{H}{L - H} = \alpha + bt \qquad (7\text{-}5)$$

The parameters α and b can then be estimated with the use of the worksheet detailed in Fig. 4-11 for calculating the constants for a simple regression model.

The results of fitting the adaptation of the logistic used by Griliches to the data for the five states in Fig. 7-4a are presented in Table 7-3, and the calculated curves are illustrated in Fig. 7-4b. It must be noticed that the curves were fitted to all the available data except in the case of one state, Wisconsin, which exhibits an extreme "tailing off" above the 90th percentile. All values above the 90th percentile were deleted in this one case. With this exception, the logistic hypothesis, as expressed in the transformation in Eq. (7-5), fits the data extremely well for each time period, particularly for Iowa and Alabama. The worst fit is for Texas, which exhibits a number of "steps," or discontinuities, in the original curve. Thus it may be concluded that the acceptance process implied by the logistic function is tenable for the dispersion of hybrid corn in the five states. In realistic terms, as the acceptors are people, it implies that once resistance to the hybrid corn innovation is overcome, the idea is quickly accepted until a few hard-core resistant farmers remain who need some time to be convinced. In Wisconsin there are, perhaps, proportionately more of these hard-core resisters than in Iowa.

The slope of the logistic function b, which in this case refers to the ln adoption ratio $H/(L - H)$ and *not* the proportional number of adopters, H, indicates the average acceptance rate for each state. The acceptance rate is highest for Iowa and lowest for Texas, but the fact that Alabama has the third

Table 7-3 REGRESSION COEFFICIENTS, CORRELA-TION COEFFICIENTS, AND YEARS FOR WHICH THE LOGISTIC CURVES WERE FIT

State	b	r	Years
Iowa	1.8429	.999	1934–1944
Wisconsin	1.5816	.985	1936–1944
Alabama	.8186	.998	1944–1958
Kentucky	.6267	.956	1938–1958
Texas	.5843	.906	1942–1958

highest acceptance rate of the five states indicates that this is not related to the date at which hybrid corn first became a noticeable feature of the landscape (the 10th percentile date). Griliches presents the view that variations in the rate of acceptance are related to the profitability of making the shift from nonhybrid to hybrid corn. Thus on the good cornlands of Iowa it was very profitable to make the shift, whereas on the poorer soils of Texas the profitability was not so apparent to the individual farmer. Although there may be a great deal of truth in Griliches' profitability thesis, there is little doubt that many other factors play a significant part, and lengthy argument has waged back and forth concerning this conclusion (Babcock, 1962). For example, the growing importance of cattle farming in the southeastern United States has undoubtedly encouraged more efficient farming in that area, and therefore hybrid corn is part of the overall change. Also, the increasing yields obtained from hybrid corn have had a feedback effect in that marginal areas have gone out of production.

Use of the logistic curve   The methods chosen for presentation have assumed that the researcher is able to estimate the ceiling L. There are methods for obtaining a solution to the logistic equation if L is not known (Nair, 1954). A method discussed by Rhodes (1940) is an iterative procedure which requires the observations of the independent variable to be drawn at equal incremental intervals. The problem with this, and other similar methods, is not simply that it requires equal incremental intervals, but that it apparently can lead to very poor estimates of a, and therefore bad fits for some data. In these cases, Day (1963) suggests that a be so chosen that the curve is *forced* through one or more observations. The suggestion is, therefore, that if there is some reasonable method of estimating L (as there usually is in human geography), this iterative procedure should be avoided so as to make forcing unnecessary.

Thus the two methods developed for fitting the logistic curve to a series of data require knowledge of the ceiling limit L. In the symbols in Eq. (7-1), these estimating equations are

$$\ln \left(\frac{L}{Y} - 1 \right) = \ln a - bX \tag{7-6}$$

and

$$\ln \frac{Y}{L - Y} = \alpha + bX \tag{7-7}$$

Of these two equations, Eq. (7-6) seems to be the easiest to derive, use, and interpret. In the geographical context it is apparent that the logistic curve model is aspatial, for it does not, of itself, subsume any spatial operator. The use of the curve by Griliches involves spatial comparisons, for the logistics of states are compared, but this use ignores the actual spatial diffusion within the states. Furthermore, the diffusion processes implied by the logistic model, as detailed by Cassetti (1969), are exceedingly simplistic, and the model is not capable of incorporating more complex behavioral characteristics (Brown, 1968b, p. 80). However, in most situations the evidence is not available to develop more complex models, as is evidenced by the use of mean information fields derived from very simple distance-decay functions. The great advantage of the logistic curve is that it does adequately describe the spread of an innovation in developed and less developed areas (Day, 1970).

A SIMULATION MODEL OF DIFFUSION

A quantitative technique that is directly spatial and becoming increasingly important in the analysis of processes in human geography is simulation. Hagerstrand (1953) has adapted the simulation technique to geographic space in order to analyze the diffusion of an innovation over space through time. Simulation models are widely used in the physical and social sciences, and for geography this kind of model has particular appeal because it facilitates spatial-temporal analysis. Morrill (1963) has used simulation models to analyze the spatial distribution of towns in Sweden, Bowden (1965) has used them to test certain behavioral assumptions concerning the spread of irrigation in the western part of the United States, and Morrill (1965) has again used this particular research approach to examine various hypotheses concerning the spread of ghettos within urban areas.

A geographic or spatial simulation begins with a given distribution of acceptors (people) who have already accepted the innovation. Rules are then developed which are thought to govern (control) the ensuing spread of the innovation. All other factors which might influence the spread of the innovation, but which are not included as rules, are considered to interact randomly. This last aspect is particularly important, for the random element also attempts to represent reality by suggesting that within a given framework of rules there is a stochastic element of behavior, an observation which has been made most provocatively by Rogers (1967). The next stage is to develop a series of game operations which control the working of the simulation model itself, and then to generate the diffusion of the innovation within this framework. Finally, a comparison is made between the generated distributions and some later actual distribution in order to discern other factors that might be important but which were ignored in the formation of the first set of rules.

A Model Developed by Hagerstrand

Hagerstrand (1953, 1967) applied the simulation technique to an analysis of the diffusion of a government subsidy program among the farmers within and surrounding the district of Asby, Sweden. The subsidy was introduced in 1928 and was designed to encourage farmers to improve their pastures and to discourage

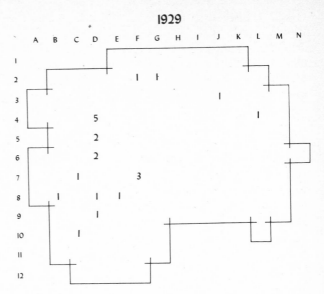

FIGURE 7-5
The distribution of acceptors of a farm subsidy, Asby and surrounding districts,
Sweden, 1929. (*From Hagerstrand*, 1953, *p.* 62.)

them from allowing their cattle to forage in the open woodland. The dispersal
of acceptors in Asby and surrounding districts in 1929 is illustrated in Fig. 7-5,
and this serves as the starting distribution for Hagerstrand. The map (Fig. 7-5)
has been gridded into cells, each of which measures 5 × 5 kilometers, and the
numbers on the map represent the number of farmers in each cell who have
accepted the farm subsidy. The year-by-year diffusion of the innovation to
1932 is presented in Fig. 7-7 and the maps indicate that the idea spread around
the original nucleus of acceptors. This suggests that one of the basic controls
of the spread of the innovation involves factors influencing contact between
farmers.

Mean information field   It is postulated that the possibility of contact between
farmers is influenced by the distance separating them. Thus, Hagerstrand is
concerned with developing some spatial representation of the probability of
contact between individuals over space, and to achieve this he uses migration
data as a surrogate to determine the friction of distance on social contacts
within the area. The migration data are used to calculate a distance decay function (see Fig. 4-8 and p. 83 in Chap. 4), and this curve is then used to define the
mean information field for the Asby area.

The distance-decay function suggests that the probability of the word-of-mouth spread of an innovation should be much higher for near neighbors than for distant neighbors. In spatial terms, one can therefore imagine an area (called a "field") containing probabilities of receiving information from the central point in the field, and this is operationally defined as the mean information field. For the Asby area a mean information field can be obtained by taking the distance-decay curve in Fig. 4-8a and rotating this around 360°, though better fits calculated with different forms of curvilinear transformation could be used (Morrill and Pitts, 1967, p. 418). This would, in effect, present the probability of a location's receiving a migrant from the center of the field. But under the assumption that the individual's perception of distance for social contacts is the same as for migration, it will also represent the probability of a person at a given location experiencing word-of-mouth contact with a person living at the center of the field.

To calculate the mean information field for the Asby district, Hagerstrand divided a 25 × 25 kilometer area into a regular lattice of twenty-five square cells, each cell measuring 5 × 5 kilometers (the same size as the grid used in Figs. 7-5 and 7-7). By rotating the Asby local-migration distance-decay function over 360°, with the origin set at the center point of the center cell, Hagerstrand was able to determine point values for the center of each cell (Fig. 7-6a). For example, a cell with a center point 10 kilometers from the center point of the center cell would have a value of .167, which can be read either from Fig. 4-8b or, more accurately, from Fig. 4-8a. These point values are in households per square kilometer, and they are translated to the number of households per cell by multiplying by 25, for each cell has an area of 25 kilometers. A 10-kilometer point value would therefore become .167 × 25 = 4.17 (Fig. 7-6b). The center-cell value cannot be obtained from the distance decay function because the logarithmic curve grossly overestimates at short distances. As a consequence, the center-cell value is obtained by using the actual number of migrations within this area.

Probabilities of contact for each cell with respect to the center cell can then be calculated by dividing each cell value by the sum of all values. A cell with a center point 10 kilometers from the center point of the center cell would therefore have a probability of

$$P_i = \frac{V_i}{\sum\limits_{i=1}^{25} V_i} = \frac{4.17}{248.24} = .0168$$

where V_i = point value of ith cell

P_i = probability of ith cell's having contact with the center cell

The twenty-five cell probabilities (Fig. 7-6c) can then be accumulated (in any sequence) from .0001 to 1.0000, so that the interval in each cell is determined

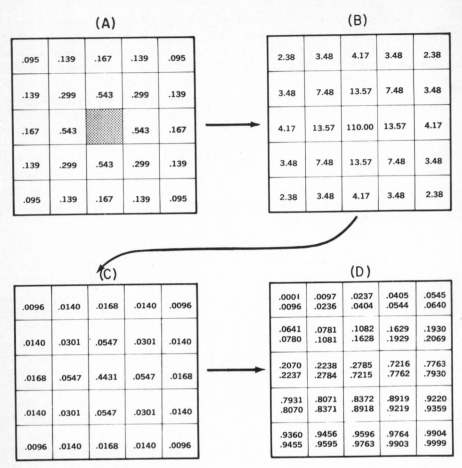

FIGURE 7-6
Stages in the calculation of the mean information field of the Asby area.

by its respective probability (Fig. 7-6*d*). This last procedure makes it possible to use random numbers to represent the random process, though it is to be noted that the slight rounding error results in a cumulation to .9999.

Rules of the simulation Hagerstrand (1953) has developed a number of simulations, each successive model being more complex than the former, and computer programs for these have been prepared by Pitts (1965) and extended to an irregular lattice in a later report (Pitts, 1967). In this discussion only the second simulation model of Hagerstrand will be examined, for the first simulation was based upon a purely random hypothesis. The area in which the simulation of the diffusion of a farm subsidy program is to take place is that presented in Fig. 7-5. The surface of this area is assumed to be uniform in all respects, which, as far as this model is concerned, means that the population is presumed to be evenly distributed and the transport surface is assumed to be "uniform." The latter assumption implies that all contacts can be made equally easily in any direction. The area can therefore be regarded as an unbiased gaming table with an equal number of potential acceptors in each cell.

There are four game operations and rules which govern the process of diffusion in the model:

1 There is one person, or a given distribution of persons, who is a carrier of the idea at the start. This given distribution is presented in Fig. 7-5 for 1929.

2 The mechanism for spreading information is systematized by stipulating that the information is transmitted at constant intervals (known as "generation intervals") when the information is imparted by word-of-mouth contact at pairwise meetings by a "teller."

3 When a carrier has told a noncarrier, the information is immediately accepted. This means that the number of acceptors should increase geometrically, which for the Asby example suggests a rate of increase as follows: 22, 44, 88, 176, ... However, this progression will not be fully in evidence because some tellings may take place beyond the boundary of the Asby area. Also, during a generation interval, two tellers might pass the information to the same receiver, or one teller might pass the information to another carrier—situations that are likely to occur increasingly as the number of tellers increases.

4 The probability of a carrier and another person's being paired depends on the distance between the two, and this probability is defined by the empirically determined mean information field for that area.

With the above rules and the starting distribution, the simulation can now commence. The accumulated probabilities (Fig. 7-6*d*) provide the position of a receiver when each four-digit random number is drawn in sequence from a table of random numbers. The accumulated mean information field acts as a "floating grid," the center of which is placed over each teller at each generation. For the first generation the center of Fig. 7-6*d* is placed over cell F2 in Fig. 7-5. The first random number is .7986, which falls in the interval .7931 to .8070 on the floating grid. Thus one person receives the information in cell D3. The floating grid moves and then centers over G2, and the second random number is used. This number is .9347, which falls in the interval .9220 to .9359. This

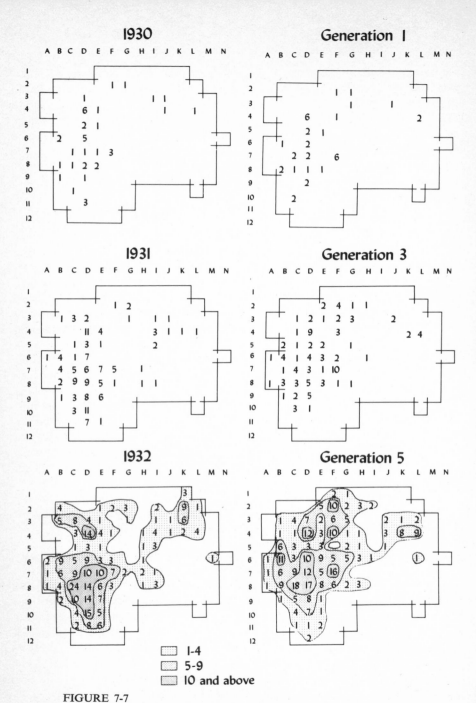

FIGURE 7-7
A comparison between Hagerstrand's second simulation model and the actual
diffusion of the decision to accept a farm subsidy. (*From Hagerstrand, 1967,
pp. 17 and 23.*)

means that one person receives (and therefore accepts) the information in a cell to the southwest of the teller, that is, in cell I3. The procedure continues with twenty additional random numbers used in sequence until the first generation is completed (Fig. 7-7, 1930).

Comparison between the simulation and the real-world pattern   A comparison between the second simulation of Hagerstrand and the development of the real-world pattern is illustrated in Fig. 7-7. For three real-world time periods, five simulation generations were necessary to produce comparable numbers of acceptors. As a consequence, only the comparative generations are presented: generation 1 to compare with 1930, generation 3 to compare with 1931, and generation 5 to compare with 1932. In gross terms, the processes in the simulation yield rather similar distributions at each time period. The distribution, for example, in 1931 is particularly dependent on the distribution in 1930, and the distance decay rate maintains the original 1929 concentration in the western part of the area. A visual comparison of the simulated and actual distributions for 1932 reveals the development of some differences, for the actual pattern appears to be more concentrated in the south and west than the simulated. These differences may well be due to the rigidity of the assumptions, or rules. The population of the area is not distributed evenly, and the number of acceptors in a cell is obviously related to the number of possible acceptors, so that the total number of acceptors at each period in time should conform to a logistic trend. Furthermore, there is not a uniform transport surface, and people do not tend to accept new ideas immediately. These assumptions are relaxed by Hagerstrand (1953) in a third model.

The visual comparison of generation 5 with the 1932 actual distribution raises the important geostatistical question of whether the two maps are significantly similar. There are a number of methods that have been used or could be suggested, such as planes of best fit (Robinson and Caroe, 1967), the use of simple correlation (Taaffe et al., 1963), comparison of the parameters of conformant trend surfaces, or multivariate-multiple-regression procedures (Anderson, 1958). One technique that has been tested in this particular context has been reported by Anderson (1965, pp. 10–11), who applies two- and three-color contiguity ratios (Dacey, 1968) to test whether the actual pattern is as possible an outcome of the model as in generation 5. For example, in the two-color case each cell containing one or more farms adopting the subsidy is colored black, and those cells with no adopters are labeled white. The maps are then overlain, and the number of black-on-black, white-on-white, and black-on- (or under) white cells are recorded. The statistical question is now whether the number of joins in each category, and particularly the black-white joins, is significantly greater than would occur if both patterns were random. Anderson (1965) concludes that the black-white pattern has a definite nonrandom element in its arrangement, but suggests that more sophisticated tests are desirable.

MARKOV CHAIN MODELS

Although Markov chain models are fairly easy to explain with simple examples, the mathematical basis for the technique is fairly complex and has been detailed exhaustively in the literature (Kemeny and Snell, 1960; Bharucha-Reid, 1960). Much of this work is based on the desire of researchers to develop models that incorporate learning processes (Golledge and Brown, 1967), for the technique makes explicit use of the information received at some past time to determine a situation more recent. For example, consider a sequence of two events arranged in the following manner (Bush and Mosteller, 1955):

$$AAABAABAAAAABAAABA$$

This sequence starts with an A, and the rule was formulated that the probability of a B following an A is .5, and of a B following a B is 0. Thus the probability of an A following a B is unity, and that of an A following an A is .5. These probabilities can be expressed in matrix form as

(Follows)

$$\text{(Begins)} \begin{array}{c} \\ A \\ B \end{array} \begin{array}{cc} A & B \\ \begin{bmatrix} .5 & .5 \\ 1.0 & .0 \end{bmatrix} \end{array} \qquad \text{(Example 1)}$$

with the starting point being a letter on the rows. This example introduces several important concepts concerning Markov chains, the most important being the notion of *dependency*, for each event in the sequence above depends upon the event immediately prior to it. The nature of this dependency is expressed within a framework of probabilities, and the Markov chain sequence depends directly upon the nature of the framework and the probabilities within it.

The Markov Chain Framework

The limits of the framework are defined by a set of states, $s_1, s_2, s_3, \ldots, s_i, \ldots, s_j, \ldots, s_n$, which in the example above are defined as A and B, for the sequence was in either of these states at a given time period. The states can be defined in many ways, such as classes, groups, or categories of one kind or another. For example, in Clark's (1965) study the states are equally spaced class intervals of contract rents; Marble (1964) and Bourne (1969a) define them as discrete classes of land use; and Rose (1970) uses categories of commercial retail activities. The states are ordered, and they remain as defined and ordered for each time period in the study. Sometimes the order itself has a particular meaning which is inherent in the sequence. In Clark's (1965) study the order of the states implies a sequence of low-cost rents to high-cost rents, whereas in Rose's (1970) analysis the sequence of the states (professional, personal, financial, eating and drinking, and so forth) does not, of itself, imply any particular scaling.

An item can be in one and only one of these states at a given time, and it moves successively within a state or from one state to another in constant intervals. Each of these moves is referred to (jargonistically) as a step, and the probability that the item moves from s_i to s_j depends only on the states s_i that it occupied before the step. These steps are called *transition probabilities* p_{ij}, and they give the probability that an item will move from s_i to s_j for every ordered pair of states. The one-step transition probabilities for an ordered set of states s_1, s_2, and s_3 can, therefore, be expressed in matrix form as

$$t \begin{cases} s_1 \\ s_2 \\ s_3 \end{cases} \overbrace{\begin{matrix} s_1 & s_2 & s_3 \end{matrix}}^{t+1} \begin{bmatrix} p_{11} & p_{12} & p_{13} \\ p_{21} & p_{22} & p_{23} \\ p_{31} & p_{32} & p_{33} \end{bmatrix} \qquad \text{(Example 2)}$$

where the probability that an item in state s_1 in time period t will be in s_3 in time period $t + 1$ is p_{13}; and the probability that an item in state s_2 in time period t will be in s_3 in time period $t + 1$ is p_{23}.

Thus, not only is a matrix of transition probabilities required, but also the distribution of the item (or items) among the various states at the beginning time period. If the movement of just one item is being traced, then the initial starting state will be given by a vector of binary coded numbers. For example, if the item is in state s_2 at time period t, this can be indicated by the vector

$$[s_1 \quad s_2 \quad s_3] = [0 \quad 1 \quad 0] \qquad \text{(Example 3)}$$

Alternatively, a number of items may be distributed among the various states at time period t. This type of distribution is frequently depicted in terms of proportions. For example, if 20 percent of the items are in state s_1; 45 percent in s_2; and 35 percent in s_3, the initial starting vector is

$$[.20 \quad .45 \quad .35]$$

The starting vector is determined empirically, but the transition probability matrix can be determined in a number of ways.

Transition probability matrices   Every transition probability matrix exhibits the same set of properties. First, the sum of the elements in any row must equal unity. Thus, in row 2 of Example 2 above, $p_{21} + p_{22} + p_{23} = 1$, and the same applies to rows 1 and 3. Secondly, the elements of the matrix must be nonnegative, that is, they can be zero or greater than zero. Thirdly, the elements on the diagonal of each transition probability matrix indicate the probability of

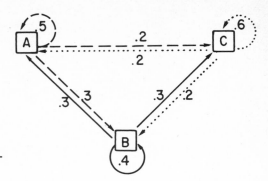

FIGURE 7-8
The probable destination of trips orig-
inating from three distinct locations.

an item's staying in the same state at each step. Conversely, the elements
off the diagonal indicate the probability of a change in state at each step. Each
row of each matrix is a probability vector indicating the probable state of an
item in any particular state s_j at the termination of one step. In this context,
a mean information field is obviously a probability vector.

Brown (1964) mentions three groups of methods that could be used to
calculate a transition probability matrix. The first, and least likely to be used,
is a set of simultaneous equations with each unknown in the equations corresponding to an element in the transition probability matrix, and each equation
referring to a particular time period. Therefore, for large transition probability
matrices, large equations are needed, which require information at many
different time periods. This procedure sounds cumbersome and *is* cumbersome,
and it is for this reason that it is least likely to be used.

A second method requires knowledge of some good (persuasive) theoretical
formulation of the probable degree of connection between associated pairs of
states at different time periods, and then calibration of the probabilities on the
basis of this formulation. As an illustration of this type of procedure an example,
suggested by Horton and Shuldiner (1966), of possible tripmaking behavior
with respect to three spatially distinct land uses will be used. The relative
position of the three distinct land uses is indicated in Fig. 7-8, and the tripmaker
is located on any one of these three spaces. At each time period the tripmaker
must leave the parcel of "land use" on which he happens to be located at that
time, and must go to one of the other two *or* return to the parcel which he just
left. The theory, which is based on notions of distance decay and the friction
of distance, is that the probable destination for each trip depends on the distances between each land-use space. Thus, if the tripmaker is located at A, the
probability of his going to B is .3, and the probability of his ending at C, which

is slightly farther, is .2. The probability of his returning to A (which would require little effort) is .5. Similar sets of probabilities for the parcels of land use at B and C are indicated in Fig. 7-8, and can be placed in the form of a transition probability matrix as follows:

$$
\begin{array}{c}
 \quad A \quad B \quad C \quad \text{Sum} \\
\begin{array}{c} A \\ B \\ C \end{array}
\left[
\begin{array}{ccc}
.5 & .3 & .2 \\
.3 & .4 & .3 \\
.2 & .2 & .6
\end{array}
\right]
\begin{array}{c} 1.0 \\ 1.0 \\ 1.0 \end{array}
\end{array}
\qquad \text{(Example 4)}
$$

A third method is either to calibrate the matrix directly from the data or to estimate the probabilities from analogous or similar sets of data. In the Hagerstrand (1953) case, for example, the probability vector of the mean information field for the diffusion of an innovation in agriculture is estimated from data on migration. Marriage distances, telephone data, and so forth, are other forms of flow information which can be used as surrogates (Harvey, 1967). Frequently, sufficient information is available to calculate the matrices from the actual data, as is exemplified most recently by the work of Bourne (1969b), Rose (1970), and Morley and Thornes (1972).

Construction of a transition probability matrix to examine the filtering process in Kingston This third method calls for the construction of a tally matrix from which the transition probability matrix is derived. As an example of the operation of such a procedure the construction of a transition probability matrix to examine the filtering process in housing in Kingston between 1958 and 1963 will be described. The filtering principle suggests that decrease in the real price of housing relative to housing quality over time makes possible an upward filtering of lower-income groups into better-quality housing. On the other hand, if the real price of housing relative to housing quality is increasing over time the possibility of upward filtering of lower-income families into better-quality housing is severely limited, and in fact downward filtering may occur. In other words, higher socioeconomic groups may occupy the housing formerly occupied by those of lower income or rank (Yeates and Garner, 1971, pp. 284–285).

To examine whether filtering, and which type (upward or downward), or stability has occurred in Kingston, Ontario, Canada, Kirkland (1969) has examined the occupancy of 2,495, or approximately 15 percent, of the homes in Kingston for 1958 and 1963. The head of household of each of these homes is classified by occupation into one of seven groupings, unskilled, service, craft, clerical, sales, managerial, professional; and these groups are ordered according to the *average income* of each as indicated by the 1961 census of Canada. Thus, a house can be classified by the socioeconomic position of its occupant in 1958 and 1963, and the states are defined by the occupational groupings. If a home has filtered down from being occupied by a professional head of house in 1958 to being occupied by a service worker in 1963, then the operational definition is that upward filtering has occurred in that the lower-income family now occupies a home formerly occupied by a higher-income family.

A tally matrix of the occupancy of each of these 2,495 homes can therefore be constructed quite meaningfully with these ordered states. From Table 7-4 it can be learned that 64 that were occupied by craftsmen in 1958 were occupied by unskilled workers in 1963, 95 were occupied by service workers, 337 remained in the occupancy of craftsmen, 13 were occupied by clerical workers, 22 by sales people, 29 by those in managerial occupations, and 8 by those in the professions. A filtering upward of families into homes previously occupied by families of higher economic status is, therefore, indicated by entries to the left of the diagonal; and a filtering downward of families into homes of those previously occupied by families of lower economic status is indicated by entries to the right of the diagonal. Thus, 179 of the homes that were occupied by unskilled workers in 1958 were still occupied by unskilled workers in 1963; 62 were occupied by service workers; 39 by craftsmen; 7 by clerical workers; 18 by sales people; 10 by those in managerial occupations; and 5 by those in the professions.

While a certain proportion of these changes may well be the result of errors in classification due to imperfections in the original data (voter enumeration lists), it is assumed that the errors offset each other, and that the overall matrix is a good summary of filtering in Kingston during this period. The tally matrix can be converted into a transitional probability matrix by presenting each element as a proportion of the total number of homes in each row. Thus, element p_{11} is $\frac{179}{320} = .559$; and p_{47} is $\frac{13}{138} = .094$. The result of these calcula-

Table 7-4   TALLY MATRIX OF THE OCCUPANCY OF 2,495 HOMES IN KINGSTON IN 1958 AND 1963

1958 state	1963 state							
	1	2	3	4	5	6	7	Total
1 Unskilled	179	62	39	7	18	10	5	320
2 Service	116	359	103	31	32	12	18	671
3 Craft	64	95	337	13	22	29	8	568
4 Clerical	11	23	12	66	7	6	13	138
5 Sales	27	40	25	15	96	18	23	244
6 Managerial	10	24	19	12	23	146	17	251
7 Professional	6	25	21	9	20	15	207	303
Total	413	628	556	153	218	236	291	2,495

SOURCE: Data supplied by J. S. Kirkland.

tions for each element in the matrix is presented in Table 7-5, and the elements of each row indicate the probability that an item in s_i in 1958 will be in s_j in 1963. The elements on the diagonal indicate stability, and it is interesting to note that stability is greatest for the highest economic groups, and apparently lowest for those in which classification problems were the greatest.

Some comments concerning transitional probability matrices   At this stage in the discussion at least two comments are in order on transitional probability matrices. First, if any element on the diagonal were unity, the state to which it pertains would be an *absorbing state*, for it would be impossible for any element to leave that state at any stage in the chain. For example, if element p_{33} in Table 7-5 were 1.00, all houses occupied by craftsmen in 1958 would be occupied by craftsmen in 1963. Secondly, if there were no data for one state, then that state would be inaccessible, and other states would not be accessible from that state, for all elements of the row would be zero. It is obvious that absorbing states and states for which all the transitional probabilities are zero are not permissible for an effective Markov chain model. Both situations can be avoided either by deleting the appropriate state, or by combining them with other states.

The Use of Markov Chains for Simulations and Projections

The transition probability matrix is the basis for the use of Markov chains for simulation and projection purposes (Krumbein, 1967), if it is assumed that the probabilities in the matrix are an adequate representation of the sequence of events through time. As an initial example of the use of the matrix for these purposes, the hypothetical case of movement of an individual among three different land uses will provide an illustration (Example 4). Suppose that the

Table 7-5   TRANSITION PROBABILITY MATRIX FOR HOMES IN KINGSTON, 1958 TO 1963, BASED ON TABLE 7-4

1958 state	1963 state							
	1	2	3	4	5	6	7	Total
1	55.9	19.4	12.2	2.2	5.6	3.1	1.6	100.0
2	17.3	53.4	15.4	4.6	4.8	1.8	2.7	100.0
3	11.3	16.7	59.3	2.3	3.9	5.1	1.4	100.0
4	8.0	16.7	8.7	47.8	5.1	4.3	9.4	100.0
5	11.1	16.4	10.2	6.1	39.4	7.4	9.4	100.0
6	4.0	9.5	7.6	4.8	9.2	58.1	6.8	100.0
7	2.0	8.3	6.9	3.0	6.6	5.0	68.2	100.0

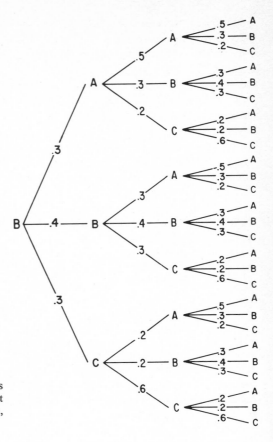

FIGURE 7-9
A tree diagram indicating the various paths along which a move beginning at B may end at state A, B, or C in one, two, or three steps.

individual starts on land use B, a situation which is depicted by the initial-stage vector in Example 3. What is the probability of his ending up at B after one trip, or step? Obviously it is .4. What is the probability of his ending at B after two moves, or steps? He could end up at B by three routes, through A, B, and C, and these are indicated in the tree diagram in Fig. 7-9. The probability of his ending at B after two steps can be traced along this diagram as the sum of the *conditional probabilities* of all paths that terminate at B. These are

$$(.3)(.3) + (.4)(.4) + (.3)(.2) = .31$$

The probability of his ending at B after three steps is, therefore,

$$(.3)(.5)(.3) + (.3)(.3)(.4) + (.3)(.2)(.2) + (.4)(.3)(.3) + (.4)(.4)(.4)$$
$$+ (.4)(.3)(.2) + (.3)(.2)(.3) + (.3)(.2)(.4) + (.3)(.6)(.2) = .295$$

The calculation of these probabilities is obviously a very lengthy and repetitive procedure after two steps, particularly if the probability of an item beginning in *any* state s_i and ending in *any* state s_j is desired. From our knowledge of matrix multiplication it will be observed that the procedure outlined above for one element can be achieved for all elements by simple matrix multiplication. The probability of any item in state s_i being in state s_j after two steps is simply the square of the matrix

$$\mathbf{P}^2 = \begin{bmatrix} .5 & .3 & .2 \\ .3 & .4 & .3 \\ .2 & .2 & .6 \end{bmatrix} \cdot \begin{bmatrix} .5 & .3 & .2 \\ .3 & .4 & .3 \\ .2 & .2 & .6 \end{bmatrix} = \begin{bmatrix} .38 & .31 & .31 \\ .33 & .31 & .36 \\ .28 & .26 & .46 \end{bmatrix}$$

which can be expressed more succinctly as $\mathbf{P} \cdot \mathbf{P} = \mathbf{P}^2$. Thus the probability that any item in state s_i will be in state s_j after three steps is $\mathbf{P} \cdot \mathbf{P} \cdot \mathbf{P} = \mathbf{P}^2 \cdot \mathbf{P} = \mathbf{P}^3$, and after four steps it is $\mathbf{P} \cdot \mathbf{P} \cdot \mathbf{P} \cdot \mathbf{P} = \mathbf{P}^3 \cdot \mathbf{P} = \mathbf{P}^4$, and after n steps it is $P^{n-1} \cdot \mathbf{P} = \mathbf{P}^n$. This procedure is known as *powering the matrix*, and it is a simple operation to perform on any computer.

The results of powering the matrix in Example 4 from $\mathbf{P}^1$ to $\mathbf{P}^9$ are indicated in Table 7-6. These computations were performed on an IBM 360-65, as are many of the other smaller exercises in this volume, with the use of a programming language (APL) which is particularly suited to matrix operations and computer-aided instruction procedures (Yeates and Nicholson, 1969). It is to be noted that in the last stages of powering, the elements of the matrix become similar to the associated elements in the matrix immediately prior to it. In other words, $\mathbf{P}^7$ is almost the same as $\mathbf{P}^8$, and $\mathbf{P}^8$ is scarcely different from $\mathbf{P}^9$. This convergence of the matrices occurs usually after six or seven steps, and the property has important repercussions when the procedure is used for projections.

The Kingston example   The tally matrix (Table 7-4) and transition probability matrix (Table 7-5) can be used to project the distribution of homes among the various occupational groupings at future time periods, if it is assumed that the population of homes within the system remains constant. The initial vector can be derived from the last column of Table 7-4, which gives the total number of homes in the sample in 1958 occupied by the various states. This vector can be expressed in percentage terms as

$$\mathbf{K}_t = \begin{bmatrix} 12.8 & 26.9 & 22.8 & 5.5 & 9.8 & 10.1 & 12.1 \end{bmatrix}$$

Given the transition probability matrix described in Table 7-5, which will be designated $\mathbf{H}^1$, what will be the projected distribution for 1968? (For the matrix $\mathbf{H}^1$ is estimated on the basis of a five-year interval.) If

$$\underset{1 \times 7}{[\mathbf{K}_t]} \cdot \underset{7 \times 7}{[\mathbf{H}^1]} = \underset{1 \times 7}{[\mathbf{K}_{t+1}]}$$

the period $t + 1$ conforms to 1963, and so K_{t+1} replicates the actual 1963 situation, which is detailed in raw figures in the last row of Table 7-4.

Since 1968 is K_{t+2},

$$[K_{t+2}] = [K_t \cdot H^2]$$
$$= [18.2 \quad 24.7 \quad 22.1 \quad 6.3 \quad 8.4 \quad 9.1 \quad 11.2]$$

This K_{t+2} vector conforms very closely to the actual situation for the sample of houses, which was

$$[18.4 \quad 26.2 \quad 22.4 \quad 6.0 \quad 7.3 \quad 8.4 \quad 11.3]$$

The chain for seven time periods is listed in Table 7-7, and it is to be noted that the projected vector converges after the fifth projection. This is to be expected because the transition probability matrix itself usually converges after the fifth or sixth powering, as has been demonstrated in the previous section. The vector

Table 7-6   THE RESULTS OF POWERING THE MATRIX P FROM P^1 TO P^9

$$P^1 = \begin{bmatrix} .5 & .3 & .2 \\ .3 & .4 & .3 \\ .2 & .2 & .6 \end{bmatrix}$$

$$P^2 = \begin{bmatrix} .38 & .31 & .31 \\ .33 & .31 & .36 \\ .28 & .26 & .46 \end{bmatrix}$$

$$P^3 = \begin{bmatrix} .345 & .300 & .355 \\ .330 & .295 & .375 \\ .310 & .280 & .410 \end{bmatrix}$$

$$P^4 = \begin{bmatrix} .3335 & .2945 & .3720 \\ .3285 & .2920 & .3795 \\ .3210 & .2870 & .3920 \end{bmatrix}$$

$$P^5 = \begin{bmatrix} .32950 & .29225 & .37825 \\ .32775 & .29125 & .38100 \\ .32500 & .28950 & .38550 \end{bmatrix}$$

$$P^6 = \begin{bmatrix} .328075 & .291400 & .380525 \\ .327450 & .291025 & .381525 \\ .326450 & .290400 & .383150 \end{bmatrix}$$

$$P^7 = \begin{bmatrix} .3275625 & .2910875 & .3813500 \\ .3273375 & .2909500 & .3817125 \\ .3269750 & .2907250 & .3823000 \end{bmatrix}$$

$$P^8 = \begin{bmatrix} .32737750 & .29097375 & .38164875 \\ .32729625 & .29092375 & .38178000 \\ .32716500 & .29084250 & .38199250 \end{bmatrix}$$

$$P^9 = \begin{bmatrix} .327310625 & .290932500 & .381756875 \\ .327281250 & .290914375 & .381804375 \\ .327233750 & .290885000 & .381881250 \end{bmatrix}$$

of convergence is termed the *unique fixed-point probability vector of* **H**, and it can be regarded as a state of equilibrium. The unique fixed-point probability vector of **H**, $\mathbf{K}_u$, is

$$\mathbf{K}_u = [19.7 \quad 24.9 \quad 22.0 \quad 6.3 \quad 8.1 \quad 8.6 \quad 10.4]$$

and the vector of differences between this and $\mathbf{K}_t$,

$$[+6.9 \quad -2.0 \quad -.8 \quad +.8 \quad -1.7 \quad -1.5 \quad -1.6]$$

suggests an upward filtering, particularly of unskilled workers, into homes previously occupied by the higher-ranked economic groups.

The discussion thus far has been limited to first-order Markov chains, that is, a situation at time period t which exerts a dominant influence on the situation at period $t + 1$. Markov chains can also be long-memory events, where a situation at time period t may exert, for example, a dominant influence on $t + 5$. This form of model is described as a fifth-order Markov chain. In a sense, the Kingston filtering example, though couched in terms of a first-order chain, could be regarded as a long-memory model because the transition probability matrix is defined over a number of years. Furthermore, growth can be incorporated in certain situations by adding the growth factors to the elements on the diagonal of the transition probability matrix (Rogers and Miller, 1967). Thus, in the conceptual range of models extending from the purely random [Hagerstrand's (1953) first simulation model] to the purely deterministic (the transportation problem), the Markov chain model occupies an intermediary position (Harvey, 1967); for though it is developed within a framework of probabilities, the chain sequence is deterministic in nature.

Table 7-7 THE MARKOV CHAIN PREDICTION OF THE DISTRIBUTION OF HOMES AMONG THE VARIOUS OCCUPATIONAL GROUPINGS IN KINGSTON, $\mathbf{K}_{t+1}$ TO $\mathbf{K}_{t+7}$

Time	Unskilled	Service	Craft	Clerical	Sales	Managerial	Professional
$\mathbf{K}_t$	12.8	26.9	22.8	5.5	9.8	10.1	12.1
$\mathbf{K}_{t+1}$	16.5	25.2	22.3	6.1	8.7	9.5	11.7
$\mathbf{K}_{t+2}$	18.2	24.7	22.1	6.3	8.4	9.1	11.2
$\mathbf{K}_{t+3}$	19.0	24.7	22.0	6.3	8.2	8.9	10.9
$\mathbf{K}_{t+4}$	19.3	24.7	22.0	6.3	8.2	8.8	10.7
$\mathbf{K}_{t+5}$	19.5	24.8	22.0	6.3	8.2	8.7	10.5
$\mathbf{K}_{t+6}$	19.7	24.8	22.0	6.3	8.2	8.6	10.4
$\mathbf{K}_{t+7}$	19.7	24.9	22.0	6.3	8.1	8.6	10.4

8

NONPARAMETRIC STATISTICS

In the discussion of various forms of measurement in Chap. 1, it was indicated that in many situations in human geography nominal and rank-ordered scales are frequently the only type of measurement that can be obtained. Though several of the examples in the preceding chapters have made use of variables that are either nominally scaled or rank-ordered, they have been treated as if they were measured on an interval or ratio scale so that they could be included in models that required the calculation of means, variances, and standard deviations. A number of statistical techniques have been developed which do not make use of parameters of this kind, and these are called "nonparametric" techniques (Siegel, 1956). Many of these techniques make use of the ranking of data or grouping of observation units as well as simple dichotomous scaling (Kendall, 1955). As a consequence, nonparametric techniques are useful tools either when the data can only be nominally scaled or rank-ordered, or when the data are so untrustworthy that only a rank order can be inferred. Furthermore, if the data derived from a sample are nonnormal and cannot be normalized by any readily interpretable transformation, the use of nonparametric techniques may again be most appropriate. The methods described in this chapter will be concerned directly with nonparametric correlation techniques and goodness-of-fit tests.

NONPARAMETRIC CORRELATION TECHNIQUES

As the data that are of concern in this chapter refer to variables that are measured on either nominal or ordinal scales, it is appropriate that the correlation techniques described pertain separately to variables calibrated according to these different forms of measurement. Though there are a number of correlation techniques that could be used (Siegel, 1956, pp. 195–239), the discussion will focus upon one technique that is useful for nominally scaled variables, and two techniques that are useful for ordinally scaled variables. Only one of these techniques has experienced widespread use in human geography, and this is, perhaps, due more to the lack of attention devoted to nonparametric techniques in general than to any fundamental disutility of any of them for geographic research.

The Correlation of Nominally Scaled Variables

A statistic which is commonly used for correlating nominally scaled variables is the *contingency coefficient*. The calculation of this coefficient will be described for data obtained from surveys of homes in two Canadian urban areas, Winnipeg and Kingston. In each of these urban areas, 100 homes have been selected at random, and each home has been classified according to the type of residence in which the home is located, and the stage in the life cycle of the family which occupies that home. Both type of residence and stage in the life cycle are nominally scaled variables. If the home occupies a single-family residence, or one unit of a duplex or row of townhouses, the home is classified as occupying a single-family residence. If the home is in a house converted into apartments, or in a low- or high-rise apartment building, then the home is classified as occupying a multifamily residence. Thus the first variable describing the type of residency of the home is nominally scaled by whether it occupies a single or multifamily structure. The second variable defines life cycle stage by whether or not the family has children.

    The data can be grouped into a 2 × 2 square table, where the information for Winnipeg is listed in regular type and that for Kingston in italics (Table 8-1). The research seeks to determine whether the home occupancy situation in Winnipeg is similar to that in Kingston. The contingency coefficient c is calculated on the basis of the differences between the frequencies in each group. Therefore, the larger the difference between the values, the higher the coefficient. The coefficient is defined as

$$c = \sqrt{\frac{\chi^2}{N + \chi^2}} \tag{8-1}$$

The chi-square (χ^2) value in the equation is calculated as

$$\chi^2 = \sum_{i=1}^{r} \sum_{j=1}^{c} \frac{O_{ij} - E_{ij}}{E_{ij}} \tag{8-2}$$

where r = number of rows
   c = number of columns
   O = observed frequency
   E = expected frequency

In this particular case the observed frequencies are defined by the Winnipeg sample data, and the expected frequencies are defined by the Kingston sample data.

The procedure for calculating χ^2 is detailed in Table 8-2. It will be noted that a very slight difference in value of χ^2 would be calculated if Kingston were compared against Winnipeg rather than Winnipeg against Kingston. By substituting χ^2 value in Eq. (8-1), the contingency coefficient is estimated to be

$$c = \sqrt{\frac{4.35}{100 + 4.35}} = \sqrt{.04} = .2$$

Table 8-1   THE FREQUENCY OF OCCURRENCE OF FAMILIES WITH AND WITHOUT CHILDREN IN SINGLE- AND MULTIFAMILY RESIDENCES IN WINNIPEG (1969) AND KINGSTON (1970)

	Single family		Multifamily		Total	
With children	(a) 66	60	(b) 13	20	79	80
Without children	(c) 13	10	(d) 8	10	21	20
Total	79	70	21	30	100	100

Table 8-2   PROCEDURE FOR CALCULATING χ^2 FOR THE WINNIPEG AND KINGSTON SAMPLE DATA

Cell	Winnipeg	Kingston	W − K	(W − K)^2	$\dfrac{(W - K)^2}{K}$
a	66	60	6	36	.60
b	13	20	−7	49	2.45
c	13	10	3	9	.90
d	8	10	−2	4	.40
Total	100	100			4.35

If the data for the two urban areas were perfectly correlated, c would equal zero, but the value of c when the data are perfectly uncorrelated varies.

Comments concerning the contingency coefficient The fact that the value of c for completely uncorrelated data varies limits the use of the coefficient severely. For example, the upper limit of c for a 2×2 table is .707, and for a 3×3 table it is .816 (Siegel, 1956, p. 201). Thus it is possible to compare contingency coefficients for tables of the same dimension, but it is not possible to compare them if they are derived from tables of different dimensions. The coefficient itself cannot be used in the same way as Pearson's r; that is, it cannot be manipulated to indicate the proportion of the variation in one set of data that is associated with another. Furthermore, the sampling distribution of c is mathematically very complex to compute, and so normally the significance of the degree of association between the sets of data is usually calculated by using the sampling distribution of χ^2, a statistic that is estimated "on the way" to estimating c.

Chi Square

The value of χ^2 for the Winnipeg-Kingston random sample of homes is calculated to be 4.35. If there were perfect agreement between the two sets of data, χ^2 would be zero. The question that arises, therefore, is whether the calculated value is significantly different from zero, the null hypothesis being that any difference between the two sets of data is simply the product of sampling error, for both are drawn from the same population. Assume that the distribution of homes of families with and without children among single- and multifamily residences were distributed in exactly the same way in the two cities. If a large number of random samples were drawn, each of 100 homes, it would be possible to estimate a large number of chi-square values within the framework of Tables 8-1 and 8-2. These chi-square values could be grouped into a histogram, and a continuous curve could be fitted to the grouped discrete data rather in the same way that a normal curve can be fitted to the discrete binomial distribution.

The theoretical distribution of χ^2 values varies according to the dimensions of the table for which the values are calculated. The greater the number of cells, the closer the theoretical distribution approaches a normal distribution. The "size" of the table is indicated by the number of degrees of freedom pertaining to it. Though the degrees of freedom appropriate to tables of this type are discussed at greater length later in the chapter, a sufficient explanation at this stage is that they are equal to the minimum number of cell values that need to be known to calculate all the others (provided that the row and column totals are given). The number of degrees of freedom is given by the product of $(r-1)(c-1)$, which in the Winnipeg-Kingston example is calculated to be $(2-1)(2-1)$, which is unity.

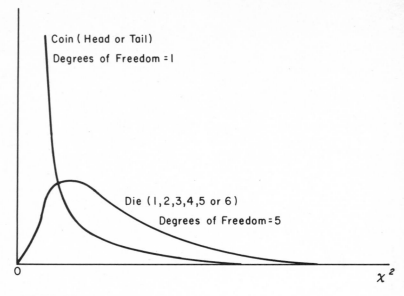

FIGURE 8-1
The sampling distribution of χ^2 for degrees of freedom 1 and 5 generated from throws of a six-sided die. (*From Yeomans*, 1968*b*, *p.* 278.)

The shapes of the chi-square continuous curves for degrees of freedom 1 and 5 are indicated in Fig. 8-1. The critical values of χ^2 at the 95 and 99 percent confidence levels are listed in Table 8-3, and the fact that discrete data are compared with critical values derived from continuous distributions is of little practical concern provided that the expected frequencies in all the cells are at least 5 (Hoel, 1960, p. 161). As the chi-square distribution approaches the normal distribution for degrees of freedom greater than 30, the table of critical values of areas under the normal curve can be used, providing that it is remembered that the χ^2 test is a one-tailed test. For these large degrees of freedom the value of χ^2 is transformed into a normal standard deviate by the expression

$$\sqrt{2\chi^2} - \sqrt{2 \text{ (degrees of freedom)} - 1}$$

Having discussed, very briefly, the χ^2 test of significance, we are now in a position to apply this test to the calculated contingency coefficient for the Winnipeg-Kingston data. The null hypothesis is that there is no difference between the two samples, but this means that when the contingency coefficient is being tested, the hypothesis is that *c is greater* than zero. The chosen confidence level is 0.95, for which the critical value of χ^2 with 1 degree of freedom is 3.841. The 95 percent confidence level has been chosen because the researcher wishes to avoid making a Type I error in the contingency coefficient, which would be very easy to do in this instance because the calculated χ^2 lies between the critical values of χ^2 at the 95 and 99 percent confidence levels. The lower limit is chosen because the samples are so small, relative to the number of homes in the two cities, that it would be unwise to be overconfident and accept a hypothesis that would have interesting theoretical implications concerning the similarity of the towns. Thus at the 95 percent confidence level the null hypothesis is rejected, and it is inferred that the contingency coefficient is significantly different from zero. This implies that the home occupancy situation in Winnipeg is not similar to that in Kingston on the basis of the evidence from these rather limited samples.

THE CORRELATION OF ORDINALLY SCALED VARIABLES

In this section Spearman's rank correlation coefficient r_s and Kendall's rank correlation coefficient τ are used to determine the existence of an association between variables that are *regarded* as ordinally scaled. The data are listed in Table 8-4, and though the method of measurement implies a ratio and interval scaling, it is considered that the basis on which many of the data have been described is so suspect that the most the data can convey is the relative position

Table 8-3   CRITICAL VALUES OF χ^2 AT THE 95 AND 99 PERCENT CONFIDENCE LEVEL

Degrees of freedom	$\chi^2_{0.95}$	$\chi^2_{0.99}$
1	3.841	6.635
2	5.991	9.210
3	7.815	11.341
4	9.488	13.277
5	11.070	15.086
6	12.592	16.812
7	14.067	18.475
8	15.507	20.090
9	16.919	21.666
10	18.307	23.209
15	24.996	30.578
20	31.410	37.566
25	37.652	44.314
30	43.773	50.892

SOURCE: Extracts from Fisher and Yates (1943, table 4).

of each country to the other countries for either variable. The hypothesis to be tested is a reformulation of *Engel's law* of consumption, which suggests that poor families tend to spend a much higher percentage of their incomes on food than do richer families. This observation has been reformulated at the country level of aggregation to suggest that, on the average, the inhabitants of poorer countries tend to spend a higher proportion of their incomes on food and beverages than those in richer countries do. The hypothesis, therefore, is that there should be an *inverse* relation between the two variables, measured on what is considered an ordinal scale, for sixteen randomly chosen countries in 1961.

Spearman's Rank-Correlation Coefficient

The Spearman rank-correlation coefficient is probably the best known and most used of all the nonparametric correlation techniques. The relative position of each observation for each variable is ranked, and the technique determines the correlation between the ranks. It is derived from one of the expressions of the simple correlation coefficient [Eq. (4-21) and Fig. 4-11] in which the X and Y variables are expressed in terms of deviations. This derivation is detailed in

Table 8-4   EXPENDITURES ON FOOD AND BEVERAGES AND PER CAPITA INCOME FOR SIXTEEN RANDOMLY SELECTED COUNTRIES, 1961

Country	Percentage spent on food and beverages	PCI 1961, U.S. dollars
Thailand	48.1	101
Spain	39.5	321
Australia	30.3	1,475
Belgium	32.3	1,348
Jordan	58.9	126
Norway	33.6	1,223
United States	24.3	2,790
Luxembourg	39.8	1,604
Ecuador	51.2	159
Italy	50.2	623
France	38.3	1,203
Honduras	53.6	180
South Vietnam	47.7	111
Ireland	44.7	570
Puerto Rico	33.6	643
Malta	41.2	501

SOURCE: United Nations, "Statistical Yearbook," 1961.

Siegel (1956, pp. 203–204), and the most convenient formula for estimating the nonparametric equivalent of the Pearsonian correlation coefficient is

$$r_s = 1 - \frac{6 \sum\limits_{i=1}^{N} d^2}{N^3 - N} \tag{8-3}$$

Like the simple correlation coefficient, Spearman's r_s varies between -1 (perfect negative correlation), 0 (no correlation), and $+1$ (perfect positive correlation). But, unlike the simple correlation coefficient, it cannot be squared to provide an estimate of the degree of explanation.

In Table 8-5 are listed the ranks of each country for each variable. The difference between the ranks for each observation is calculated, d, squared, d^2, and then summed for all observations. Substituting these figures in Eq. (8-3),

$$r_s = 1 - \frac{6(1,227.45)}{(16)^3 - 16} = 1 - \frac{7,364.70}{4,080} = -.81$$

The calculated value of r_s is to be compared with the absolute value of -1 for perfect negative correlation, but as the data pertain to a random sample, the question arises whether it is significantly different from zero.

Testing the significance of r_s   The null hypothesis is that there is no relation between the two variables, a situation that would be demonstrated by an r_s of .0.

Table 8-5   THE CALCULATION OF $\sum d^2$ FOR THE RANK-ORDERED DATA IN TABLE 8-4

Country	Rank percentage of income spent on food and beverages	Rank of PCI	Difference d	d^2
Jordan	1	14	-13	169
Honduras	2	12	-10	100
Ecuador	3	13	-10	100
Italy	4	8	-4	16
Thailand	5	16	-11	121
South Vietnam	6	15	-9	81
Ireland	7	10	-3	9
Malta	8	9	-1	1
Luxembourg	9	2	7	49
Spain	10	11	-1	1
France	11	6	5	25
Norway	12.5	5	7.5	56.2
Puerto Rico	12.5	7	5.5	30.25
Belgium	14	4	10	100
Australia	15	3	12	144
United States	16	1	15	225
Total				1,227.45

In order to test the significance of the calculated r_s we have to know the distribution of all possible r_s's that could be calculated from the ranking of the sixteen randomly drawn observations. This can be obtained by calculating r_s for all possible permutations of rankings of the sixteen observations for the two variables. If this is done, a frequency distribution of the r_s is obtained, and the value of r_s which includes 95 and 99 percent of all the possible permutations can be determined. This critical value is listed in Table 8-6 as .43 at the 95 percent confidence level and .60 at the 99 percent level, along with the critical values of selected sample sizes from 4 to 30. Thus at both the 95 and 99 percent confidence levels r_s tests as being significantly different from zero, and the null hypothesis is rejected. As it is also negative, the research hypothesis, which is that the percentage of total income on food is inversely related to PCI, is supported.

An alternative procedure for testing the significance of r_s has been suggested by Kendall (1955). This procedure applies only when N is 10 or larger, and it makes use of the fact that the distribution of r_s for large samples (greater than 10) approaches the family of distributions of t. Thus, for large samples, any particular r_s can be transformed to a value of t,

$$t = r_s \sqrt{\frac{N - 2}{1 - r_s^2}} \qquad\qquad (8\text{-}4)$$

Table 8-6   CRITICAL VALUES OF THE SPEARMAN RANK-CORRELATION COEFFICIENT (ONE-TAILED TEST)

Sample size N	Significance level	
	.95	.99
4	1.00	
5	.90	1.00
6	.83	.94
7	.71	.89
8	.64	.83
9	.60	.78
10	.56	.75
12	.51	.71
14	.46	.65
16	.43	.60
18	.40	.56
20	.38	.53
25	.33	.47
30	.31	.43

SOURCE: Adapted from Olds (1938, 1949).

where the critical value of t is to be determined with $N - 2$ degrees of freedom. Applying this procedure to the calculated r_s,

$$t = -.81 \sqrt{\frac{16 - 2}{1 - (-.81)^2}} = -5.17$$

From Table 3-3 it can be discerned that 5.17 is much larger than the critical value of t at both the 95 and 99 percent confidence levels.

Kendall's Tau

Kendall's τ can be used to calculate the correlation between two sets of data that are rank-ordered in a fashion exactly the same as required for Spearman's r_s. The measure is constructed entirely differently, however, and this different procedure is, of itself, exceedingly interesting. It is based upon a comparison of the actual number of conformant pairwise orders in the rankings with the maximum number of pairwise orders that would be achieved if the rankings were exactly the same. The value of τ can assume any number between -1, 0, and 1, with unity's, indicating perfect positive association between the rankings and -1's indicating perfect negative association.

The procedure for calculating τ can be explained best with a simple example. A random sample of four countries has been selected from the random sample of sixteen listed in Table 8-4. The countries chosen are Ecuador a, Luxembourg b, Jordan c, and Belgium d. The rankings for these are as follows:

Country	a	b	c	d
Percentage spent on food and beverages	2	3	1	4
PCI	3	1	4	2

If the order of the countries is rearranged from lowest rank to highest for the percent spent on food and beverages, the analysis can concentrate on the degree to which the numerical order of the ranks of PCI proceeds in the same fashion.

Country	c	a	b	d
Percentage spent on food and beverages	1	2	3	4
PCI	4	3	1	2

The logical sequence demonstrated by the first row is that for any pair of countries, and there are six possible combinations, the country to the right is always of lower rank than the country on the left.

Let us now examine the situation with respect to the second row of ranks, scoring a pair which conforms to the logical sequence of the first row as $+1$, and a pair that does not as -1. The maximum number of possible pairs of countries and associated scores are $c, a = -1$; $c, b = -1$; $c, d = -1$; $a, b = -1$; $a, d = -1$; $b, d = +1$. These scores sum to -4. The maximum

possible total that could have been achieved if the second row had had the ranking of the first row would have been 6. The degree of association between the
two rows is indicated by the ratio between the actual total of scores of the second
row to the maximum possible total which is demonstrated by the first. Thus

$$\tau = \frac{\text{actual total of scores}}{\text{maximum possible total}}$$

$$= \frac{-4}{6} = -.67 \tag{8-5}$$

The maximum possible total is, in effect, the number of ways in which four
things can be taken two at a time, and in the notation of probability theory, it
is indicated by $\binom{4}{2}$, or in general terms $\binom{N}{2}$. This general expression can be
evaluated as $N(N-1)/2$.

The application of Kendall's tau to large data sets   At this juncture it
may be interesting to apply the procedure outlined above to the calculation of τ
for the entire data set listed in Table 8-5, which can thus be presented as follows:

a	b	c	d	e	f	g	h	i	j	k	l	m	n	o	p
1	2	3	4	5	6	7	8	9	10	11	12.5	12.5	14	15	16
14	12	13	8	16	15	10	9	2	11	6	5	7	4	3	1

Table 8-7   SCORES FOR CALCULATING KENDALL'S τ FOR THE DATA
IN TABLE 8-5

	b	c	d	e	f	g	h	i	j	k	l	m	n	o	p	Sum
a	−1	−1	−1	+1	+1	−1	−1	−1	−1	−1	−1	−1	−1	−1	−1	−11
b		+1	−1	+1	+1	−1	−1	−1	−1	−1	−1	−1	−1	−1	−1	−8
c			−1	+1	+1	−1	−1	−1	−1	−1	−1	−1	−1	−1	−1	−9
d				+1	+1	+1	+1	−1	+1	−1	−1	−1	−1	−1	−1	−2
e					−1	−1	−1	−1	−1	−1	−1	−1	−1	−1	−1	−11
f						−1	−1	−1	−1	−1	−1	−1	−1	−1	−1	−10
g							−1	−1	+1	−1	−1	−1	−1	−1	−1	−7
h								−1	+1	−1	−1	−1	−1	−1	−1	−6
i									+1	+1	+1	+1	+1	+1	−1	+5
j										−1	−1	−1	−1	−1	−1	−6
k											−1	+1	−1	−1	−1	−3
l												+1	−1	−1	−1	−2
m													−1	−1	−1	−3
n														−1	−1	−2
o															−1	−1
Total																−76

Arrange the countries in matrix form, and list the scores for each pair as elements of the upper half of the matrix. These are presented in Table 8-7, and the sum of the scores is calculated to be -76. The maximum possible total is $16(16 - 1)/2 = 120$. Therefore,

$$\tau = \frac{-76}{120} = -.63$$

which is remarkably close to the value of τ estimated from the sample of four. Of course, it is different from r_s calculated for the same set of data, but this is to be expected as the methods of calculation are entirely different.

Testing the significance of τ In order to calculate the critical values of τ associated with the various confidence levels, it is necessary to know the distribution of τ, which can be interpreted as a desire to know all possible values of τ for a particular sample size. The method for determining this is the same as for r_s. If the rankings for one variable are written in logical ascending sequence, then all that need be known is all the possible rankings of the second variable that can be associated with the first. For $N = 4$ there are $N!$ or $4 \times 3 \times 2 \times 1 = 24$ possible combinations of rankings. If all these possible rankings for the second variable are compared with the first variable, and 24 values of τ computed, the number of occurrences of each value of τ can be determined. Thus, when $N = 4$, seven possible values of τ can arise, and the frequency of occurrence of each of these is $-1, 1; -.67, 3; -.33, 5; 0, 6; .33, 5; .67, 3; 1, 1$. Thus the value of $-.67$ computed in the example of the sample of four countries could have occurred theoretically $\frac{3}{24}$ or 12.5 percent of the time purely from a chance ordering. Therefore, with $N = 4$, it could be concluded that a $\tau = -.67$ could have occurred by chance alone.

For large N the method outlined for testing the significance of τ becomes extremely cumbersome. Fortunately, Kendall (1955) has shown that when N is larger than 8, the theoretical distribution of all possible values of τ approaches the normal distribution. By using the null hypothesis, τ may be transformed into a normal standard deviate as follows:

$$z = \frac{\tau}{\sqrt{2(2N + 5)/9N(N - 1)}} \tag{8-6}$$

Substituting the calculated value of τ, $-.63$, in the example pertaining to a random sample of sixteen countries, outlined above, the following is obtained

$$z = \frac{-.63}{\sqrt{\frac{74}{2,160}}} = \frac{-.63}{.18} = -3.5$$

As this value of z is greater than the critical value of z at the 99 percent confidence level (Table 2-5), it can be concluded from a two-tailed test that we are 99 percent sure that a value of τ as high as $-.63$ could not have occurred merely by chance alone. Thus, the null hypothesis is rejected and the research hypothesis that the two variables are negatively associated can be inferred.

The Intercorrelation between Several Sets of Rankings

Thus far the discussion has been concerned with establishing a measure of correlation between two sets of rankings. In this section the discussion is extended to a consideration of a measure of multiple correlation between several sets of rankings. There are two methods that could be used. One uses an application of the Spearman rank correlation technique, and the other Kendall's coefficient of concordance. The first of these is simply an averaging technique. Spearman's r_s is calculated for all possible pairs of sets of rankings, all the r_s values are then summed and the average is determined. This measure, $r_{s,av}$, which can vary between -1, 0, and $+1$, is then an index of the degree of association between the variables.

The second suggested method, Kendall's coefficient of concordance, W, is an index of the degree of variation of the ranks from absolute disagreement. As such, it varies between 0 and 1, unity being complete agreement, and zero absolute disagreement. The construction of W will be described because it is the simplest to compute, and from it can also be derived $r_{s,av}$. Also, significance tests have been developed for W.

The data used to illustrate the computation of W pertain to various characteristics of the population of ten randomly chosen countries. The characteristics are per capita income, the percentage of the total population of a country enrolled in postprimary education, and general accessibility within the country as indicated by railroad mileage density. The sample has been drawn from Ginsberg (1961), and the research hypothesis is that there should be some significant association between these three variables because they are all, in a sense, indices of relative economic development. The scores of the countries for each variable have been ranked, and these ranks are presented in the $N \times c$ ($N = 10$, $c = 3$) data matrix within Table 8-8, with the rankings for the first variable listed in numerical sequence.

Coefficient of concordance   The first step in the construction of W is to determine the general ranking of each country for each variable. This can be obtained by summing the ranks across each row, $\sum_{j=1}^{3} r_j$; for Norway, for example, this sum is $3 + 7 + 7 = 17$. Now, what would be the sum for Norway if there were *absolute agreement* in the rankings? It would be $3 + 3 + 3 = 9 = 3c$. Alternatively, what would be the sum for Norway if there were *absolute disagreement*? Kendall suggests that it would be the mean of the sum of the row sums, that is, $\sum_{i=1}^{10} \sum_{j=1}^{3} r_{ij}/N$, which is 16.7. Thus, if the difference between the row sum and this mean value were small, the disagreement between the three sets of rankings would be great. The corollary to this is that the larger the difference, the greater the degree of association. The sum of these differences squared, S, will thus give a measure of agreement between all three rankings, because the larger the sum, the greater the level of agreement.

The value of S can then be adjusted to lie between 0 and 1 by dividing it by the maximum possible sum of squared deviations. This can be calculated by determining the sum of the rankings for each row if there is perfect agreement —for Norway it is $3c$, for Spain $7c$, and so forth—and then following the procedure as detailed above for the calculation of S. A quicker way of calculating this value is to use the formula $c^2(N^3 - N)/12$. Thus the coefficient of concordance, W, is

$$W = \frac{S}{c^2(N^3 - N)/12} \qquad (8\text{-}7)$$

Substituting the data from Table 8-8 in Eq. (8-7), we obtain

$$W = \frac{570.5}{3^2(10^3 - 10)/12} = \frac{570.5}{742.50} = .77$$

The calculated W lies very close to 1, but the question now arises whether it is large enough to indicate general agreement among the rankings, given the number of variables and the sample size.

Testing the significance of W   The significance of W can be tested through

Table 8-8   THE RANKINGS OF THREE VARIABLES FOR A RANDOM SAMPLE OF TEN COUNTRIES, AND THE STEPS IN THE CALCULATION OF S IN KENDALL'S COEFFICIENT OF CONCORDANCE

Country	Rank PCI	Education	Accessi-bility	Sums	Mean	Difference	d^2
United States	1	2	5	8	16.5	−8.5	72.25
Belgium	2	3	1	6	16.5	−10.5	110.25
Norway	3	7	7	17	16.5	.5	.25
France	4	5	3	12	16.5	−4.5	20.25
Puerto Rico	5	1	2	8	16.5	−8.5	72.25
Ireland	6	8	4	18	16.5	1.5	2.25
Spain	7	4	6	17	16.5	.5	.25
Ecuador	8	10	9	27	16.5	10.5	110.25
Jordan	9	6	10	25	16.5	8.5	72.25
Thailand	10	9	8	27	16.5	10.5	110.25
Total				165			$S = 570.5$

the sampling distribution of S in a manner similar to those outlined above for τ and r_s. For any particular N and c all possible values of S for all combinations of ranks can be determined, and a frequency distribution obtained. In the case of $N = 4$ and $c = 3$, for example, there are $(N!)^c$, or 13,824 possible combinations of ranks. A frequency distribution of the 13,824 possible values of S can, therefore, be established, and the critical values of S for any set of confidence levels determined. This is, obviously, a very time-consuming procedure, and it is fortunate that the critical values of S at the 95 and 99 percent confidence levels have been calculated for N from 3 to 7 and for c from 3 to 20. Examples of these values are presented in Table 8-9.

In those more numerous cases where N is larger than 7, the distribution outlined above can be transformed into the chi-square distribution with $N - 1$ degrees of freedom. This transformation is

$$\chi^2 = \frac{S}{cN(N + 1)/12} = c(N - 1)W \tag{8-8}$$

Substituting the coefficient of concordance of .82 in Eq. (8-8), we obtain

$$\chi^2 = 3(9)(.77) = 20.79$$

From Table 8-3 it can be determined that with 9 degrees of freedom a W of .82 is significant at both the 95 and 99 percent confidence levels. Thus the null hypothesis of no agreement between the rankings can be rejected, and the research hypothesis can be inferred.

Comments concerning $r_{s,av}$ Kendall (1955) has also demonstrated that the coefficient of concordance can be used as a shortcut to the calculation of $r_{s,av}$.

Table 8-9   **CRITICAL VALUES OF S AT THE 95 AND 99 PERCENT CONFIDENCE LEVEL***

	Values of N								
c	3		4		5		6		7	
3					64.4	75.6	103.9	122.8	157.3	185.6
4			49.5	61.4	88.4	109.3	143.3	176.2	217.0	265.0
5			62.6	80.5	112.3	142.8	182.4	229.4	276.2	343.8
6			75.7	99.5	136.1	176.1	221.4	282.4	335.2	422.6
8	48.1	66.8	101.7	137.4	183.7	242.7	299.0	388.3	453.1	579.9
10	60.0	85.1	127.8	175.3	231.2	309.1	376.7	494.0	571.0	737.0
15	89.8	131.0	192.9	269.8	349.8	475.2	570.5	758.2	864.9	1,129.5
20	119.7	177.0	258.0	364.2	468.5	641.2	764.4	1,022.2	1,158.7	1,521.9

*Shown in italic type.
SOURCE: Critical values selected from Friedman (1940).

The formula for the calculation of $r_{s,\text{av}}$ using W is

$$r_{s,\text{av}} = \frac{cW - 1}{c - 1} \tag{8-9}$$

Substituting the data from Table 8-8 in Eq. (8-9),

$$r_{s,\text{av}} = \frac{3(.82) - 1}{3 - 1} = .73$$

It will be noticed that $r_{s,\text{av}}$ can assume any value between -1, 0, and $+1$. The interpretation of $r_{s,\text{av}}$, therefore, requires a little consideration if Eq. (8-9) is used as an estimator. The upper limit $+1$ indicates absolute agreement between the rankings, but the area of no significant agreement varies in a zone that includes 0 and -1. For example, the zone of no significant agreement for $r_{s,\text{av}}$ at the 95 percent confidence level extends in this particular case from $+.45$ to $-.50$, for these values are the equivalent of corresponding nonsignificant scores of W equal to $.63$ and 0. The significance of $r_{s,\text{av}}$ must, therefore, be tested by using the significance test for W.

GOODNESS-OF-FIT TESTS

A second, and extremely important, use in human geography of nonparametric techniques is for tests of goodness of fit. In this section the discussion will focus upon the Kolmogorov-Smirnov test and the previously described chi-square test. Both these can be used to test whether a perceived nominal or ordinally measured distribution is significantly similar to, or different from, some theoretical distribution. This theoretical distribution can be regarded as a "strawman" which would give the distribution if certain hypothesized principles were followed in the real world. Thus the tests can be used to determine the degree to which an actual distribution based on some empirical information departs from the distribution that would be achieved if the real world acted in accordance with the principles enunciated by the theoretical model. Some considerable care, therefore, has to be taken not only with the choice of the test itself but also with the structuring of the model, matters which will be discussed further in the examples in the ensuing sections.

Contingency Tables

The word "contingency" has been used previously with respect to c which is derived from data set forth in a certain tabular form. The contingency table is, in fact, a specific kind of table which can be used to establish a theoretical distribution that could be expected on the basis of empirical information. The actual distribution can then be compared with this expected distribution by using the χ^2 test. As an illustration of the procedures, data will be used derived from an expanded sample of the Kingston home-survey data discussed previously in this chapter. This information is obtained from a random sample of 175 homes for which two variables, single family or multifamily and with children or without children, have been measured with a nominal scaling. The hypothesis to be examined is that there is no relation between type of home occupied and stage-in-life cycle of the family. The research hypothesis, of course, is that there is a relation (Yeates, 1972a).

The data are presented in the form of a square 2 × 2 table as follows:

		Single family	Multifamily	Total
With children	(a)	115	(b) 23	138
Without children	(c)	22	(d) 15	37
Total		137	38	175

The table indicates that 115 out of 138 families with children live in single-family homes, whereas 22 out of 37 families without children live in single-family homes. The question that arises is what would be the expected distribution of families among homes if there were no relation between the type of home occupied and the stage in life cycle of the family. This expectation can be calculated if the table is viewed as one in which the elements are *contingent* upon the distributions indicated by the marginal totals. Thus, if the sample contains 175 families and 138 of these are with children, it could be expected that $\frac{138}{175}$, or 78.8 percent, of the families living in single-family homes would be with children. As the number of single-family homes is 137, it would, therefore, be expected that $(.788)(137) = 108$ families with children would live in single-family homes. An alternative, and shorter, method of calculation would, of course, be $(138)(137)/175 = 108$. Following this procedure, the number of families without children that one would expect to find in single-family homes is $(138)(37)/175 = 29$. Also, the number of families with children that one would expect to find in multifamily homes is $(138)(38)/175 = 30$; and the number of families without children that one would expect to find in multifamily homes is $(38)(37)/175 = 8$.

The expected table if there were no relation between type of home occupied and stage of life cycle in the family would, therefore, be as follows:

		Single family	Multifamily	Total
With children	(a)	108	(b) 30	138
Without children	(c)	29	(d) 8	37
Total		137	38	175

where each element within the table is contingent upon the ratios calculated from the marginal totals. It is for this reason that a type of table which will yield calculations of this kind is known as a "contingency table." The table from which c can be calculated is obviously one form of contingency table, and it is for this reason that c is described as a *contingency coefficient*.

The actual values can now be compared with the expected values by using the χ^2 test to determine whether the observed, O, and expected, E, distributions are significantly similar, and thus whether the observed elements are no different from those that would be expected on the basis of the totals. The level of significance chosen is the 99 percent confidence level because the researcher wishes to reject the null hypothesis, and thus infer the research hypothesis, only if the evidence is powerful. The calculation of χ^2, in the manner of Table 8-2, is as follows:

Cell	Observed	Expected	O − E	(O − E)²	$\frac{(O-E)^2}{E}$
a	115	108	7	49	.45
b	23	30	−7	49	1.63
c	22	29	−7	49	1.69
d	15	8	7	49	6.13
Total	175	175	0		9.90

The table of critical values of χ^2 (Table 8-3) is entered with $(r-1)(c-1)$ degrees of freedom, because, as previously explained, if the marginal totals are known, the expected elements can all be calculated even if a number of elements on each row and column are unknown. Thus in a 2 × 2 table, if the marginal totals are known, only one element need be calculated, for the rest can be derived from that by addition and subtraction. Likewise, in a 3 × 4 table, if six appropriately chosen elements have already been calculated, the other six can be derived from these and the marginals. Therefore, the number of degrees of freedom for a 3 × 4 table are $(3-1)(4-1) = 6$. The calculated χ^2 of 9.90 is, as a consequence, to be compared with a critical value of χ^2 at the 99 percent confidence level of 6.635. As the calculated χ^2 exceeds this, the null hypothesis is rejected and the research hypothesis inferred.

The direction of the association can also be determined from the pattern of differences between the observed and expected values. The direction of the association is important because the χ^2 test is, after all, a one-tailed test. There are more families with children than expected living in single-family residences, and also more families without children than expected living in multifamily residences. Conversely, there are fewer families with children than expected living in multifamily dwellings, and fewer families without children than expected living in single-family residences. Thus it is evident that families with children tend to gravitate, probably out of definite preference, toward single-family residences, but more than expected of those without children locate in multifamily dwellings. This association is important to human geography because the different types of residences have very definite spatial locations (Berry and Rees, 1969).

The Chi-Square Test for Normality

A very important and well-known use of the χ^2 test is for establishing whether a particular distribution is normal. In this case, the ratio or intervally measured data are presented in the form of a frequency distribution, and this is compared with a theoretical distribution that has been constructed by using the standard deviation and the mean of the empirical data as parameters. The procedure for constructing a "strawman" normal distribution based on the standard deviation and the mean of an actual empirical distribution has been detailed in Chap. 2 and Table 2-6. The expected values listed in the last column of Table 2-5 are the frequencies that would be expected in each interval used if the data were normally distributed. Thus if the original data can be defined as the observed values, and the normally distributed data as the expected values, the distributions can be compared by using the null hypothesis. The null hypothesis in this case states that there is no significant difference between the two distributions, and that any difference that may have occurred is simply due to chance sampling errors from observations chosen randomly from a normally distributed population.

The procedures used in the χ^2 test for normality are detailed in Table 8-10, and χ^2 is calculated to be 13.14. The null hypothesis is to be tested at the 95 percent confidence level, and the table of critical values of χ^2 is to be entered with $N - 3$ degrees of freedom. One degree of freedom is lost because if $N - 1$ expected frequencies are known (N being the number of intervals), the last can be calculated from knowledge of the others and the total number of observations. Two more degrees of freedom are lost because the expected distribution in effect makes use of the standard deviation and mean of the sample as estimates of the population parameters. The critical value of χ^2 with $12 - 3$ degrees of freedom is 16.919, and as 13.14 is less than this value, the null hypothesis is accepted.

At this juncture it is important to note two characteristics of Table 8-10. In the first place, the χ^2 test, which calculates values row by row, can be very much affected by a large "deviation^2/E" in one or two rows. In Table 8-10 this is in row 11, and other examples can be noted in various tables previously in the chapter. This is an important property of the χ^2 test in general for it permits the researcher to determine the exact source of greatest variation. The second point to notice is that in this particular example the great source of variation in row 11 is the result of division by a very small expected value. The observation has been made previously in this chapter that the test should always have expected values of about 5 in each interval or group, and the results of not having met this requirement are clearly illustrated by row 11 in Table 8-10. The solution for this problem is, of course, to group the data so that the smallest value in any one interval is not too far removed from 5, and this has been done in Table 8-11. The recalculated χ^2 is 2.52, and the critical value at the 95 percent confidence level with $7 - 3$ degrees of freedom is 9.488. Thus the null hypothesis is again accepted, for the calculated χ^2 is much less than the critical χ^2.

Table 8-10   CHI-SQUARE TEST FOR NORMALITY OF DATA LISTED IN TABLES 2-3 AND 2-6

Interval	Observed	Expected	Deviation	Deviation^2	Deviation^2/E
1	0	.9	−.9	.81	.90
2	3	1.5	1.5	2.25	1.50
3	2	3.1	−1.1	1.21	.39
4	5	5.0	0	.00	.00
5	6	6.6	−.6	.36	.05
6	9	7.0	2.0	4.00	.57
7	8	6.2	1.8	3.24	.52
8	2	4.4	−2.4	5.76	1.31
9	2	2.5	−.5 •	.25	.10
10	0	1.2	−1.2	1.44	1.20
11	2	.4	1.6	2.56	6.40
12	0	.2	−.2	.04	.20
Total	39	39.0			13.14

Table 8-11   CHI-SQUARE TEST FOR NORMALITY OF DATA LISTED IN TABLES 2-3 AND 2-6 WITH THE INTERVALS REGROUPED

Interval	Observed	Expected	Deviation	Deviation^2	Deviation^2/E
1, 2, 3	5	5.5	−.5	.25	.05
4	5	5.0	.0	.00	.00
5	6	6.6	−.6	.36	.05
6	9	7.0	2.0	4.00	.57
7	8	6.2	1.8	3.24	.52
8	2	4.4	−2.4	5.76	1.31
9, 10, 11, 12	4	4.3	.3	.09	.02
Total	39	39.0			2.52

Table 8-12 THE CALCULATION OF THE KOLMOGOROV-SMIRNOV STATISTIC

	Observed			Expected			
Interval	Frequency	Proportion	Cumulated	Frequency	Proportion	Cumulated	Difference
1	0	.000	.000	.9	.023	.023	.023
2	3	.076	.076	1.5	.038	.061	.015
3	2	.051	.121	3.1	.079	.140	.019
4	5	.129	.256	5.0	.129	.269	.013
5	6	.154	.410	6.6	.169	.438	.028
6	9	.231	.641	7.0	.180	.618	.023
7	8	.206	.847	6.2	.159	.777	.070
8	2	.051	.898	4.4	.113	.890	.008
9	2	.051	.949	2.5	.064	.954	.005
10	0	.000	.949	1.2	.031	.985	.036
11	2	.051	1.000	.4	.010	.995	.005
12	0	.000	1.000	.2	.005	1.000	.000

The Kolmogorov-Smirnov Test

An alternative test to chi square is the Kolmogorov-Smirnov (K-S) test, which is based on the principle that one expects the cumulated frequency distributions of two samples to be similar if they are random samples drawn from the same population. The test takes advantage of situations in which there can be some logical ordering of intervals so that the profiles of the frequency distributions can be compared. Unlike the χ^2 test there is no limitation on the number of observations or the size of each interval or group. Furthermore the statistic may be calculated very easily. It does not, however, indicate the individual sources of variation as clearly as the χ^2 statistic, but it is much more useful for small samples because it does not have a minimum frequency restriction for any particular interval.

The method of construction and relative advantage of this statistic may be indicated most clearly for the data presented in Table 8-10, where the minimum frequency restriction of the χ^2 test made that test inappropriate. Obviously, when intervals have to be combined, a certain amount of information is lost, and the K-S test requires no such combinations. First, both sets of data are ordered in an internally logical sequence (Table 8-12). Second, each frequency is expressed as a proportion of N, which in this case is 39. Third, the proportions are accumulated. Fourth, the absolute values of the differences between the accumulated proportions for each row are calculated. The largest of these differences is designated D, and this is .070.

The theoretical distribution of all possible D's calculated for all sample sizes is known (Siegel, 1955, p. 48), and so the critical limits of D at the 95 and 99 percent confidence limits can be determined. These critical limits, for a two-tailed test, for $N = 10$ to 35 are listed in Table 8-13, where it is noted that for samples greater than 35 the critical limit can be calculated by dividing the coefficients 1.36 or 1.63 by the square root of N. In this particular case the critical limit at the 95 percent confidence level would be $1.36/\sqrt{39} = .218$, and as the calculated D of .07 is much less than this, the null hypothesis of no difference between the two distributions can be accepted.

Thus far, the K-S test has been explained, and a significance test described for these situations in which the sample sizes of the two distributions are exactly the same. If the sample sizes are *large and not the same*, the same procedure can be used for calculating D, but a different significance test which pools the two sample sizes must be used. This test makes use of the fact that the sampling distribution of D can be transformed into the chi-square distribution as follows:

$$\chi^2 = 4D^2 \frac{N_1 N_2}{N_1 + N_2} \qquad (8\text{-}10)$$

This transformation can be used only when the size of each of the samples is greater than 40. The critical values of chi square are determined with $N - 2$ degrees of freedom, and care must be taken to remember that a one-tailed test is involved.

In conclusion it must be mentioned that an area in human geography in which goodness-of-fit tests have been used a great deal is the analysis of cell frequencies derived from spatial probability models (Dacey, 1964a and b; Rogers, 1969a), which, of themselves, are considered beyond the scope of this particular volume. For example, if the researcher hypothesizes that a given spatial pattern, such as the distribution of grocery stores within a defined part of an urban area (Getis, 1964), could have arisen through some random process, then he may well use a Poisson model in a cell or quadrat framework to test this notion. The cell (urn) frequencies of the actual distribution can then be compared with those derived from the simulated pattern, which incorporates the hypothesized process using the chi-square or the Kolmogorov-Smirnov test. The problem with this type of approach is that many hypothesized probability models may be proved to fit the actual frequency distribution extremely well (Rogers, 1969b), and the researcher thus has to be extremely sure of his theoretical base to select definitely one particular model as the most appropriate.

Table 8-13 CRITICAL VALUES OF D AT THE 95 AND 99 PER-CENT CONFIDENCE LEVELS IN THE KOLMO-GOROV-SMIRNOV TEST

N	Confidence level 95%	99%
10	.410	.490
11	.391	.468
12	.375	.450
13	.361	.433
14	.349	.418
15	.338	.404
16	.328	.392
17	.318	.381
18	.309	.371
19	.301	.363
20	.294	.356
25	.27	.32
30	.24	.29
35	.23	.27
Over 35	$1.36/\sqrt{N}$	$1.63/\sqrt{N}$

SOURCE: Massey (1951).

9

FACTORIAL ANALYSIS

Probably the most widely used technique in human geography during the past ten years has been factorial analysis. The methodology of factorial analysis was introduced on a persuasive scale to human geographers through its application by B. J. L. Berry and his colleagues in a variety of geographic situations. These include an investigation into the basic dimensions of economic development (Berry, 1960), multivariate regional classification (Berry, 1961; Ahmad, 1965), determination of the various roles played by unplanned retail nucleations in the commercial structure of Chicago (Berry, 1963; Simmons, 1964), and more recently, extension of social area analysis through the procedures of factorial urban ecology (Berry and Rees, 1969; Berry, 1971). Though this widespread application, which must have resulted in the publication of many hundreds of articles using factorial analysis, has not resulted in widespread uncritical acceptance of many of the results from studies using these procedures (King, 1969), nevertheless, the methodology now forms a basic tool in the kit of techniques available to the geographer. The fact that this is not an isolated phenomenon in geography, but is part of a more general application in many of the social sciences, which is yielding very important results, is attested to by Rummel (1967, p. 455), who states, "factor analysis and the complementary multiple regression model are initiating a scientific revolution in the social sciences as profound and far-reaching as that developed by the calculus in physics." Though this may be an overstatement of the important claims of the methodology, it nevertheless underlines the general importance of the technique beyond the immediate confines of the geographic discipline.

All the studies mentioned above use one of two basically similar procedures, one of which is called *principal-components analysis* and the other *factor analysis*. The differences between the two procedures are many and varied, the mathematical differences being discussed at some length in such standard texts as Cattell (1952), Fruchter (1954), and Harman (1960). At the outset, the basic difference between the two can be expressed verbally as an observation that component analysis assumes that all the variation in a given population is contained within the variables used to define that population, whereas factor analysis assumes that only part of the variation in a given population is contained within the variables used to define that population. These two different assumptions lead to a much more deterministic approach if principal-components analysis is used, and a much more flexible experimental approach if factor analysis is used.

Factorial analysis is concerned with discussing the underlying structure exhibited by a group of variables. For example, assume that a researcher wishes to determine the basic underlying structure of the social geography of an urban area. This area can be subdivided into six data units or census tracts, and the social geography is defined by six variables or socioeconomic characteristics. The proportion of the population of each census tract in each variable is listed in Table 9-1, where, for example, it is indicated that in census tract 1, in 1971, 10 percent of the population is Roman Catholic; 8 percent is bilingual; 2 percent of the male wage earners earns less than $4,000; only 9 percent of the house-

Table 9-1   HYPOTHETICAL SOCIOECONOMIC DATA PERTAINING TO AN URBAN AREA, 1971

				Percentage		
Census tract	Roman Catholic	Bilingual	Under $4,000	Fewer than two autos	Managerial and professional	Without high school diploma
1	10	8	2	9	13	4
2	11	9	30	35	36	39
3	17	10	38	37	70	21
4	36	11	46	49	72	55
5	80	9	69	66	81	57
6	90	40	81	68	83	87

holds has fewer than two automobiles apiece; 13 percent of the male labor force is classified as professional and managerial; and only 4 percent of the working force is without a high school diploma.

These data can be viewed in two ways. Either the variation in data between the rows can be analyzed, or the variation in data between the columns. For example, if the concern is to compare census tracts, a matrix of correlation coefficients of each census tract with the five other census tracts for the six variables would indicate the degree of correlation, or similarity, among each pair of tracts. Alternatively, if the concern is to compare the variation in spatial distribution between the variables, a matrix of correlation coefficients of each variable with every other variable would summarize the degree of similarity between each pair of characteristics. A comparison between rows results in a Q-mode factorial analysis, whereas a comparison between columns results in an R-mode factorial analysis. In this particular case, the concern is to analyze the variation in spatial distribution between the variables, so an R-mode factorial analysis is required.

A common method of comparing spatial distributions used by geographers is map comparison through overlays. The six variables would thus yield six maps, and the maps can be compared visually. The researcher would ask himself, To what extent do these six maps tell the same story? and, What is the story? Though it may be easy to compare two or three maps visually, it is extremely difficult to compare more than that number, particularly if the degree of variation within each map is large. Thus, it would be pleasant if there were procedures that could use a quantitative measure of association such as the correlation coefficient to determine the "story" told by the six maps. Factorial analysis provides such a set of procedures that use the correlation coefficient matrix to enable the researcher to discern quantitatively the basic patterns or dimensions ("stories") described by the data. In principal-components analysis it is assumed that the six variables describe all the socioeconomic variation in the urban area, whereas in factor analysis it is assumed that only a part of the variation is described by the six variables.

PRINCIPAL–COMPONENTS ANALYSIS

The first step in principal-components analysis, and in factor analysis models, is the calculation of a correlation coefficient matrix. This is obtained by transforming the data matrix $\underset{n \times m}{X}$ into a matrix of standard scores $\underset{n \times m}{Z}$ (Table 9-2), and from this is calculated the correlation coefficient matrix

$$\underset{m \times m}{R} = (\underset{m \times n}{Z^T} \cdot \underset{n \times m}{Z} / \underset{1 \times 1}{N})$$

This matrix (Table 9-3) indicates the degree of intercorrelation between all the variables, elements along the diagonal indicating the total variation in the population of socioeconomic variables represented by the data. In the principal-components analysis model this variance is indicated by a set of unities on the diagonal, and so the total variation in the population of socioeconomic variables is considered to be represented by the six listed variables. The total variation is defined as $\sum r_{ij}$ for all $i = j$, or the sum of the elements on the diagonals, which is 6.0. The problem, therefore, becomes one of finding a measure that summarizes the main dimensions of variation among the variables and that furthermore indicates the way in which the variables are grouped together. In the latter sense, factorial analysis is similar to linkage analysis.

Table 9-2   STANDARD-SCORE MATRIX FOR THE DATA LISTED IN TABLE 9-1

Census tract	Roman Catholic	Bilingual	Percentage Under $4,000	Fewer than two autos	Managerial and professional	Without high school diploma
1	−0.9386	−0.5284	−1.6395	−1.7412	−1.7868	−1.4906
2	−0.9079	−0.4471	−0.5542	−0.4477	−0.8953	−0.1798
3	−0.7239	−0.3658	−0.2441	−0.3482	0.4224	−0.8539
4	−0.1411	−0.2845	0.0658	0.2487	0.5000	0.4194
5	1.2085	−0.4471	0.9573	1.0945	0.8488	0.4943
6	1.5153	2.0731	1.4224	1.1940	0.9263	1.6179

TABLE 9-3   CORRELATION COEFFICIENT MATRIX FOR DATA IN TABLES 9-1 AND 9-2

Variable	1	2	3	4	5	6
1 Roman Catholic percentage of population	1.0000	0.6816	0.9199	0.8948	0.7566	0.8597
2 Bilingual percentage of population	0.6816	1.0000	0.6640	0.5646	0.4638	0.7505
3 Head-of-household percentage earning less than $4,000	0.9199	0.6640	1.0000	0.9887	0.9143	0.9226
4 Family percentage with fewer than two autos	0.8948	0.5646	0.9887	1.0000	0.9176	0.9205
5 Male worker percentage in managerial and professional occupations	0.7566	0.4638	0.9143	0.9176	1.0000	0.7638
6 Worker percentage without a high school diploma	0.8597	0.7505	0.9226	0.9205	0.7638	1.0000

Correlate with table 2

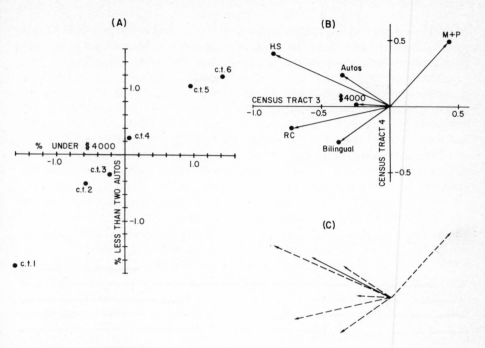

FIGURE 9-1
A pictorial representation of a resolution vector: (*a*) a scatter diagram, (*b*) a
vector space, (*c*) the resolution vector.

    The conception of factorial analysis can be explained most clearly through
a geometric interpretation of the procedures. In correlation analysis the basic
form of a relation can be discerned from a scattergram relating the two variables.
For example, Fig. 9-1*a* indicates the relation between the percentage of the
heads of households earning less than $4,000 and the percentage of families
with fewer than two autos for the six census tracts in the standardized data
matrix, Table 9-2. The six points fall almost along a straight line, and the
correlation coefficient .9887 indicates that the two variables are almost perfectly
correlated. Thus variable 3 tells almost the same story as variable 4 about the
spatial variation of the data over the six census tracts. The question that therefore arises is how many stories are told by the six variables measured in the six
census tracts.
    The answer to this question requires a grouping that focuses upon the
socioeconomic variables as observations, and the census tracts as variables.
For example, in Fig. 9-1*b* the six socioeconomic variables are plotted in the
standardized space for census tracts 3 and 4. Within this "two-space" there

seems to be one cluster of points containing five variables on the left-hand side of the diagram, and one variable (managerial and professional percentage) in the top right-hand portion of the diagram. Thus, for just two census tracts, five variables seem to be closely clustered and one does not. Of course, if it were possible to draw a diagram with six axes, that is, in "six-space," the relative position of all the variables measured for all the census tracts could be determined. However, as such a diagram is impossible to construct, the discussion will continue with respect to two observations, or census tracts.

The next step is to estimate the closeness of the variables in the two-space. A method for achieving this is to draw a line between the origin 0, 0 and the variables. This line is a *vector* representation of the data, and if the six variables were plotted in an imaginary space defined by the six census tracts, the thrusts of each of the vectors would describe a *vector space* containing all the information in the standardized data matrix. The vectors can then be used to measure the degree of association between the variables because the *angle* between the vectors indicates the degree of association. For example, if the angle between two vectors were 0°, there would be a perfect relation because the vectors would "lie" on top of each other. On the other hand, if the angle between the two were 90°, they would be orthogonal and this would indicate no relation. If the angle between two vectors were 180°, there would be a perfect negative relation, for the direction of the thrust vector of one variable would be negatively complemented by the thrust vector of the other.

Thus a matrix of angles could be prepared from the two-space diagram in Fig. 9-1*b* of every vector against every other, and the result would be a symmetrical 6×6 matrix with angles of 0 and 180° off the diagonal. The *cosine* of these angles varies between -1, 0, and 1, the cosine of 0°, for example, being 1, cos 40° being .70, cos 90° being 0, and cos 140° being $-.70$. The cosines of the angles are, in fact, the correlation coefficients between the variables, and so though it is impossible to draw a diagram in six-space and measure the angles, it is possible to calculate what they would be simply by calculating the correlation coefficient matrix for the variables being analyzed. Of course, if we were concerned with a *Q*-mode analysis, the coefficients would be calculated for the census tracts that are imagined plotted in the six-space defined by the socioeconomic variables.

The principal-component procedure, which attempts to discern *all* the underlying dimensions existent within the data matrix, begins by calculating that dimension which accounts for the greatest proportion of the total variation. Pictorially, this first dimension is that vector which when fitted to the cluster of vectors (all six) in Fig. 9-1*b* explains the largest amount of variation. A physics analogy of this "best-fit" vector is the *resolution vector* for expressing the mean thrust and direction of the six vectors. The length and direction of the suggested first resolution vector for the two-space example in Fig. 9-1*b* is presented in Fig. 9-1*c*, and this is described as the "principal component," or "first factor," or "basic underlying dimension." If it could be estimated geometrically in six-space, it would be the principal component of the data matrix in Table 9-1.

The resolution vector is, of course, a mathematical artifact, and it can be interpreted only with respect to the original variables. As it can be regarded as the best-fit vector, its interpretation, naturally, relates to the degree to which it represents the variables. This degree of representation can be estimated from the association between each of the original six vectors and the resolution vector, which can be determined from the angles between each of the vectors and the resolution vector. The cosine of these angles will give the correlation coefficient between each respective variable and the abstract mathematical component, and in the language of factorial analysis this coefficient is referred to as a *factor loading*. The square of these correlation coefficients, or factor loadings, will indicate the proportion of variation in the variables that is associated with the variation in the component, and the sum of the squared factor loadings (which is referred to as an *eigenvalue*) is used to determine the proportion of total variation summarized by this component.

The Centroid Method

At this juncture it may be interesting to detail some computations that are undertaken to calculate the first component for the example data. The procedure used is the centroid method, which is a fairly easy method to perform on a desk calculator if there are few variables and they are mostly positively correlated. The method was developed originally for factor analysis models as there are more simple procedures available for principal-components analysis (Holzinger and Harman, 1941), but as the method can be used for *both* types of factorial analysis, it will be described here. Of course, more efficient and theoretically sound solution procedures have been developed (such as the principal-axis method) and are used in most computer programs (Rummel, 1970), but these are not so easy to illustrate if the problem is to be solved "by hand" for demonstration purposes. The centroid solution, in effect, approximates the solution that is derived from the more optimal principal-axis method.

The centroid method requires as input a correlation coefficient matrix, for it is this which effectively summarizes the similarities between the variables. This requirement is uniform for all solution procedures in factorial analysis. If a principal-components analysis is required, the assumption that all the variation in the population is represented by the socioeconomic variables used is indexed by the retention of unities on the diagonal. This assumption also implies that there are no unique factors or errors. Thus the unities already present along the main diagonal of the correlation matrix listed in Table 9-3 are retained, and the solution obtained by the centroid method will be a principal-components solution. The modification to this matrix that is necessary for a factor analysis solution will be indicated in a later section.

The components, being mathematical artifacts, are defined with respect to the factor loadings. Thus, in the present example six factor loadings have to be calculated, one for each variable. These loadings can be obtained for the first component directly from the correlation coefficient matrix (Table 9-3). First, it is necessary to calculate the total of the correlation coefficients for each row of the matrix S_i

$$S_i = \sum_{j=1}^{6} r_{ij} \quad i = 1, 2, 3, 4, 5, 6 \tag{9-1}$$

and, from Table 9-3, these are estimated to be

$S_1 = 5.1126$ *SUM OF ROWS OF TABLE 9.3*

$S_2 = 4.1245$

$S_3 = 5.4095$

$S_4 = 5.2862$

$S_5 = 4.8161$

$S_6 = 5.2171$

The same totals will be obtained if the coefficients are summed down the columns because the matrix is symmetrical. It is to be noted that the closer the correlation coefficients approach perfect positive correlation, the closer will the total for each row be to the total variation, which, as has been indicated previously, is 6.

These S_i values are, in fact, measures of association between the variables and the first principal component, but in order to represent them as correlation coefficient indices varying between -1, 0, and $+1$, they have to be modified. This necessary modification is achieved by scaling them with respect to the square root of the sum of the S_i. Thus

$$T = \sum_{i=1}^{6} S_i = 29.9660 \quad \text{\textit{Sum of all } } S_i \tag{9-2}$$

and the loading for each variable is

$$a_i = \frac{S_i}{\sqrt{T}} \tag{9-3}$$

For the example being discussed, the loadings are estimated to be

$a_1 = \frac{5.1126}{5.479} = .9331$

$a_2 = \frac{4.1245}{5.479} = .7527$

$a_3 = \frac{5.4095}{5.479} = .9873$

$a_4 = \frac{5.2862}{5.479} = .9648$

$a_5 = \frac{4.8161}{5.479} = .8790$

$a_6 = \frac{5.2171}{5.479} = .9521$

As these a_i are interpreted as correlation coefficients, they indicate that all the variables are strongly associated with the first component, but that variable 3 is the most correlated, followed by variables 4, 6, 1, 5, and 2.

The eigenvalue, or sum of the squared factor loadings, for the first component is, therefore, $(.9331)^2 + (.7527)^2 + (.9873)^2 + (.9648)^2 + (.8790)^2 + (.9521)^2 = 5.0220$. The total variation is 6, so the first component explains $\frac{5.0220}{6} \times 100 = 83.7$ percent of the variation in the original data matrix, leaving 16.3 percent unexplained. The question that now remains concerns the way in which this unexplained variation is distributed among the variables, and whether this unexplained variation forms a relatively large second component. It is obvious that the variables most explained by the first component leave little variation to be associated with a second component, but variables 2 and 5, which have only 57 and 77 percent of their respective variations associated with the first, may well form the nucleus of a second common component. Furthermore, just as the first component describes the largest common dimension of variation in the correlation coefficient matrix, so does the second component describe the largest common dimension of variation remaining in the matrix. Thus the concern is now to calculate the residual coefficient matrix pertaining to the variables after the variation described by the first component is extracted.

First residual coefficient matrix The first step is to construct from the loadings the correlation coefficient matrix that would have existed had the first component completely exhausted all the variation in the original data matrix. If the vector $\mathbf{A}_{6 \times 1}$ is regarded as the vector of loadings, this matrix can be obtained from the multiplication of $\mathbf{A}$ by its transpose

$$\underset{6 \times 1}{\mathbf{A}} \cdot \underset{1 \times 6}{\mathbf{A}^T} = \underset{6 \times 6}{\mathbf{Q}}$$

where each element of $\mathbf{Q}$ is the product of two loadings. For example,

$$q_{11} = (.9331)(.9331) = .8707$$
$$q_{14} = q_{41} = (.9331)(.9648) = .9002$$
$$q_{35} = q_{53} = (.9873)(.8790) = .8678$$

and the entire set of elements of $\mathbf{Q}$ are listed in Table 9-4. The second step is to subtract the symmetrical matrix $\mathbf{Q}$ from the matrix $\mathbf{R}$ to obtain the first factor residual matrix. The results of this simple element-by-element subtraction procedure is presented in matrix form as Table 9-5, where it is to be noticed that this matrix is also symmetrical. *What is matrix R?*

Second factor (or component) Although the first factor residual matrix has now been obtained, it *cannot* be used in its present form without some readjustment. The need for this is apparent if the $_1S_i$ values are calculated for Table 9-5 (the prefix 1 indicates that the S_i values pertain to the first factor matrix). The $_1S_i$ values are

$$_1S_1 = .0096$$
$$_1S_2 = .0082$$
$$_1S_3 = .0104$$
$$_1S_4 = .0099$$
$$_1S_5 = .0090$$
$$_1S_6 = .0104$$

and it is apparent that with these scores the second component stands little chance of maximizing its explanatory contribution, for the greatest residual variance lies with variables 2 and 5 *not* 3 and 6. In effect, then, the resolution vector must be "forced" in the direction of the maximum possible explanation of the residual variance, and this is achieved in the centroid procedure by a *reflection*, or *change in signs*, of the variables.

The reflecting procedure is extremely pedantic and is explained in detail

Table 9-4 THE PRODUCT MATRIX Q

Variable	1	2	3	4	5	6
1	.8707	.7023	.9212	.9002	.8202	.8884
2	.7023	.5665	.7431	.7262	.6616	.7166
3	.9212	.7431	.9748	.9525	.8678	.9397
4	.9002	.7262	.9525	.9308	.8480	.9186
5	.8202	.6616	.8678	.8480	.7726	.8369
6	.8884	.8166	.9397	.9186	.8369	.9065

Table 9-5 FIRST FACTOR RESIDUAL MATRIX

Variable	1	2	3	4	5	6
1	.1293	−.0207	−.0013	−.0054	−.0636	−.0287
2	−.0207	.4335	−.0791	−.1616	−.1978	.0339
3	−.0013	−.0791	.0252	.0362	.0465	−.0171
4	−.0054	−.1616	.0362	.0692	.0696	.0019
5	−.0636	−.1978	.0465	.0696	.2274	−.0731
6	−.0287	.0339	−.0171	.0019	−.0731	.0935

by Holzinger and Harman (1941, pp. 361–365). The steps can be detailed for this particular case as follows:

1 Write down the pattern of signs of the coefficients in the first factor residual matrix. These are:

Variable	1	2	3	4	5	6
1	+	−	−	−	−	−
2	−	+	−	−	−	+
3	−	−	+	+	+	−
4	−	−	+	+	+	+
5	−	−	+	+	+	−
6	−	+	−	+	−	+
Total negatives	5	4	3	2	3	3

2 Determine the total number of negative signs for each variable.
3 If there are no variables with $m/2 = \frac{6}{2} = 3$ or more coefficients with negative signs, no reflection is necessary.
4 But, if there is a variable, or there are variables, with $m/2$ or more negative signs, choose the variable with the largest number of negatives, and reflect that first. If two or more variables have the same number of negatives, reflect the variable with the largest residual sum first.
5 Variable 1 has five coefficients with negative signs, so that variable is reflected first. Reverse all the signs in the column and row for variable 1 *except* that pertaining to the coefficient on the diagonal (which, in effect, is reversed twice). This reflection yields:

Variable	1	2	3	4	5	6
1	+	[+	+	+	+	+]
2	+⌉	+	−	−	−	+
3	+	−	+	+	+	−
4	+	−	+	+	+	+
5	+	−	+	+	+	−
6	+⌋	+	−	+	−	+
Total negatives	0	3	2	1	2	2

where the coefficients that are reflected are enclosed in square brackets.
6 Determine the total number of negative signs for each variable following the first reflection.
7 If there is a variable, or are variables, with $m/2$ or more negative signs, reflect that with the largest number of negatives. Variable 2, with three negative signs, is, thus, reflected by reversing all the signs in both the column and row for variable 2 (except that pertaining to the coefficient on the diagonal). This second reflection yields:

Variable	1	2	3	4	5	6
1	+	[−]	+	+	+	+
2	[−]	+	[+	+	+	−]
3	+	⎡+⎤	+	+	+	−
4	+	⎢+⎥	+	+	+	+
5	+	⎢+⎥	+	+	+	−
6	+	⎣−⎦	−	+	−	+
Total negatives	1	2	1	0	1	3

where the coefficients that are reflected are enclosed in square brackets.

8 Determine the total number of negative signs for each variable following the second reflection, and repeat step 7, but this time for variable 6. This third reflection yields:

Variable	1	2	3	4	5	6
1	+	−	+	+	+	⎡−⎤
2	−	+	+	+	+	⎢+⎥
3	+	+	+	+	+	⎢+⎥
4	+	+	+	+	+	⎢−⎥
5	+	+	+	+	+	⎣+⎦
6	[−	+	+	−	+]	+
Total negatives	2	1	0	1	0	2

where the coefficients that are reflected are enclosed in square brackets.

9 As there are no variables with $m/2$ or more negative signs, the reflection procedure is complete.

The signs can now be substituted for the original ones in Table 9-5, and the full reflected residual matrix is listed in Table 9-6.

Second factor coefficients The second factor, or component as it is in this case, can now be calculated from Table 9-6 in exactly the same way as the first

Table 9-6 THE REFLECTED RESIDUAL MATRIX

Variable	1	2	3	4	5	6
1	+.1293	−.0207	+.0013	+.0054	+.0636	−.0287
2	−.0207	+.4335	+.0791	+.1616	+.1978	+.0339
3	+.0013	+.0791	+.0252	+.0362	+.0465	+.0171
4	+.0054	+.1616	+.0362	+.0692	+.0696	−.0019
5	+.0636	+.1978	+.0465	+.0696	+.2274	+.0731
6	−.0287	+.0339	+.0171	−.0019	+.0731	+.0935
$_{1R}S_i$	.1502	.8852	.2054	.3401	.6780	.1870

component is extracted from Table 9-3. The $_{1R}S_i$ values are calculated to be:

$$_{1R}S_1 = .1502$$
$$_{1R}S_2 = .8852$$
$$_{1R}S_3 = .2054$$
$$_{1R}S_4 = .3401$$
$$_{1R}S_5 = .6780$$
$$_{1R}S_6 = .1870$$

where the prefix $1R$ indicates that the S_i values pertain to the reflected first factor residual matrix. The value of $_{1R}T$ is therefore 2.4459; so, from Eq. (9-3), the second factor coefficients, or loadings, are

$$_2a_1 = \frac{.1502}{\sqrt{2.4459}} = .0960$$

$$_2a_2 = \frac{.8852}{\sqrt{2.4459}} = .5660$$

$$_2a_3 = \frac{.2054}{\sqrt{2.4459}} = .1313$$

$$_2a_4 = \frac{.3401}{\sqrt{2.4459}} = .2175$$

$$_2a_5 = \frac{.6780}{\sqrt{2.4459}} = .4335$$

$$_2a_6 = \frac{.1870}{\sqrt{2.4459}} = .1196$$

where the prefix 2 indicates that the a_i loadings pertain to the intercorrelations of the variables with the second component.

But, as three of these coefficients are, in fact, constructed on the basis of some variables for which the residual coefficient signs have been reflected, this has to be indexed by reflecting the signs of those factor coefficients. Thus the second factor coefficients, or loadings, become

$$-_2a_1 = -.0960$$
$$-_2a_2 = -.5660$$
$$_2a_3 = .1313$$
$$_2a_4 = 2.175$$
$$_2a_5 = .4335$$
$$-_2a_6 = -.1196$$

This indexing is important not only because it is a necessary product of the reflecting procedure, but also because it provides a check on the calculations, for when the corrected signs are applied to the $_{1R}S_i$ values, they should sum to zero (to be exact, they sum to .0011, which is fairly close given the rounding errors).

The eigenvalue, or sum of the squared factor loadings, for the second component is, therefore, $(-.0960)^2 + (-.5660)^2 + (.1313)^2 + (.2175)^2 + (.4335)^2 + (-.1196)^2 = .5963$. Thus, the proportion of the total variation explained or summarized by the second component is $\frac{.5963}{6} \times 100 = 9.94$ percent. The variation summarized by the first two components is, therefore, $83.7 + 9.94 = 93.64$ percent, leaving 6.36 percent as an unexplained residual. There are two rather interesting features that could be noted at this juncture concerning this second component. The first is that the reflection procedure has, in fact, extracted the greatest contributory explanation from variables 2 and 5— the ones that load least on the first component. Second, the signs of these two larger loadings are opposite to each other, so that they delineate a dimension that is bipolar. These loadings reveal some interesting details which will be interpreted later.

The "Cutoff" Point in Principal-Components Analysis

The question now arises whether a third component, or underlying dimension, should be calculated. If it were to be calculated, the procedures would be exactly the same as those outlined for the determination of the second component. A Q matrix would have to be calculated from the corrected second factor coefficients; this would then be subtracted from the reflected first residual matrix to form a second residual matrix. The second residual matrix would be reflected so that the third component would summarize as large a proportion of the remaining variance as possible, and from this the loadings and eigenvalues would be calculated. If there were any remaining variance, a fourth, fifth, and perhaps even a sixth component would need to be determined. The maximum number of possible components is equal to six, the number of variables, because the maximum number of possible independent stories is assumed represented by the six variables.

Thus, in theory, the number of components extracted equals the number of original variables. The results of a principal-components analysis of the correlation coefficient matrix for Florida listed in Table 4-3, and discussed in Chap. 4, illustrate some interesting results of this method of component extraction. In this example an R-mode analysis of twenty-one variables for sixty-seven counties reveals twenty-one components. The principal component, or the first dominant underlying dimension, accounts for 33 percent of the total

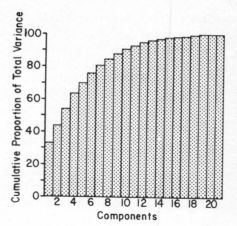

FIGURE 9-2
The components determined from a principal-components analysis of twenty-one variables concerning the economic geography of Florida. (*From Yeates, 1964, p. 15.*)

variation. The second accounts for 13 percent, and the third for nearly 10 percent. Thus, the first three components account for well over one-half of the total variation in the 67×21 data matrix summarized by the correlation coefficient matrix. As each successive component is extracted, the explanation that it contributes decreases so that the last few components account for a minute proportion of the total variation. A cumulated ogive curve illustrating this gradual reduction in explanation is presented in Fig. 9-2, and this diagram indicates that whereas the first ten components extracted account for 92 percent of the total variation, the last eleven account for only 8 percent.

As the variation accounted for by over half the components is so small, the problem of cutoff is vital, because many of the components may consist of errors that have been incurred in the original measurement of the data. An extensive survey of the various methods for determining the number of dimensions for both principal-components and factor analysis models is presented by Rummel (1970, pp. 349–367). He describes criteria based on inference, mathematics, and rules of thumb. The plethora of different types of tests is so overwhelming that perhaps the author will be forgiven if a few (that have been used in geography) are suggested. One, which was originally proposed by Kaiser (1960), and is based on Guttman's weakest lower bound, is that all components having an eigenvalue of less than unity should be excluded. Though this has some sound mathematical base, it must be used with caution, particularly if there are a number of components that have an eigenvalue around 1. Another much used criterion, which King (1969 p. 174), also, suggests, is that all components contributing less than 5 percent to the overall explanation should be excluded on the basis that any component explaining less than this proportion must contain a large random-error variance. An alternative procedure is to examine the graphic distribution of the component variances (such as those represented in Fig. 9-2) and find a marked break of slope, or discontinuity, which would seem to divide the more significant components from those less significant.

Probably the best suggestion is that the researcher should use all the above criteria, in concert with an intelligent appraisal of the meaning of the components, to arrive at an inclusion of the most meaningful dimensions. This is, of course, on the assumption that the researcher has a good idea of the direction of the research program, and has chosen the principal-components method as a logical procedure to fulfill, or contribute toward, a stated research objective. As indicated in the introductory chapter, this research objective may well be couched in some broad theoretical framework, and so the variables will have been selected to assist in achieving this objective. Thus the researcher would have a reasonable a priori understanding of the types of components and loadings that might emerge. The procedures that are used to interpret these mathematical artifacts, known as components, are, therefore, extremely important.

The Interpretation of the Principal-Components Solution

The components can be interpreted only in terms of the variables from which they are constituted. For example, in the principal-components analysis of the six socioeconomic variables cited above, the relative "mix" of each of the six variables with respect to the two components is indicated by the correlation of each variable with each component. These correlations, or loadings, can be used to interpret the components in verbal descriptive terms. The principal component, because it accounts for nearly 84 percent of the variation in the data matrix, is naturally correlated quite highly with each of the six variables. These loadings are presented rank-ordered from high to low in Table 9-7. The highest loading, .9873, indicates that 97.5 percent of the variance over the census tracts in the proportion of heads of households earning less than $4,000 per year is associated with this dimension; whereas the lowest loading, .7527, indicates that 56.7 percent of variance in the proportion of the population that is bilingual is associated with this component. Thus the principal story suggested by the six variables is one of great similarity between the variables, and the verbal descriptive label given to this overwhelmingly important dimension could be "socioeconomic homogeneity."

All the loadings of the variables on this first component are positive. This is to be expected if all the correlation coefficients in the original correlation coefficient matrix are positive. If some of the correlation coefficients are negative, then it is quite likely that some of the loadings will be negative, and a bipolar first component will be quite probable. More probable, however, is

Table 9-7 LOADINGS AND ADEQUACY OF THE PRINCIPAL-COMPONENTS SOLUTION

No. Variable name	Loadings		Explanation			Adequacy of the solution
	Component 1	Component 2	Component 1	Component 2	Variance	
3 Percentage with less than $4,000	0.9873	0.1313	0.9748	0.0172	1	0.9920
4 Percentage with fewer than two autos	0.9648	0.2175	0.9308	0.0473	1	0.9781
6 Percentage without high school diploma	0.9521	−0.1196	0.9065	0.0143	1	0.9208
1 Roman Catholic percentage	0.9331	−0.0960	0.8707	0.0092	1	0.8799
5 Managerial and professional percentage	0.8790	0.4335	0.7726	0.1879	1	0.9605
2 Bilingual percentage	0.7527	−0.5660	0.5666	0.3204	1	0.8870
Eigenvalues			5.0220	0.5963		5.6183
Percentage of total variance			83.7	9.94		

a bipolar second component, which is defined as one in which a strong positive, or group of positive, loadings is offset by a strong negative, or group of negative, loadings. This is well illustrated by the second component, which, in accounting for nearly 10 percent of the variation in the original data matrix, reveals a more subtle underlying dimension. In this case a fairly strong negative loading of $-.566$ for the percentage of the population that is bilingual is partly counterbalanced by a loading of .4335 for the percentage of heads of households that are employed in managerial and professional occupations. This bipolarity, which results from the reflection procedure, therefore suggests a second dimension which could be labeled "bilingual but not managerial or professional."

The centroid factoring procedure is discontinued after the calculation of the second component because the remaining variation of 6.36 percent is not accounted for in any persuasive way by the third and subsequent components. Although the overall cumulative explanation of 93.64 percent is a good general overall indication of the adequacy of the solution, it is interesting (and possibly important) to know the degree to which the variation in the individual variables has been subsumed by the two components. A measure of this can be obtained by summing the squares of the loadings of each variable on each component and expressing this sum as a percentage. Thus, the adequacy of the solution for variable 3 is

$$[(.9873)^2 + (.1313)^2]100 = 99.2 \text{ percent}$$

and for variable 4 is

$$[(.9648)^2 + (.2175)^2]100 = 97.81 \text{ percent}$$

The variable that is least adequately accounted for (Table 9.7) is variable 1, but even in this case almost 88 percent of the variation in the variable is subsumed by the two components.

Interpreting a principal-components analysis of the Southeast United States The example concerns a principal-components analysis of fourteen variables relating to the economic geography in 1961 of over 973 counties comprising an area that is commonly defined as the Southeast United States. The original data matrix has been transformed into a standardized matrix, and from this has been derived the correlation coefficient matrix. This matrix has been factored by using the principal-components procedure described above. Four components only are used because at the fifth the contribution of the component drops to around 5 percent, its eigenvalue is much less than unity, and the components themselves in this case describe specific dimensions rather than general dimensions. This last point will be discussed in greater detail in the factor analysis section.

The first four components account for 73.21 percent, or nearly three-quarters, of the variation in the data matrix. Thus, three-quarters of the spatial variation exhibited by fourteen maps of these variables pertaining to the Southeast United States can be succinctly represented by four maps. The loadings of each variable on each component are listed in Table 9-8 (all figures corrected back to two decimal places), and the adequacy of the solution for each variable is also listed. The variables are rank-ordered with respect to their loadings on the principal component, which in this example accounts for 41.46 percent of the variation in the original data matrix. The loadings are very strong (above .70 or below −.70) for seven variables, and the five positive loadings appear to cluster around "urban wealth," while the two negative loadings appear to describe "rural poverty." Thus the first component appears to describe a strong urban wealth–rural poor dimension existing in general throughout the counties of the Southeast.

The second component, which accounts for 13.08 percent of the variation in the original data matrix, contains a number of variables for which the loadings are strong (between .5 and .7); and on the positive side these consist of variables relating to the size of the county and its agricultural production, while on the negative side this is counterbalanced by a variable relating to manufacturing. Thus this second component describes a dimension that describes counties in which agriculture predominates and manufacturing is relatively absent, and for this reason it is labeled an "agricultural dimension." The third component, on which population density and average farm value are very strongly loaded, describes a dimension which obviously relates to density measured in terms of both people and pressure on land. For this reason it can be labeled a "density dimension." The fourth component is rather more interesting in that two variables, relating to manufacturing and the proportion of a county's population that is nonwhite, are strongly loaded upon it. This, therefore, is a dimension which describes counties in which heavy concentrations in manufacturing and nonwhite persons are associated. For this reason it can be labeled a "manufacturing dimension" in which, presumably, the nonwhite persons provide the basic labor force.

The interpretation of these components therefore requires a little descriptive imagination, and the resultant labels may, therefore, vary from researcher to researcher. However, if the tables of loadings are always presented, the reader can draw his own conclusions. Furthermore, if the adequacy of the solution for each variable is calculated, the reader can also judge whether some interesting dimensions may have been ignored. For example, many studies with data aggregates as observation units yield a principal component related to size because the observation units (that is, counties) vary so much in size. In this particular study no such dimension emerged, though three of the variables that are *least* adequately explained by the solution consisting of four

Table 9-8 THE SOUTHEASTERN UNITED STATES: LOADINGS AND ADEQUACY OF THE PRINCIPAL-COMPONENTS SOLUTION

Ranked variables	Loadings				Variance	Adequacy of the solution
	Component 1	Component 2	Component 3	Component 4		
Median family income	0.91	−0.27	−0.10	−0.02	1	0.92
White-collar percentage	0.87	0.09	−0.01	−0.22	1	0.82
Income per capita	0.86	−0.07	−0.01	−0.01	1	0.75
Urban percentage	0.81	0.18	−0.12	0.09	1	0.72
Population increase percentage, 1940–1960	0.72	0.10	−0.11	−0.25	1	0.60
Total population (1960)	0.69	0.32	0.07	0.08	1	0.59
Population density per sq. mile	0.57	0.12	0.73	0.16	1	0.93
Average farm value per acre	0.34	0.13	0.80	0.14	1	0.80
Area of county	0.19	0.59	−0.43	0.15	1	0.61
Total value of farm production sold	0.15	0.69	−0.23	−0.05	1	0.56
Population percentage in manufacturing	0.11	−0.63	−0.20	0.55	1	0.76
Nonwhite percentage of population	−0.18	0.46	−0.04	0.63	1	0.66
Rural farm percentage of population	−0.71	0.16	0.26	−0.24	1	0.65
Percentage earning less than $3,000	−0.87	0.30	0.17	−0.00	1	0.88
Eigenvalues	5.80	1.83	1.64	0.98	14	10.25
Percentage of total variance	41.46	13.08	11.70	6.97		

components do, in fact, relate to size. As size itself contributes little of analytical importance, the solution can be regarded as satisfactory.

Component Scores

If maps of the components are required, the scores of each observation unit on each component have to be calculated. In effect, these components can be regarded as variables that effectively summarize much of the variation in the data, and so the scores of the observations that would have yielded these components provide the data that can be utilized for a mapped spatial representation. The scores can be obtained by using the loadings as weights to modify the original standardized data. Thus, in the example of the principal-components analysis of the six socioeconomic variables for the six census tracts, Z is the standardized data matrix, and L is the matrix of component loadings, and a matrix S of component scores is required. This can be obtained by post-multiplying the matrix Z by L:

$$\underset{6 \times 6}{Z} \cdot \underset{6 \times 2}{L} = \underset{6 \times 2}{S}$$

In more general terms, if Z is the standardized data matrix of n observations and m variables, and L is the matrix of loadings of the m variables on the p components, then

$$\underset{n \times m}{Z} \cdot \underset{m \times p}{L} = \underset{n \times p}{S}$$

where S is the matrix of scores of the n observations on the p components.

Substituting the data from Table 9-2 (corrected to two decimal places) and the loadings from Table 9-7 (corrected to two decimal places) in the above equation, we obtain

$$\begin{bmatrix} -.94 & -.53 & -1.64 & -1.74 & -1.79 & -1.50 \\ -.91 & -.45 & -.55 & -.45 & -.90 & -.18 \\ -.72 & -.37 & -.24 & -.35 & .42 & -.85 \\ -.14 & -.28 & .07 & .25 & .50 & .42 \\ 1.21 & -.45 & .96 & 1.09 & .85 & .49 \\ 1.52 & 2.07 & 1.42 & 1.19 & .93 & 1.62 \end{bmatrix} \cdot \begin{bmatrix} .99 & .13 \\ .96 & .22 \\ .95 & -.12 \\ .93 & -.10 \\ .88 & .43 \\ .75 & -.57 \end{bmatrix}$$

$$= \begin{bmatrix} -7.32 & .22 \\ -3.20 & -.39 \\ -1.89 & .55 \\ .66 & -.14 \\ 3.81 & -.08 \\ 7.98 & -.16 \end{bmatrix}$$

or the component score of census tract 3 on component 2 is $(-.72)(.13) +$ $(-.37)(.22) + (-.24)(-.12) + (.35)(-.10) + (.42)(.43) + (-.85)(-.57) = .55.$ These scores are interpreted in exactly the same way as the data for the original variables. That is, the highest scores for a particular observation unit on a component indicate those units that are highest in association with that particular component, whereas the lowest scores indicate the opposite. In situations where a component is described by positive and negative loadings, as in component 2, then those census tracts with large positive scores are associated with the positive extrema of the component spectrum, whereas those census tracts with large negative scores are associated with the negative loadings on the component. Thus, census tracts 6 and 5 "contain" a great deal of component 1, whereas census tracts 1 and 2 contain rather less of component 1. Likewise, census tracts 3 and 1 score highly on the "bilingual" side of component 2, whereas census tract 2 scores noticeably on the "managerial and professional" side of that same component.

The component score matrix has been calculated for the study of the Southeast United States by using this same procedure, and the scores are presented in map form for each component in Fig. 9-3a, b, c, and d. The component score matrix has been standardized (a common procedure in all factorial analysis studies) so that the researcher may concentrate on the spatial variation of the scores of the counties for each component rather than the absolute magnitudes of the scores. The scores are mapped in three discrete intervals, two indicating scores well above and below the mean. The urban wealth–rural poor map (Fig. 9-3a) clearly reveals the urban areas of the South, which naturally score highest on this dimension. Florida, the Gulf Coast, the counties around Atlanta, and the Piedmont plateau all score highest and stand in stark contrast to the more rural areas. The agricultural dimension (Fig. 9-3b) clearly reveals the importance of the coastal plain, Florida, the old "black" belt, and the Mississippi lowlands. The density dimension (Fig. 9-3c) is not very meaningful, but it does delineate the urban areas of the south with great clarity. Finally, the manufacturing dimension (Fig. 9-3d) illustrates clearly the widespread distribution of industrial activity associated with nonwhite labor of all types through a wide belt running from the Appalachian valleys and the Piedmont through northern and central Georgia, Alabama, and Mississippi to the lower Mississippi Valley. It is noticeable that the mapped version of this fourth dimension suggests a clear distinction between this kind of widespread manufacturing and the heavier industrialization of the Gulf Coast area.

These clear distinctions are intrinsic properties of this principal-components solution. Because a certain number of variables are reflected at each successive stage in the solution in order to obtain a maximum accounting of the residual variance, the components are usually orthogonal or almost orthogonal. This property is extremely important in the interpretation of the components

FIGURE 9-3
The Southeast United States: (*a*) urban wealth–rural poor, (*b*) agricultural dimension, (*c*) density dimension, (*d*) manufacturing dimension.

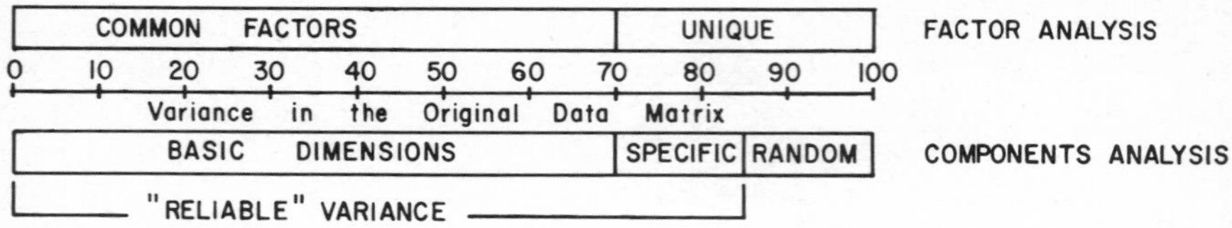

FIGURE 9-4
An interpretation of the general purpose of the principal-components and factor
analysis models.

themselves; and it also provides a useful role for the procedure as an adjunct
to other types of geographical analysis, particularly those in which independence
among variables is assumed, as in multiple-regression models. For example, in
the last case, if the requirement of independence is being grossly violated, the
researcher can construct new "variables" (or components) from the original set
by using principal components, and then use these as the independent variables
in the multiple-regression model. The calculated regression coefficients can then
be reconstituted in terms of the original variables (Riddell, 1970b).

FACTOR ANALYSIS

Most of the discussion in this chapter has focused upon the principal-components model because it is the simplest factorial procedure to explain and most
of the terminology can be transferred directly to the various factor analytic
procedures. The differences between the two general groups of models are,
however, fundamental, and in some cases they are mathematically extremely
complex. The basic difference, however, is fairly easy to comprehend in principle, though the particular interpretation of the difference postulated may well
be subject to some debate. Both models are concerned with discerning basic
dimensions in the variation of an original set of data. In the principal-components model *all* the variation is included for analysis, though in the previous
section various types of components and variance have been considered. These
types are presented diagrammatically in the components-analysis bar chart of
Fig. 9-4, where the subgroups refer to some hypothetical partitioning of the
total variance. The "basic" dimensions are the components that summarize
many general sources of variation in the original data matrix, and if the researcher is concerned only with these, he uses some acceptable cutoff threshold
plus a close examination of the loading structure to determine those components
to be included in this group. The principal component is always included in this
group, and usually two to five others. Thus in the Southeastern United States
study the basic dimensions are considered the first four.

The remaining portion of the variation is usually considered structured into components that relate primarily to specific sources of variation and to random errors. These are, of course, conceptual divisions in the principal-components case, but they undoubtedly underlie many of the applications of the principal-components procedure in the geographic literature (Carey et al., 1968; Casetti et al., 1971). The specific components usually constitute a relatively small proportion of the total variation; and they may consist of dimensions upon which one single variable is strongly loaded, or they may consist of dimensions upon which a few variables that relate to a specific aspect of the data (such as size of the observation units) are strongly loaded. In the latter case the components may be excluded, but in the former case exclusion of the components may well result in the exclusion of an important independent dimension. These two groups of dimensions together comprise the components that are generally assumed to constitute the "reliable" source of variation, because the components that remain are usually considered to constitute random sources of variation. Unfortunately, in principal-components analysis the errors may be spread among all the components, but only in the components at the residual or "scree" end of the distribution of dimensions are the errors considered to constitute almost the entire source of variation.

The factor analysis models, on the other hand, partition clearly the common sources of variation from those that may be considered unique. This division, which is illustrated in the factor analysis bar chart of Fig. 9-4, is usually assumed to be analogous with the basic and specific-plus-random dichotomy of the principal-components procedure. The assumption is not, of course, absolutely valid, for it is quite possible for a few specific and random sources of variation to be included in the basic components, and the cutoff points are usually chosen with a degree of educated subjectivity. Nevertheless, this assumption is important to understand, for it underlies much of the criticism of the use of factorial analysis in geography. The assumption that the common factors in the factor analysis model are substantially the same as the basic dimensions of the principal-components model cannot be made without careful consideration of the theoretical basis of the study as well as close analysis of the data.

In factor analysis, the division between the common and unique sources of variation is extremely important, for factor analysis models are concerned only with the common sources of variation. The models use the same information, that is, the correlation coefficient matrix, concerning interrelation among the variables. It will be recalled that the total variation in the data matrix was indexed in the principal-components analysis by the retention of unities on the diagonal. In factor analysis, these are replaced by an estimation of the proportion of the variance of that variable that is held in common with all the other variables. This estimated proportion is usually derived from a multiple correlation of each variable with the $m - 1$ other variables. Thus, if there are fourteen variables, there have to be fourteen multiple correlations calculated, each variable being regressed against the thirteen others. The estimated proportion is considered the multiple coefficient of determination, R^2, or the squared multiple correlation coefficient. Consequently, the matrix to be factored in factor analysis is the correlation coefficient matrix, the unities on the diagonal being replaced by the squared multiple correlation coefficients derived from regressing each variable against all the others.

The number of factors that are derived depends upon the total variance to be factored. This variance is indicated by the sum of the sources for each variable, which in factor analysis are referred to as "communalities" or h_j^2. Thus the total variance to be factored is $\sum_{j=1}^{m} h_j^2$. Therefore, whereas in principal-components analysis m components can be derived from m variables, in factor analysis the number to be derived is usually less than m, though it can be equal to m if $\sum h_j^2 = m$. Theoretically, as many factors should be determined as are necessary to exhaust the entire common variance. Thus the "adequacy of the solution" column in Tables 9-7 and 9-8 would be replaced by a column of h_j^2 if a factor analysis procedure were used.

Rotation

Once the communalities have been estimated and inserted in place of the unities in a correlation coefficient matrix, the factoring procedure *can* continue as outlined in the previous sections concerning principal components. If a centroid solution is used, the factors will be extracted in order of decreasing magnitude of contribution to the total variance, and the factoring procedure will continue until the last residual matrix is a zero matrix. At this point all the necessary factors have been extracted, and they can now be interpreted with respect to the loadings of each variable on each factor. The factor scores cannot be calculated in exactly the same way as component scores because "only a part of the total variance is accounted for by the common factors" (King, 1969, p. 187). Two methods for estimating factor scores are outlined in Lawley and Maxwell (1963).

One of the difficulties of using this solution procedure in factor analysis (and, therefore, principal-components analysis) is that the pattern of loadings for each component may not yield dimensions that can be easily interpreted in a geographical context. For example, in a correlation matrix where none of the coefficients are particularly large, the pattern of loadings that may occur with respect to the first factor (or principal component) may be of the same relative order of magnitude, and this may continue into the second, third, and so forth, factors. Such a situation is illustrated in Table 9-9, where the loadings are derived from a factor analysis of the common variation of fifteen variables relating to the characteristics of one hundred randomly selected houses and the families residing in them in 1969 in Winnipeg, Canada. These variables were chosen with a particular theoretical structure in mind, which was that the characteristics relating to houses should focus around dimensions concerning the "type of home" and its "quality," while those relating to families should cluster around dimensions concerning the "social status" and "stage in life cycle" of the family.

This type of hypothesis in fact implies a particular kind of factor model. The model used thus far ensures that common underlying dimensions are extracted in decreasing order of the degree to which they account for the common variation. That is not the type of model required in this instance, where the hypothesis appears to require a solution which sorts out factors around particular clusters of variables. (A nondeterministic method of achieving this (there are deterministic methods which will pick out prestated variables) is to use a *varimax rotation*. The purpose of this rotation is to place the factor axes (resolution vectors) in a unique position such that the factor can be interpreted by as large loadings as possible relating to the fewest variables possible.) Thus, if the particular theoretical structure outlined above were tenable, the variation held in common by the fifteen variables should be partitioned into four factors

Table 9-9 FACTOR LOADINGS (UNROTATED)* AND ESTIMATED COMMU-NALITIES, WINNIPEG, 1969

| Variables | Factor loadings | | | | Communalities |
	Factor 1	Factor 2	Factor 3	Factor 4	h^2
1 Total income	0.7836	0.0076	0.3722	0.2463	0.8134
2 Income, male	0.8305	0.1073	0.3067	0.0771	0.8012
3 Living condition	0.6357	0.0872	0.0324	0.3752	0.5536
4 Price of home	0.5918	0.1097	0.2170	0.1169	0.4231
5 Lot size	0.2659	0.7491	0.4158	0.1430	0.8252
6 Type of home	0.0737	0.7591	0.4426	0.0018	0.7776
7 Home ownership	0.1731	0.6547	0.2425	0.2686	0.5895
8 Family size	0.0387	0.7514	0.3157	0.3339	0.7773
9 Space ratio	0.3147	0.2736	0.4342	0.3802	0.5070
10 Age of heads of family	0.0682	0.2207	0.3409	0.4688	0.3894
11 Family age	0.1730	0.5552	0.4864	0.0749	0.5804
12 Education, male	0.6676	0.2164	0.1814	0.4551	0.7327
13 Education, female	0.6917	0.2654	0.2205	0.2913	0.6825
14 Occupation, female	0.1742	0.0463	0.4039	0.5094	0.4552
15 Occupation, male	0.6492	0.1007	0.1663	0.2199	0.5077
Eigenvalues	3.6756	2.7233	1.6218	1.3950	9.4155
Percentage of total variance	24.50	18.16	10.81	9.30	62.77

* All signs of loadings ignored because they reflect the various orders of scaling, which only confuse the interpretation.

focusing upon those variables that are considered indicators of the same general trait.

Fortunately, the unrotated solution suggests that the common variation, which constitutes $100(\sum h^2/15) = 100 \times \frac{9.4155}{15} = 62.77$ percent of the total variation, can be summarized by four dimensions. As the thrust of the hypothesis does not imply a search for general summary factors, but unique factors focusing on few variables, this unrotated solution is metamorphosed to a unique solution through a varimax rotation. The result of this varimax rotation is listed in Table 9-10. Each factor is now characterized by the existence of three or four variables with very large loadings, which are indicated by the very high factor concentrations. These factor concentrations are calculated simply by determining the proportion of the eigenvalue for each factor that is derived from the three or four variables with loadings greater than .5. As each group of variables tends to measure the same or only slightly different aspects of the postulated dimensions, the varimax rotated solution can be considered highly satisfactory.

Factor analysis solutions invariably require a rotated solution of one kind

Table 9-10 ROTATED FACTOR LOADINGS (VARIMAX ROTATION)* AND ESTIMATED COMMUNALITIES, WINNIPEG, 1969

Variables	Factor loadings				Communalities
	Factor 1	Factor 2	Factor 3	Factor 4	h^2
1 Total income	*0.8985*	0.0029	0.0444	0.0631	0.8134
2 Income, male	*0.8483*	0.1030	0.1579	0.2143	0.8012
3 Living condition	*0.6530*	0.1247	0.3191	0.0986	0.5536
4 Price of home	*0.6300*	0.0705	0.0181	0.1444	0.4231
5 Lot size	0.0824	*0.8997*	0.0135	0.0932	0.8252
6 Type of home	0.1409	*0.8586*	0.0972	0.1051	0.7776
7 Home ownership	0.1232	*0.7505*	0.0065	0.1052	0.5895
8 Family size	0.0294	0.4271	*0.7701*	0.0312	0.7773
9 Space ratio	0.2226	0.1003	*0.6521*	0.1491	0.5070
10 Age of heads of family	0.0295	0.0568	*0.5988*	0.1635	0.3894
11 Family age	0.3613	0.2894	*0.5313*	0.2893	0.5804
12 Education, male	0.3287	0.0830	0.0106	*0.7859*	0.7327
13 Education, female	0.3914	0.0683	0.1365	*0.7113*	0.6825
14 Occupation, female	0.2026	0.1489	0.0596	*0.6232*	0.4552
15 Occupation, male	0.3996	0.0537	0.0598	*0.5844*	0.5077
Eigenvalues	3.036	2.457	1.824	2.098	9.4155
Percentage of total variance	20.24	16.39	12.16	13.98	62.77
Factor concentration, %	77.44	85.88	91.00	88.32	

* All signs of loadings ignored because they reflect the various orders of scaling, which in this case confuse the interpretation rather than help. Loadings greater than 0.5 in italics.

or another. In human geography most studies using factor analysis have employed a varimax rotated solution, such as that by Ward (1969) of immigrant residential districts in the nineteenth century, but a varimax solution is not the only rotation that can be used. There are many rotations—oblique, "biquartimin," orthogonal, and so forth—and these are discussed in great detail in Rummel (1970, pp. 368–422). Few of these have, however, been used in geography. The choice of rotation is, of course, crucial in any study with factor analysis, and the researcher should take care to ensure that the rotation suits the purpose of the study. Every time a particular procedure is used, an assumption is implicit concerning the underlying structure of the variables, and the choice of an inappropriate rotation can serve to mislead rather than clarify.

SOME COMMENTS ON THE VARIOUS TYPES AND USES OF FACTORIAL ANALYSIS

The preceding discussion has focused upon an examination of two factorial analysis models and one procedure that can be used to obtain a solution. There are, of course, many types of factorial models that can be used, and the principal-components model and factor analysis procedure presented are but two of these, though they are the most commonly used in the social sciences. In fact, the factor analysis procedure described in this chapter is frequently referred to as "common" factor analysis, and the word "common" applies not only to the source of variation to which it is applied, but also to its almost universal use. The researcher can, as indicated above, vary the common-factor model by using different rotations, and can, theoretically, use different procedures for estimating the communalities. In essence, the latter alternative appears to be followed when researchers use a principal-components model to derive basic dimensions, which are then rotated (usually with a varimax rotation). A charitable interpretation of this procedure is that the researcher is calculating the communalities in retrospect after an initial principal-components screening of the data matrix!

Two other types of factorial models that should be of some considerable use in geographical research are R- and Q-mode procedures for samples, rather than for an entire population as has been implied by the discussion of the models thus far. If samples are used, significance tests are required, and these tests are based upon assumptions concerning randomness in the selection of the sampling units and normally distributed errors. If common factors are to be determined for a data matrix containing a sample of observations, *canonical factor analysis* should be employed, for this procedure provides statistics that can be used to test whether the derived factors are significant estimates of those that would have been obtained had the entire population been used. Likewise, if common factors are to be determined for a data matrix containing a sample of variables, *alpha factor analysis* should be employed, for this procedure provides statistics that can be used to test whether the derived factors are significant estimates of those that would have been obtained if the entire population of variables had been used. These two types of factorial models are discussed in some detail by Rummel (1970).

In many instances of research in human geography, such as in the numerous factorial urban ecology studies, all the data available, in terms of variables and observations, are utilized. On the other hand, studies that include samples of observations but all the variables available (such as the Winnipeg data) should use canonical analysis. In this situation, normalization of the variables is an important precondition to the analysis, for this will maximize the likelihood of the errors being normally distributed. Also, it would be pleasant if the data approximated a normal distribution in all factorial analyses even when entire populations are used, because correlation coefficients can be misleading measures of association if the variables are *highly* skewed. The pros and cons of this aspect of the correlation coefficient have been discussed in Chap. 4.

The Uses of Factorial Analysis

The various factorial analysis procedures discussed in detail or referred to in this chapter can be used for a variety of purposes. Frequently, these purposes overlap, for a given study may use the technique for several purposes simultaneously. Rather than replicate the exhaustive (and confusing) listings that are available elsewhere (Harman, 1960, pp. 6–8; Rummel, 1967, pp. 448–451), the uses discussed in this section will be with respect to specific applications in the geographical literature, and they will be limited in number. The discussion will focus upon four major uses: theory evaluation and hypothesis testing, calibration of constructs, data transformation, and intelligent exploration.

Theory evaluation and hypothesis testing   The brief discussion of the application of the scientific method to human geography in Chap. 1 has emphasized the contention that quantitative analysis can proceed efficiently and meaningfully only with a theoretical basis to a study. It is the theory which helps the researcher to form his analysis in terms of the data needed and the type of model that can be used. From this theory are deduced hypotheses which need to be tested or evaluated so that the theory may be expanded, refined, or modified. Factorial models can be used as a hypothesis-testing device for both standard statistical tests and a rather more qualitative inferential approach. For example, in the Winnipeg study referred to previously the basic constructs or dimensions underlying the units were hypothesized, and the variables were chosen to measure these hypotheses. A rotation was chosen that would reveal these constructs if they were in fact empirically tenable, and the results were encouraging (Yeates, 1972*a*). Another example lies in the area of factorial urban ecology (Rees, 1971), where the theoretical constructs by Shevky both with Williams and with Bell (1949 and 1955) concerning social status, family status (urbanization), and segregation have been refined and extended through the procedure of principal-components analysis as well as factor analysis (Murdie, 1969).

Calibration   A second, and rather important, use of factorial analysis is as a technique for effectively combining several indicators of the same general trait by a common scale, which is usually calibrated in standardized form. Golant and Burton (1970), for example, have used principal-components analysis to calibrate the meaning of a hazard. If the variables that are to be combined and scaled are clearly defined, one of two strategies can be used. Either the variables can be grouped into clusters of related variables, and the first component derived from a principal-components analysis, or the common variation of the entire data set can be factored by using the procedures of factor analysis with a varimax rotation.

Data transformation   The use of factorial procedures in a multiple-regression model to satisfy the requirements of independence among the independent variables has been referred to previously along with the interesting article by Riddell (1970*b*). In this case it is obvious that a factor analysis of only the common sources of the variation will not suffice, as the regression model is concerned with all the variation. Thus a principal-components model is required, along with an orthogonal rotation of all the basic and specific sources of variation. The identification of these components should be undertaken with great care. If the axes are then rotated so that they are 90° to each other, the dimensions will be orthogonal. Rotation would not, of course, be required if the components that were derived directly from the principal-components analysis proved generally independent. Berry has used this particular method in a multiple-regression analysis of regional development (Ginsburg, 1961).

Intelligent exploration   GIGO (garbage in, garbage out) is probably more true of factorial analysis studies than of any other statistical procedure. This is particularly so because the various methods of factorial analysis, and particularly principal-components analysis, have been used frequently for exploration into unknown domains, an example of which is the output relating to the Southeast United States. General support for this form of exploration is provided by Armstrong (1967), who argues that factor analysis can be treated as a *hypothesis-creating* technique. Given a mass of data, the various procedures of factorial ecology can be used to sort out the underlying structure in the data matrix (Hodge, 1971), and from this, hypotheses can be generated which can be tested by using more rigorous procedures. A basic observation concerning this kind of approach is that the whole analysis must be pursued intelligently; undergraduate researchers must not rush in where even professional fools fear to tread, though he and she may venture forth if they are aware of the limitations of the data and the technique chosen.

10

SPATIAL ALLOCATION MODELS

Although nearly all the discussion in the previous chapters has been concerned with the use of statistical methods and inference in human geography, the quantitative innovation has not been confined solely to the application of statistics. One type of model that has been slowly gaining in use in geography is the linear program (Scott, 1971a), particularly as it is used in spatial allocation models and the analysis of transport networks (Mackinnon and Hodgson, 1970). The name linear program is given "to any method for finding where a given linear function of several variables takes on an extreme value, and what that value is, when the variables are required to be non-negative and to satisfy further constraints of the form of linear equalities or inequalities" (Ficken, 1961, p. 1). The aim, then, is to maximize or minimize a linear function containing several variables subject to a number of constraints, one of which is that the variables not be negative. Both the *primal* equation, that is, the equation to be maximized or minimized, and the constraints must be linear, though nonlinear programming is being developed (Dorfman et al., 1958). To discuss and illustrate the type of procedures and terminology involved, a very simple linear program and a graphic solution will be presented for a two-variable example. Then the application of linear programming in spatial allocation models (Scott, 1970) will be outlined in greater detail with some specific empirical examples.

A SIMPLE LINEAR PROGRAM

For an example of the structure and notation of a linear program, consider a trivial hypothetical example concerning land reclamation and its allocation to two major uses, agricultural and urban (or nonagricultural). The reclamation of land for urban purposes, X_1, costs $400 per acre, and for agricultural uses, X_2, it costs $300. The primal problem is that the reclamation agency wishes to minimize the total cost of reclaiming the land,

$$\$400X_1 + \$300X_2 = Z = \text{minimum} \tag{10-1}$$

Obviously, this equation can be minimized by setting both X_1 and X_2 at zero, that is, reclaiming nothing, but the problem is subject to a number of constraints derived from three different groups. The first is an urban group which insists that at least 4,000 acres of land must be reclaimed for urban purposes (buildings, transportation, parks, and so forth). The second group is concerned with agriculture, and they say that at least 5,000 acres of land must be reclaimed for agricultural purposes. Finally, the third group is concerned only with reclamation per se, and they are quite disinterested in whether the land is used for agricultural or urban purposes. The last group, however, says that at least 10,000 acres in total must be reclaimed.

   The primal problem and the constraints can be written in full as follows:

$$400X_1 + 300X_2 = Z = \text{minimum} \tag{10-1}$$

subject to

$$1X_1 + 0X_2 = 4,000 \tag{10-2}$$
$$0X_1 + 1X_2 = 5,000 \tag{10-3}$$
$$1X_1 + 1X_2 = 10,000 \tag{10-4}$$

and the side condition that X_1 and $X_2 = 0$. The graphic solution to this problem is presented in Fig. 10-1. The broken lines are isolines of equal cost where different combinations of urban land and agricultural land result in the same reclamation expenditures. Thus a map of isoline costs can be envisaged covering the whole figure, but in this example, four are presented at constant cost intervals of $1,200,000. The three constraints are plotted as solid black lines, and according to these constraints, the only *feasible region* for a solution which satisfies each of the constraints is in the shaded area. Thus, there are any number of *feasible solutions* which lie in this area, but the problem requires a solution at minimum cost. This solution will be where the feasible region just touches the lowest cost isoline, which in this example is the $3,400,000 isoline. The combination of urban and agricultural land at this point reveals that 4,000 acres will be devoted to urban purposes and 6,000 acres to agricultural purposes. Thus the solution is

$$\$400(4,000) + \$300(6,000) = 3,400,000 = Z$$

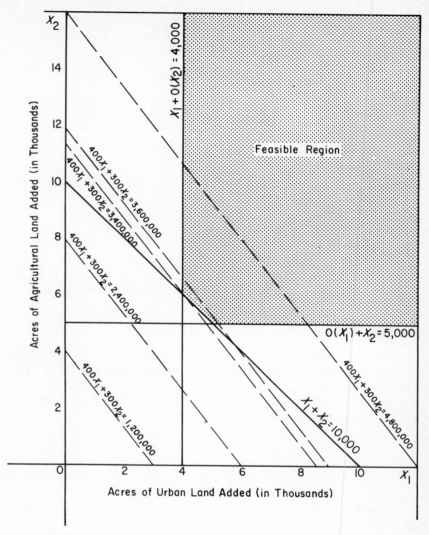

FIGURE 10-1
Graphic solution for a linear program.

Although the example illustrates the maxim that trivial problems have trivial solutions, it does demonstrate with real numbers a linear program which can be presented in general form as follows:

$$C_1 X_1 + C_2 X_2 = Z = \text{minimum} \qquad (10\text{-}5)$$

subject to

$$a_{11} X_1 + a_{12} X_2 \geq R_1 \qquad (10\text{-}6)$$

$$a_{21} X_1 + a_{22} X_2 \geq R_2 \qquad (10\text{-}7)$$

$$a_{31} X_1 + a_{32} X_2 \geq R_3 \qquad (10\text{-}8)$$

and

$$X_1, X_2 \geq 0$$

Of course, Eq. (10-5) could also be written

$$\sum_{i=1}^{2} \sum_{j=1}^{2} C_i X_j = Z$$

and the constraints could also be written in a similar concise fashion.

The Dual

For every primal problem there is a dual which can be interpreted easily in some cases, but less easily in others. If the primal problem concerns a minimization, the dual concerns a maximization, and vice versa; and the solutions to the primal and the dual yield the same result. This is an extremely important property which is utilized in the complex solution algorithms for linear programming, of which two (the northwest-corner rule and the simplex solution) are discussed later and a third (the Hungarian flow method) is mentioned briefly. The coefficients a to the constraints in the primal problem yield the coefficients to the constraints in the dual when transposed, and the inequalities, in accordance with the opposite aims of the dual, are reversed. Thus, by using the general form detailed above, and designating the unknown variables by the symbol U, the system of equations is

$$R_1 U_1 + R_2 U_2 + R_3 U_3 = Z = \text{maximum} \qquad (10\text{-}9)$$

subject to

$$a_{11} U_1 + a_{21} U_2 + a_{31} U_3 \leq C_1 \qquad (10\text{-}10)$$

$$a_{12} U_1 + a_{22} U_2 + a_{32} U_3 \leq C_2 \qquad (10\text{-}11)$$

and

$$U_1, U_2, U_3 \geq 0$$

In the example being discussed, the substitution of real numbers in the dual reveals the following set of equations:

$$4{,}000U_1 + 5{,}000U_2 + 10{,}000U_3 = Z$$

subject to

$$1U_1 + 0U_2 + 1U_3 \leq 400$$

$$0U_1 + 1U_2 + 1U_3 \leq 300$$

The U's can be determined in this example because Z is known, and there are, therefore, three equations with three unknowns. This solution yields the following values: $U_1 = 100$, $U_2 = 0$, and $U_3 = 300$. The graphic solution which provided values for X_1, X_2, and Z in the primal could also be used to solve the dual, but it would be difficult because three dimensions are involved. However, it is interesting to note that if the primal has three variables and two constraints, it can be solved by a graph more easily through its dual, which will have two variables and three constraints.

An interpretation of the U's can be presented through the fact that they must be values (or prices) of some type. The solution of the primal problem indicates that the agricultural constraint is redundant, for the requirement of this group is automatically met when the first and third constraints are met. The dual therefore suggests that the costs are actually incurred by the requirements of the urban and general reclamation groups. If the latter group is envisaged to be a government agency which is going to reclaim at least 10,000 acres of land, and then the urban and agricultural interests state their requirements, the interests of the urban group are met at an additional cost of $100 per acre, while those of the agricultural group are met at no additional cost.

THE TRANSPORTATION PROBLEM

Probably the best-known form of linear program for determining economic flows over geographic space is the transportation problem (Scott, 1971b). It will be noted from the previous discussion that the linear program, or set of statements, is normative; that is, it states an optimal condition which is to be achieved within a set of linear constraints. The transportation problem is also normative, for it states that a set of flows from a given spatial pattern of sources to a given pattern of destinations should be directed so as to minimize the total costs of transportation. This minimization is to take place, of course, within a set of constraints, and these constraints relate to the supply and the demand for the goods being shipped. The side constraint concerning the nonpossibility of negative shipments is also in effect.

An Equilibrium Pattern of Flows among Spatially Separated Markets

Assume a situation where there are four surplus-producing regions and four deficit regions all spatially separated. The four regions with surplus and the quantity of surplus can be labeled a_1, a_2, a_3, and a_4; and the four deficit regions and the quantity required are labeled b_1, b_2, b_3, and b_4. The costs of transport of goods per hundredweight between all possible combinations of pairs of sources and destinations are known (Table 10-1), and any particular cost is referred to as C_{ij}, where i refers to any one of the four sources, and j refers to any one of the four destinations. There are, therefore, sixteen possible routes, or connections, between the surplus and deficit regions; and sixteen possible sets of flows, or routes, which can be referred to as X_{ij}. The problem is, therefore, to determine the routes that are used and the volume of flow along each, consistent with the aim of minimizing the total costs of transport.

Structure of the primal equation   For all sixteen pairs the primal equation can be written as

$$15X_{11} + 33X_{12} + 24X_{13} + 2X_{14} + 16X_{21} + 9X_{22} + 15X_{23}$$

$$+ 8X_{24} + 12X_{31} + 20X_{32} + 6X_{33} + 5X_{34} + 4X_{41} + 12X_{42}$$

$$+ 10X_{43} + 18X_{44} = Z = \text{minimum}$$

which can be expressed more succinctly as

$$\sum_{i=1}^{4} \sum_{j=1}^{4} X_{ij}C_{ij} = Z = \text{minimum} \tag{10-12}$$

Table 10-1   TRANSPORT   COST   MATRIX (CENTS PER HUNDREDWEIGHT): HYPOTHETICAL DATA

Source	Destination			
	b_1	b_2	b_3	b_4
a_1	15	33	24	2
a_2	16	9	15	8
a_3	12	20	6	5
a_4	4	12	10	18

or more generally as

$$\sum_{i=1}^{n} \sum_{j=1}^{m} X_{ij} C_{ij} = Z = \text{minimum} \qquad \begin{array}{l} i = 1, 2, 3, \ldots, n \\ j = 1, 2, 3, \ldots, m \end{array} \qquad (10\text{-}13)$$

where there are n sources and m destinations.

There are two sets of constraints. The first set refers to the deficit regions and the constraints are that the deficit in each region must at least be met

$$1X_{11} + 1X_{21} + 1X_{31} + 1X_{41} \geq b_1$$
$$1X_{12} + 1X_{22} + 1X_{32} + 1X_{42} \geq b_2$$
$$1X_{13} + 1X_{23} + 1X_{33} + 1X_{43} \geq b_3$$
$$1X_{14} + 1X_{24} + 1X_{34} + 1X_{44} \geq b_4$$

which can be expressed more succinctly as

$$\sum_{i=1}^{4} X_{ij} \geq b_j \qquad j = 1, 2, 3, 4 \qquad\qquad (10\text{-}14)$$

or more generally as

$$\sum_{i=1}^{n} X_{ij} \geq b_j \qquad j = 1, 2, 3, \ldots, m \qquad\qquad (10\text{-}15)$$

The second set of constraints refers to the regions with surplus and the constraints that the amount shipped from any ith place cannot exceed the amount produced there

$$1X_{11} + 1X_{12} + 1X_{13} + 1X_{14} \leq a_1$$
$$1X_{21} + 1X_{22} + 1X_{23} + 1X_{24} \leq a_2$$
$$1X_{31} + 1X_{32} + 1X_{33} + 1X_{34} \leq a_3$$
$$1X_{41} + 1X_{42} + 1X_{43} + 1X_{44} \leq a_4$$

which can be expressed more succinctly as

$$\sum_{j=1}^{4} X_{ij} \leq a_i \qquad i = 1, 2, 3, 4 \qquad\qquad (10\text{-}16)$$

In order to have the inequality sign in Eq. (10-16) the same as in Eq. (10-14), Eq. (10-16) is usually expressed in the negative

$$-\sum_{j=1}^{4} X_{ij} \geq -a_i \qquad\qquad (10\text{-}17)$$

Table 10-2   "TABLEAU" OF PRIMAL AND DUAL VARIABLES, TRANSPORT COSTS, AND CONSTRAINTS IN THE TRANSPORTATION PROBLEM

	X_{11}	X_{12}	X_{13}	X_{14}	X_{21}	X_{22}	X_{23}	X_{24}	X_{31}	X_{32}	X_{33}	X_{34}	X_{41}	X_{42}	X_{43}	X_{44}	
u_1	1	1	1	1													$\geq -a_1$
u_2					1	1	1	1									$\geq -a_2$
u_3									1	1	1	1					$\geq -a_3$
u_4													1	1	1	1	$\geq -a_4$
v_1	1				1				1				1				$\geq b_1$
v_2		1				1				1				1			$\geq b_2$
v_3			1				1				1				1		$\geq b_3$
v_4				1				1				1				1	$\geq b_4$
	C_{11}	C_{12}	C_{13}	C_{14}	C_{21}	C_{22}	C_{23}	C_{24}	C_{31}	C_{32}	C_{33}	C_{34}	C_{41}	C_{42}	C_{43}	C_{44}	

Again, the general expression is

$$-\sum_{j=1}^{m} X_{ij} \geq -a_i \qquad i = 1, 2, 3, \ldots, n \qquad (10\text{-}18)$$

The side condition that each $X_{ij} \geq 0$ is, of course, in effect.

The tableau and the dual Equations (10-12), (10-14), and (10-16) are presented for clarification of Table 10-2. The unities within the table are coefficients that indicate where a given combination is possible. Where such a combination is not possible, there are zeros, but these have been deleted from the table. For each flow possible in the primal X_{ij}, there is an associated transport cost which has a counterposition at the base of the table. Thus progressive multiplication of each element at the top of the table with each element at the bottom and then summing across will yield Eq. (10-12). The constraints on the primal variables are listed down the right-hand side of the table and across the rows. For example, $1X_{11} + 1X_{21} + 1X_{31} + 1X_{41} \geq b_1$, as previously stated. A table of this kind is usually prepared for linear programs in order to clarify the structure of the equations, and an example of such a "tableau" can be found in Casetti (1966*b*).

Table 10-2 is of further importance because it also assists in revealing the structure of the dual. By following the pattern outlined in the previous section, and applying this to Table 10-2, if the primal solution is obtained by cross-multiplying and summing the elements at the top and bottom of the table, then the dual must be obtained by cross-multiplying and summing the elements on the right- and left-hand sides of the table (taking care with the negative a_i's). The appropriate elements on the left-hand side of the table have been designated as u's and v's. Thus, the dual is

$$-a_1 u_1 + -a_2 u_2 + -a_3 u_3 + -a_4 u_4 + v_1 b_1 + v_2 b_2 + v_3 b_3 + v_4 b_4$$
$$= Z = \text{maximum}$$

which is written more concisely as

$$-\sum_{i=1}^{4} a_i u_i + \sum_{j=1}^{4} b_j v_j = Z = \text{maximum} \qquad (10\text{-}19)$$

or more generally as

$$-\sum_{i=1}^{n} a_i u_i + \sum_{j=1}^{m} b_j v_j = Z = \text{maximum} \qquad (10\text{-}20)$$

Continuing with the pattern revealed by the table, just as the constraining quantities for the primal equation (the a_i's and the b_j's) are found at the right-hand side of the table, so will the constraining quantities for the dual be found at the bottom of the table (the C_{ij}'s). These constraints, of course, pertain to the u's and v's in the same way as the primal constraining quantities pertain to the X_{ij}'s. The unities and zeros (recall that the zeros have been deleted) are transposed, and the resultant constraint equations are

$$1v_1 - 1u_1 \leq 15 \qquad 1v_3 - 1u_1 \leq 24$$
$$1v_1 - 1u_2 \leq 16 \qquad 1v_3 - 1u_2 \leq 15$$
$$1v_1 - 1u_3 \leq 12 \qquad 1v_3 - 1u_3 \leq 6$$
$$1v_1 - 1u_4 \leq 4 \qquad 1v_3 - 1u_4 \leq 10$$
$$1v_2 - 1u_1 \leq 33 \qquad 1v_4 - 1u_1 \leq 2$$
$$1v_2 - 1u_2 \leq 9 \qquad 1v_4 - 1u_2 \leq 8$$
$$1v_2 - 1u_3 \leq 20 \qquad 1v_4 - 1u_3 \leq 5$$
$$1v_2 - 1u_4 \leq 12 \qquad 1v_4 - 1u_4 \leq 18$$

which can be written far more concisely as

$$v_j - u_i \leq C_{ij} \qquad \begin{array}{l} i = 1, 2, 3, 4 \\ j = 1, 2, 3, 4 \end{array} \qquad (10\text{-}21)$$

and more generally as

$$v_j - u_i \leq C_{ij} \qquad \begin{array}{l} i = 1, 2, 3, \ldots, n \\ j = 1, 2, 3, \ldots, m \end{array} \qquad (10\text{-}22)$$

The signs of the u_i's are negative to conform to those of the a_i's.

It is interesting at this stage to attempt an initial guess the interpretation of the u's and v's. One point is obvious: they must have some monetary value, as they are associated with transport costs which are expressed in cents. A second interesting observation is that the v's have the subscript j, which indicates that they pertain as a cost to the deficit regions, whereas the u's have the subscript i, which indicates that they apply as a cost to the regions with surplus.

Table 10-3 SUPPLY AND DEMAND FOR PRODUCT k, IN HUNDRED-WEIGHT, BY REGION

Region	Supply	Demand
a_1	6,000	
a_2	3,000	
a_3	6,000	
a_4	7,000	
b_1		5,000
b_2		6,000
b_3		7,000
b_4		4,000
Total	22,000	22,000

What these costs mean and why they are related to the C_{ij}'s requires a discussion in the context of a more specific example.

Special case of equalities Suppose that the actual surpluses for a product k for each a_i and the actual deficits for each b_j are as listed in Table 10-3. In this special case,

$$\sum_{i=1}^{4} a_i = \sum_{j=1}^{4} b_j$$

or, the total supply equals the total demand. As a consequence, the inequalities of the constraints summarized in Eqs. (10-14), (10-17), and (10-21) become equalities, and the series of equations, or program, for the primal and the dual can be rewritten as follows:

Primal

$$\sum_{i=1}^{4} \sum_{j=1}^{4} X_{ij}C_{ij} = Z = \text{minimum} \tag{10-12}$$

subject to

$$\sum_{i=1}^{4} a_i = \sum_{j=1}^{4} b_j$$

with the constraints being

$$\sum_{i=1}^{4} X_{ij} = b_j \tag{10-23}$$

$$-\sum_{j=1}^{4} X_{ij} = -a_i \tag{10-24}$$

and

$$X_{ij} \geq 0$$

Dual

$$\sum_{j=1}^{4} b_j v_j - \sum_{i=1}^{4} a_i u_i = Z = \text{maximum} \tag{10-25}$$

with the constraints being

$$v_j - u_i = C_{ij} \tag{10-26}$$

when the system is in equilibrium

$$\sum_{i=1}^{4} \sum_{j=1}^{4} X_{ij}C_{ij} = \sum_{j=1}^{4} b_j v_j - \sum_{i=1}^{4} a_i u_i \tag{10-27}$$

A simple system of this kind can be solved in an iterative procedure with an algorithm known as the "northwest corner rule" (Churchman et al., 1957, pp. 283–295).

Northwest corner rule   Linear programs are usually solved by algorithms of one kind or another. Both the northwest corner rule and the "simplex method" are algorithms, or procedures or rules, for solving the large number of equations needed in the operational use of linear programming. Before 1947 there were no general algorithms for solving general linear programs, but a simple one for solving the transportation problem had been developed by Hitchcock (1941) when he was working on British and American merchant shipping problems during the early part of the Second World War. In 1947, Dantzig (1951), as a result of work in planning air force activities, developed a procedure known as the simplex method for solving more general linear programs having linear inequalities.

The principles behind the use of the northwest corner rule are fairly simple but exhausting to explain even in the case of four origins and four destinations. As a consequence, the discussion will concentrate on an explanation of the principles and stages in the procedure, but a repetitive explanation of each iteration will be avoided. Accounts of small problems solved with up to five iterations are exhaustively detailed in Churchman et al. (1957) and Scott (1971b). The algorithm is undertaken with the data (Tables 10-1 and 10-3) which are

Table 10-4 THE BASIC OR FIRST FEASIBLE SOLUTION

Transport costs in *cents* (italic), shipments in thousands of hundredweight

		Destinations				
		b_1	b_2	b_3	b_4	Supply
Sources	a_1	5 *15*	1 *33*	*24*	*3*	6
	a_2	*16*	3 *9*	*15*	*8*	3
	a_3	*12*	2 *20*	4 *6*	*5*	6
	a_4	*4*	*12*	3 *10*	4 *8*	7
	Demand	5	6	7	4	22

formally presented in a tableau as in Table 10-4. The sources are listed down the left-hand column, and the total supply from each source down the right-hand column. The destinations are listed along the top row, and the demand at each destination along the bottom row. The transport costs between each source and destination are detailed in italics within the appropriate cell for each pair.

The procedure begins with the establishment of a basic, or first, feasible solution. This is obtained by making an allocation of k beginning in the north-west corner, that is, between a_1 and b_1. As the total supply from a_1 is 6 and the total demand at b_1 is 5, 5 (in thousands of hundredweight) of k is sent from a_1 to b_1, and a further 1 is pedantically assigned to b_2, which exhausts the supply to a_1. The demand at b_2 is now only partially fulfilled; so the procedure, continuing from the northwest, proceeds to exhaust the supply at a_2 by allocat-ing 3 to b_2, and finally fulfills the demand at b_2 by assigning 2 from a_3. Now that the demand at b_2 is fulfilled, the supply at a_3 can be exhausted by continuing in this structured steplike procedure and assigning 4 from a_3 to b_3, which, how-ever, only results in a partial fulfillment of the requirement at b_3. The demand at b_3 is met by assigning 3 from a_4, and the supply at a_4 is exhausted and the demand at b_4 met by finally allocating the remainder to it from a_4. This first feasible solution results in a total transport cost of \$2,610, and the allocations are written in italic type within each cell.

The question now arises whether this first feasible solution is also the optimal solution. If it is not, then the additional question arises concerning a structured strategy for improving upon it. The test for optimality makes use of the constraints on the dual, which have been succinctly expressed as

$$v_j - u_i = C_{ij} \tag{10-26}$$

which can also be written

$$u_i = v_j - C_{ij}$$

or

$$v_j = C_{ij} + u_i$$

Using these dual constraints, calculate the u_i and v_j for the first feasible solution. To do this, the value of one u_i or v_j must be assumed, and in this particular algorithm, the value of u_1 is set at zero. Thus,

$$v_1 = 15 + 0 = 15$$
$$v_2 = 33 + 0 = 33$$
$$u_2 = 33 - 9 = 24$$
$$u_3 = 33 - 20 = 13$$
$$v_3 = 6 + 13 = 19$$
$$u_4 = 19 - 10 = 9$$
$$v_4 = 8 + 9 = 17$$

These v's and u's can, of course, be evaluated only with respect to the cells, or routes, to which a flow has been assigned.

The u's and v's, which are sometimes referred to as *shadow prices*, can then be used to evaluate the *opportunity costs*, or costs of not using the unused routes. It is important to note that the terms "shadow price" and "opportunity cost" have particular and very limited meanings in the jargon of linear programming. They are, in fact, unfortunate terms because they have different connotations for the economics-oriented geographer. The opportunity costs c_{ij} for the unused routes can be calculated for each unused route by using Eq. (10-26), where the c_{ij} will be equal to, or less than, the corresponding C_{ij} if the basic solution is optimal. The c_{ij} are calculated as (with the appropriate C_{ij} in parentheses)

$$c_{13} = 19 - 0 = 19 \qquad (24)$$
$$c_{14} = 17 - 0 = 17 \qquad (32)$$
$$c_{21} = 15 - 24 = -9 \qquad (16)$$
$$c_{23} = 19 - 24 = -5 \qquad (15)$$
$$c_{24} = 17 - 24 = -7 \qquad (8)$$
$$c_{31} = 15 - 13 = 2 \qquad (12)$$
$$c_{34} = 17 - 13 = 4 \qquad (5)$$
$$c_{41} = 15 - 9 = 6 \qquad (4)$$
$$c_{42} = 33 - 9 = 24 \qquad (12)$$

Thus the initial question concerning the optimality of the first feasible solution is easily answered: It is not optimal, for some c_{ij} are considerably larger than the corresponding C_{ij}. The second question concerning a strategy for making improvements can now be answered.

Calculate the difference between the c_{ij} and C_{ij} where the opportunity cost is *larger* than the transport cost. The cell with the largest difference is then termed the *pivot cell*, around which an improved feasible solution can be structured. This cell is obviously the route with flows from a_4 to b_2, or cell [4,2], and adjustments to the original set of routes are made in the tableau at right angles (or orthogonally) so that a flow occurs from a_4 to b_2. Thus if cell [4,2] is given a flow of 2, the surplus capacity of a_4 is exceeded, and an adjustment has to be made in the same row (that is, orthogonally to [4,2]) to correct this imbalance. This can be achieved by subtracting 2 from the flow in cell [4,3]. The result of this adjustment is that the demand at b_3 is now not met. An adjustment in the same column (again, orthogonally) to a route which has a flow of 2 will correct this, and thus cell [3,3] is increased to 6. Unfortunately, the capacity of a_3 is now exceeded by 2, but this can be corrected by an adjustment in the same row which reduces the flow in cell [3,2] by 2. This closes out the iteration as no more readjustments need be made to balance the amounts supplied and the quantities demanded.

It is to be noted that if a positive change is made in a given column, then the iteration resulting from that change will always close in that same column. As a matter of information, it should also be noted that the number of routes along which a flow will occur will invariably be $n + m - 1$, which in this case is 7. This can be proved mathematically but will not be demonstrated in this discussion. It is, however, a useful item to remember as it is one means of checking the feasibility of a particular iteration. In this case, the second iteration concludes with seven routes, one new one being added and one deleted. The fact that this second iteration is an improvement over the first is demonstrated by the new Z of $2,370.

The optimality of the second feasible solution can now be checked by using the opportunity cost procedure described above. If it is not optimal, a new pivot cell is chosen and the same orthogonal adjustment procedure is followed. The third iteration is then tested for optimality, and if it is not optimal, the orthogonal adjustment procedure is repeated again. The iterations continue until such time as the derived opportunity costs for the unused routes are all less than their associated transport costs. When this state has been achieved, the optimal solution has been attained.

Optimal solution The optimum solution is, in fact, one in which the total costs of transportation, Z, are $1,590. The actual pattern of flows is presented in Fig. 10-2, and a tableau indicating the exact details of the optimum as Table 10-5. This tableau is of interest because it facilitates the estimation of the u's and v's for the optimum. As indicated previously, to calculate these shadow prices one of the u_i's or v_j's has to be known. As an aid to future interpretation, set the u_i for the route farthest away from any b_1 equal to zero. In this example it happens to be u_1, for the transport cost is highest between a_1 and b_1. By using Eq. (10-26), with its two alternatives, and the assumption that $u_1 = 0$, it can be calculated that

$$v_1 = 15 + 0 = 15$$
$$v_4 = 2 + 0 = 2$$
$$u_4 = 15 - 4 = 11$$
$$v_2 = 12 + 11 = 23$$
$$v_3 = 10 + 11 = 21$$
$$u_3 = 21 - 6 = 15$$
$$u_2 = 23 - 9 = 14$$

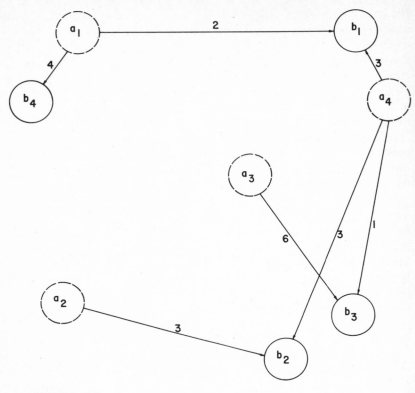

FIGURE 10-2
The actual connections between surplus and deficit regions in the minimum cost
solution.

As a check on the optimality of the solution, these shadow prices can be substituted in Eq. (10-25) to determine whether the equilibrium situation represented
by Eq. (10-27) exists. The result of this substitution is

$$\sum_{j=1}^{4} b_j v_j - \sum_{i=1}^{4} a_i u_i = \$3,680 - \$2,090 = \$1,590$$

which is, of course, exactly the same as that obtained in the primal solution.

The shadow prices in linear programs can be difficult to interpret, though
in this particular problem we do know that they are monetary values (in cents)
pertaining to the origins and destinations. Frequently, they can have very
interesting public policy implications with respect to pricing (Garrison and
Marble, 1958). In this problem, as the shadow prices relate to transport costs
which, in turn, are some function of the distance between the sources and the

destinations, an interpretation suggested by Stevens (1961) may be appropriate. His suggestion is that the u's may be interpreted in terms of economic rent (Wheeler, 1970). As an example, take the relative location as measured by transport costs of all four suppliers to one destination, b_2. From Eq. (10-26),

$$v_2^* - u_1^* = 33$$
$$v_2^* - u_2^* = 9$$
$$v_2^* - u_3^* = 20$$
$$v_2^* - u_4^* = 12$$

where the symbol * indicates that these are values relating to one particular destination, and not equilibrium shadow prices.

By using the concept of economic rent, the economic rent of the place farthest from b_2 will be zero, and if u_1^* is set at zero, v_2^* is 33. Therefore,

$$u_1^* = 0$$
$$u_2^* = 33 - 9 = 24$$
$$u_3^* = 33 - 20 = 13$$
$$u_4^* = 33 - 12 = 21$$

Table 10-5   THE OPTIMUM SOLUTION

Transport costs in *cents* (italic), shipments in thousands of hundredweight

		Destinations				
		b_1	b_2	b_3	b_4	Supply
Sources	a_1	2 15	33	24	4 2	6
	a_2	16	3 9	15	8	3
	a_3	12	20	6 6	5	6
	a_4	3 4	3 12	1 10	8	7
	Demand	5	6	7	4	22

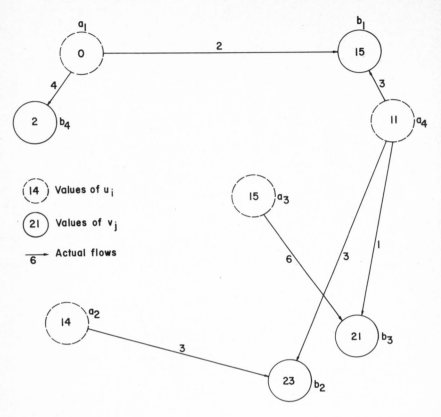

FIGURE 10-3
The shadow prices at the surplus and deficit regions in the minimum cost solution.

In this situation the u_i^*'s can be interpreted as representing an economic rent surface with respect to b_2. The equilibrium shadow price u_i's can, therefore, be interpreted as representing economic rent values for gross accessibility of all the surplus regions to all the deficit regions, taking into account the various quantities that need to be shipped. Thus, the highest economic rent value is at a_3, which is located fairly equidistant to all the destinations; the next highest is at a_2, which has the smallest surplus of all the sending regions; next comes a_4, which has a large surplus which has to be sent to three destinations; and the lowest is a_1, which is farthest from all four destinations (Fig. 10-3). Extending the analogy further, the v_j values may also be interpreted in terms of economic rent, but this time, with respect to the gross accessibility of the destinations to the four suppliers. The b_2 destination region is most accessible in terms of transport costs, and is followed by b_3, b_1, and b_4.

Price differentials between the deficit regions Now that an optimal system of flows, based on minimizing total transport costs, has been established, it is possible to determine the retail price differentials between the receiving places. The price at each receiving place is equal to the cost of production at the producing point plus the transport costs. To simplify the problem, it is assumed that the shippers' profit is subsumed in the price at the producing point and that the costs of production and the profit margins of each producer are exactly the same per unit of output. Therefore, as the price at each producing point per unit of product k is the same for each producer, the value of output at each producing point can be set at zero, for the price differentials at the receiving places will be determined solely by variations in transport costs. Consequently, the price at each receiving place will be the average transport costs incurred to suffice the demand. For example, at b_1 the demand is met by importing 3,000 hundredweight of k from a_4 at 15 cents per hundredweight. The average transport cost at b_1 is, therefore,

$$\frac{2,000(15) + 3,000(4)}{5,000} = \frac{42,000}{5,000} = 8.4 \text{ cents per hundredweight}$$

Following the same calculation procedure, it can be determined that the average transport cost at b_2 will be 10.5 cents per hundredweight; at b_3 it will be 6.6 cents per hundredweight; and at b_1 it will be 2 cents per hundredweight. In effect then, under a planned system of trade which minimizes total transport costs, prices will be lowest at b_4, next lowest at b_3, next to highest at b_1, and highest at b_2.

The model discussed has, therefore, provided a mechanism for determining the direction of trade and variations in prices under certain very rigid conditions. Not only are total supply and total demand equal, but they are also predetermined and price-inelastic. Also the transport cost rates are fixed per unit of hundredweight regardless of volume, and competition between regions is not permitted. However, it is possible to extend the model to include both demand and supply functions which may include situations where demand increases as price decreases and supply increases as price increases (G. C. Judge et al., 1964). Furthermore, models have also been constructed to allow transport costs per unit over a route to diminish as the flow increases, and to take into account the resultant competitive conditions (Mandell and Tweeten, 1971). Models of this kind are within the family of *spatial price equilibrium* models, and one of the earliest studies in human geography using this type of analysis was undertaken by Morrill and Garrison (1960) in a study of the interregional trade in wheat and the flow in the United States.

Distance Minimization

One important, and developing, interest of human geographers and regional planners lies in the application of quantitative techniques to determine the economic efficiency (Teitz, 1968) and political sensitivity (Jenkins and Shepherd, 1972) of the location of public service facilities, and the form and shape of the regions surrounding the facilities (Massam, 1972). One of the classic early studies using an intuitive transportation problem type of approach was that of Godlund (1961), who provided a structure for selecting the most appropriate sites for the location of regional hospitals in Sweden by maximizing their accessibility to the total population being served. His solution was, in effect, to locate the hospitals so that the total distance of the population to the hospitals was at a minimum. This type of approach is presented by Morrill (1967) in a formal transportation problem model for the service areas of physicians, and a similar application is used in a later study (but published earlier) of the spatial efficiency of high school districts in Grant County, Wisconsin, in 1961 (Yeates, 1963). In this rural area, eight of the thirteen schools serving the county were built within the ten years prior to 1961, and a number of school districts were subdivided and reaggregated. Many of these new schools are built on the edge of the towns and between towns, and the students from the surrounding area are transported to the schools by bus. The research question that arises is whether the hinterlands of the schools are drawn in the most efficient manner possible.

Definition of spatial efficiency   The conceptual problem is to define the word "efficient" as it pertains to a spatial problem of this kind. This conceptual problem can be resolved if it is assumed that, as many of the students have to be transported to school by bus, the spatial efficiency is achieved if the students are transported to school as cheaply as possible (and, it is hoped, in the minimum aggregate time). Therefore, any configuration of school hinterland boundaries that does not yield the minimum aggregate of transport costs can be defined as nonefficient.

In this sense, spatial efficiency can be expressed in a linear programming of the transportation problem, where the total costs of transport are to be minimized. Equation (10-13) can, therefore, be rewritten as

$$\sum_{i=1}^{n} \sum_{j=1}^{m} S_{ij} C_{ij} = Z = \text{minimum}$$

where S_{ij} = student to be transported from any ith pickup point to jth high school

C_{ij} = transport cost incurred in bussing student from any ith pickup point to any jth high school

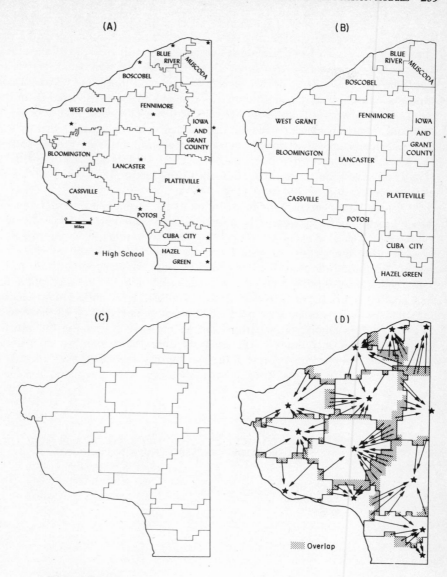

FIGURE 10-4
High school districts in Grant County, Wisconsin, 1961: (*a*) the actual districts,
(*b*) the modified actual districts, (*c*) the spatially efficient set of boundaries, (*d*) the
overlap between the modified actual set of boundaries and the spatially efficient
set of boundaries.

The address integer j can be any of the thirteen high schools serving Grant County. In order to have boundaries comparable with those existing in 1961 (Fig. 10-4a), the capacity of a high school is set at the number of pupils the school has in 1961. The address integer i refers to a mile-square section containing a figure indicating the number of students to be transported from that section. Thus, when the students are assigned to a particular high school, the mile-square section in which they are contained is also assigned. In this way, the hinterlands are constructed mile-square section by mile-square section. Therefore, for comparative purposes, the actual 1961 boundaries depicted in Fig. 10-4a have been redrawn to conform to the section lines which define the level of aggregation of this study (Fig. 10-4b).

All the data necessary for the solution of the problem are written out in a rather lengthy table, a summary of which is presented in symbolic form as Table 10-6. The $n \times m$ transport costs C_{ij} entered in this table are represented by measuring the airline distance from the center of each cell to each high school. Straight airline distances are used because the transport surface in this part of Wisconsin is fairly homogeneous (each section line is a road), and actual transport costs are difficult to determine. If all the 1,160 mile-square sections with zero or more students are used, 15,080 distances (1,160 $\times$ 13) have to be measured. This laborious procedure can be reduced by making the obvious assignments and including in the analysis only the remaining mile-square sections that contain one or more students. By this procedure, the data matrix is reduced to 293 $\times$ 13, and the number of distances to be calculated becomes a mere 3,809.

Table 10-6   FORMAT OF THE INPUT DATA FOR THE HIGH SCHOOL TRANSPORTATION PROBLEM

Location of students	High schools						Number of students at each location
	1	2	3	$\cdots$ j	$\cdots$	m	
1	C_{11}	C_{12}	C_{13}	$\cdots$ C_{1j}	$\cdots$	C_{1m}	a_1
2	C_{21}	C_{22}	C_{23}	$\cdots$ C_{2j}	$\cdots$	C_{2m}	a_2
3	C_{31}	C_{32}	C_{33}	$\cdots$ C_{3j}	$\cdots$	C_{3m}	a_3
$\cdots$							$\cdots$
i	C_{i1}	C_{i2}	C_{i3}	$\cdots$ C_{ij}	$\cdots$	C_{im}	a_i
$\cdots$							
n	C_{n1}	C_{n2}	C_{n3}	$\cdots$ C_{nj}	$\cdots$	C_{nm}	a_n
Number of students in each high school	b_1	b_2	b_3	$\cdots$ b_j	$\cdots$	b_m	

Solution   The form of the data and the assumptions outlined above yield a *simple* transportation problem. The solution is to find that set of flows where

$$\sum_{i=1}^{293} \sum_{j=1}^{13} S_{ij}C_{ij} = Z = \text{minimum}$$

subject to

$$\sum_{i=1}^{293} a_i = \sum_{j=1}^{13} b_j$$

with the constraints being

$$\sum_{j=1}^{13} S_{ij} = a_i \qquad i = 1, 2, 3, \ldots, 293$$

$$\sum_{i=1}^{293} S_{ij} = b_j \qquad j = 1, 2, 3, \ldots, 13$$

and the side condition being

$$S_{ij} \geq 0$$

where a_i = number of students in ith mile-square section

b_j = number of students in jth high school

In this instance the problem is solved by the Hungarian flow method suggested by Ford and Fulkerson (1962). Whereas in the northwest corner algorithm the solution is obtained by progressively replacing one feasible solution, or non-optimal solution, by another in an iterative manner until the optimal is achieved, the flow method only arrives at a feasible solution at the very end of the procedure. That is, throughout the iterations, the conditions $\sum_{j=1}^{13} S_{ij} = a_i$ and $\sum_{i=1}^{293} S_{ij} = b_j$ are not fulfilled until the end, when a feasible solution is derived which is also the optimal. The high school hinterland problem was solved in 123 iterations, which required 4.5 minutes of computer time.

The minimum-cost solution results in the spatially efficient school districts illustrated in Fig. 10-4c. The map of overlap between the spatially efficient set of boundaries and the modified actual set of boundaries (Fig. 10-4d) indicates the degree to which spatial efficiency existed in the 1961 school districts in Grant County. Of the 293 mile-square sections used in the analysis, 209 lie in the overlap zone. As it is assumed that the obvious assignments made are spatially efficient, this means that 209 out of 1,160 should be reassigned to achieve spatial efficiency. Therefore, it can be concluded that the high school districts of Grant County, according to the 1961 distribution of high school students, are 18 percent spatially inefficient. This inefficiency probably costs the county school system about $4,000 per year. Of course, if the location of the schools could be changed, the saving would be even greater, but this kind of decision can be made only when the facility is about to be built.

THE SIMPLEX SOLUTION

The simplex method is the best known and most used algorithm for solving linear programs. An extensive review of the historical evolution of linear programming is given in Dantzig (1963), and the simplex solution is explained in detail in most standard works on linear programming (Dorfman et al., 1958; Hadley, 1962). Most of these explanations are quite complex, so in this section, the discussion will focus upon the basic principles of the procedure. This explanation will, it is hoped, permit the researcher to understand the principles behind the various computer programs and assembly program packages that have been developed over the past years for the solution of large problems by computers.

The discussion revolves around the extremely trivial problem outlined in the first section of this chapter. It will be recalled that the primal problem is

$$400X_1 + 300X_2 = Z = \text{minimum} \tag{10-1}$$

the constraints being

$$1X_1 + 0X_2 \geq 4,000 \tag{10-2}$$

$$0X_1 + 1X_2 \geq 5,000 \tag{10-3}$$

$$1X_1 + 1X_2 \geq 10,000 \tag{10-4}$$

with the side condition that $X_1, X_2 \geq 0$.

The graphic solution to this problem is presented in Fig. 10-1, where the unknown values of X_1 and X_2 are determined to be 4,000 and 6,000. This solution is based upon the definition of a feasible solution space as indicated by the constraints, and the simplex method uses this procedure algebraically in a similar fashion.

The Algorithm

The simplex method begins by transforming the inequalities in the constraints to equalities. In this particular case, the inequalities are "greater than" ($>$), and so each equation can be transformed into an equality by the subtraction of an unknown quantity. Thus

$$1X_1 + 0X_2 - 1S_1 \qquad\qquad = 4 \tag{10-28}$$

$$0X_1 + 1X_2 \qquad - 1S_2 \quad = 5 \tag{10-29}$$

$$1X_1 + 1X_2 \qquad\qquad - 1S_3 = 10 \tag{10-30}$$

where the numbers on the right-hand side of the equations are in thousands. The variables that have been added are called "slack variables," and are appropriately denoted by the symbol S. It should be noted that if the inequalities were of the "less than or equal to" ($\leq$) types, then the constraint equations would have been transformed to equalities by the addition of *positive* slack variables. The detached coefficients pertaining to the variables and slack variables in the constraints can now be written in standard form as in Table 10-7.

Equations (10-28), (10-29), and (10-30) present a system in which there are five unknowns, but only three equations. In this type of situation there will be a solution if two of the unknowns are zero, for then there will be three equations with three unknowns. If there were three unknowns and three equations, the unknown variables could, of course, be determined by the method of simultaneous equations. Alternatively, if there were q equations with q unknowns and q is large, the unknowns could be determined more efficiently by the matrix methods described in Chap. 5. In this example, the strategy is to reduce the number of variables in the system of equations by two in all possible combinations, and to solve for the other three. The number of possible ways of assigning two variables to be zero, and thus providing three equations with three unknowns, is $\binom{5}{2}$ or $5(5 - 1)/2 = 10$, and these can be listed as follows:

Solution	X_1	X_2	S_1	S_2	S_3
1	0	0			
2	0		0		
3	0			0	
4	0				0
5		0	0		
6		0		0	
7		0			0
8			0	0	
9			0		0
10				0	0

where the zeros indicate the variables to be deleted and the blanks indicate those that are to remain.

Thus, a *basis* equation consists of three variables that are *permitted* to be nonzero (though this does not mean that they are all necessarily nonzero), and

Table 10-7 **COEFFICIENTS FOR THE VARIABLES AND SLACK VARIABLES**

Constraint	Variables		Slack variables			Limit
	X_1	X_2	S_1	S_2	S_3	
1	1	0	−1	0	0	4
2	0	1	0	−1	0	5
3	1	0	0	0	−0	10

there are, therefore, ten possible bases, or basic equations. The ten systems of three equations with three unknowns are solved by using the method of simultaneous equations, and the values of the estimated coefficients for each of these ten solutions are listed in Table 10-8. For example, consider the procedure used to estimate the coefficients for solution 8

$$1X_1 + 0X_2 - 0S_3 = 4$$
$$0X_1 + 1X_2 - 0S_3 = 5$$
$$1X_1 + 1X_2 - 1S_3 = 10$$

Obviously, $X_1 = 4$, $X_2 = 5$, and $S_3 = 4 + 5 - 10 = -1$. Parenthetically, it may be noted that the reason such a simple example with a simple set of coefficients being chosen was to make these ten separate, simultaneous calculations so easy for the reader.

Table 10-8 can now be scanned to determine which of these ten basic solutions are *feasible basic solutions*. The side condition $X_1, X_2 \geq 0$ must also apply to the slack variables, as these have been entered into the constraint equations to behave on a par with the original variables, and must, therefore, be subject to the same restrictions. Thus, all those solutions in which a negative coefficient appears are "not on," as they correspond to solutions that are not feasible. Only solutions 9 and 10 are basic feasible solutions, and the values of X_1 and X_2 correspond to the limiting vertices in Fig. 10-5. In fact, the number of basic feasible solutions derived by this method will always correspond to the number of vertices defining the graphic solution space. Of course, in this example, the fact that two of the constraints disappear to infinity severely limits the number of possible vertices.

The next step is, in effect, to compare the vertices and determine which pair of X_1 and X_2 values yields the minimum solution. Algebraically, this is

Table 10-8   THE RESULTS OF ASSIGNING TWO VARIABLES TO BE ZERO AND SOLVING FOR THE OTHER THREE

Solution	X_1	X_2	S_1	S_2	S_3	Vertex
1	0	0	−4	−5	−10	Not on
2	0	∞	0	−5	−10	Not on
3	0	5	−4	0	−5	Not on
4	0	10	−4	5	0	Not on
5	4	0	0	−5	−14	Not on
6	∞	0	−4	0	−10	Not on
7	10	0	6	−5	0	Not on
8	4	5	0	0	−1	Not on
9	4	6	0	1	0	A
10	5	5	1	0	0	B

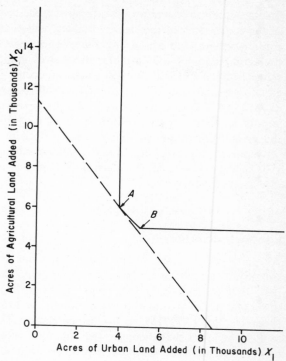

FIGURE 10-5
Sample of constraints for the simplex example (extracted from Fig. 10-1).

achieved from the two basic feasible solutions, which indicate, from solutions 9 and 10, that X_1 and X_2 are either 4,000 and 6,000 or 5,000 and 5,000. If these two sets of solutions are substituted in Eq. (10-1), it can be discerned that solution 9 provides the minimum-cost solution. This procedure requires, then, that all the basic feasible solutions be evaluated in terms of the primal program, and the one which minimizes Z (or maximizes Z) is the appropriate answer. A check on the calculations can, of course, be achieved by substituting this estimate of Z in the system defined by the dual and its constraints and determining whether the constraints are satisfied with that value of Z.

A Comment

This discussion of the basic simplex procedure has, of course, used a number of simplifications to circumvent problems, and these are evident in the limited number of equations and the binary nature of the constraint coefficients. A further situation has been finessed by a procedure which has ignored the signs of the coefficients of the slack variables, which are all negative and, therefore, could never provide a basic feasible solution. This procedure has focused upon the actual signs of the variables themselves, and thus, in essence, ignored the sign of the coefficients. This situation occurs always with greater-than-or-equal-to constraints, and is usually solved in large systems by using *artificial variables*, which are slack variables with positive coefficients. These artificial variables are then forced out of the basis by giving them very large "costs" in the primal equations, so that the basis remains feasible without them. This procedure is, however, one of many refinements in the simplex method (Ficken, 1961) and does not alter the general principles of the algorithm which have been discussed in this section.

CONCLUSION

As a conclusion to this chapter, which has introduced the researcher in human geography to some of the basic ideas and principles for solving linear programs, it is, perhaps, instructive to consider some of the advantages and disadvantages of these types of spatial allocation models, and to point to the current "state of the art." Scott (1971b), in his rather elegant discussion of spatial allocation models, suggests that there are two main advantages and two disadvantages of this type of analysis. One major problem, which is concealed, but nevertheless there in the study of high school districting, is the *indivisibility* among the variables. The allocation model assigns the units from a source to a destination by assuming that each variable is infinitely divisible. In the Grant County study, the assignment was mile-square section by mile-square section, and an algorithm is used in the flow method to avoid dividing these units. Thus the problem can be avoided, but it requires special additional procedures, such as integer programming or others that lie beyond linear programming per se.

The second disadvantage is also fairly crucial and relates to the assumption of linearity. This is a particular difficulty in studies of manufacturing, where costs are related to volume, and economies of scale are very real. Thus a problem such as that envisaged by Beckmann and Marschak (1955) is somewhat unreal not only because it is difficult to envisage a solution, but because it ignores technical economies of scale and assumes that output is linearly related to the quantity of inputs. The problem of linearity can be overcome by using quadratic programming methods, and it can also be overcome in the more complex types of spatial price equilibrium models.

A major advantage of spatial allocation models as discussed in this chapter is that they can be used to achieve a stated objective that may well be to the public good. For example, if the movement of goods within a country can be planned so as to minimize the total costs of transport (Goldman, 1958), then this could well be to the public good. Furthermore, if public facilities could be located so as to maximize their service to society, then this too would be a great asset (ReVelle and Swain, 1970). The difficulty with this type of normative approach in public planning is that it requires, for its implementation, the power to plan. The kind of power to plan envisaged by this type (normative) of approach to planning is usually available only in socialist democracies or those influenced by some variety of dictatorial government.

Concomitantly, models of this kind can yield valuable insights into the theoretical workings of an economic system, for they can be used to indicate what would be, or could be, under clearly defined hypothetical conditions. Theoretical models of this type have been extensively reviewed by Garrison (1959a and b; 1960) and Isard (1960), and an interpretation of the dual in terms of Von Thunen's theory of economic rent has been outlined earlier in the chapter. These models can also be used to establish ideal conditions of "what should be," under certain stated conditions, and the real world can be compared with them to gain further insights. This type of comparison can be couched in terms of primitive cost-benefit analysis, particularly if social welfare conditions are incorporated (Pearce, 1971).

The new types of linear programming that are being developed, such as quadratic, dynamic, and heuristic programming, which fall within the rubric *combinational programming*, have been reviewed concisely for geographers and planners by Scott (1971a). These methods and their present and potential applications point to linear programming as an exciting, but complex, area of quantitative analysis in human geography. The procedures can be made to tackle very real problems involving networks, nodes, and flows and so suggest an entertaining intellectual framework for analyzing geographical systems. It is to this task that some of the future developments in quantitative geography must be directed.

REFERENCES

ACKOFF, R. L., S. K. GUPTA, and J. S. MINAS (1962): "Scientific Method," New York: Wiley.

AHMAD, Q. (1965): Indian Cities: Characteristics and Correlates, *Dep. Geogr., Res. Paper* 105, Chicago: The University of Chicago.

ALEXANDERSSON, G. (1956): "The Industrial Structure of American Cities," Lincoln: University of Nebraska Press.

ANDERSON, D. (1965): Three Computer Programs for Contiguity Measures, *Dep. Geogr., Tech. Rep.* 5, Evanston, Ill.: Northwestern University.

ANDERSON, T. W. (1958): "Introduction to Multivariate Statistical Analysis," New York: Wiley.

ARKIN, H., and R. R. COLTON (1962): "Tables for Statisticians," New York: Barnes & Noble.

ARMSTRONG, J. C. (1967): The Derivation of Theory by Factor Analysis or Tom Swift and His Electronic Factor Analysis Machine, Am. Stat., 21:17–21.

BABCOCK, J. M. (1962): Adoption of Hybrid Corn: A Comment, Rural Sociol., 27: 332–338.

BACHI, R. (1963): Standard Distance Measures and Related Methods for Spatial Analysis, Papers Proc. Reg. Sci. Assoc., 10:83–132.

BARTON, B., and W. R. TOBLER (1971): A Spectral Analysis of Innovation Diffusion, Geog. Anal., 3:195–199.

BECKERMAN, W. (1956): Distance and the Pattern of Inter-European Trade, Rev. Econ. Stat., 38:31–40.

BECKMAN, M. J., and T. MARSHAK (1955): An Activity Analysis Approach to Location Theory, Kyklos, 8:125–141.

BERKSON, J. (1953): A Statistically Precise and Relatively Simple Method of Estimating the Bio-assay with Quantal Response, Based on the Logistic Function, J. Am. Stat. Assoc., 48:565–599.

BERRY, B. J. L. (ed.) (1971): Comparative Factorial Ecology, Econ. Geogr., 47 (Supl.):2.

BERRY, B. J. L. (1964): Approaches to Regional Analysis: A Synthesis, Ann. Assoc. Am. Geogr., 5:2–11.

BERRY, B. J. L. (1963): Commercial Structure and Commercial Blight, Dep. Geogr., Res. Paper 105, Chicago: The University of Chicago.

BERRY, B. J. L. (1962): "Sampling, Coding and Storing Flood Plain Data," U.S. Dept. Agr., Agr. Handbook 237.

BERRY, B. J. L. (1961): A Method for Deriving Multi-Factor Uniform Regions, Przegl. Geogr., 56:551–569.

BERRY, B. J. L. (1960): An Inductive Approach to the Regionalization of Economic Development," in N. GINSBERG (ed.): "Essays on Geography and Economic Development," Chicago: The University of Chicago Press.

BERRY, B. J. L., and A. BAKER (1968): in B. J. L. BERRY and D. F. MARBLE (eds.): "Spatial Analysis," pp. 91–100, Englewood Cliffs, N.J.: Prentice-Hall.

BERRY, B. J. L., and P. REES (1969): The Factorial Ecology of Calcutta, Am. J. Sociol., 74:445–491.

BHARUCHA-REID, A. T. (1960): "Elements of the Theory of Markov Processes and Their Applications," New York: McGraw-Hill.

BIRCH, J. W. (1964): The Delimitation of Farming-type Regions with Special Reference to the Isle of Man, Trans. Inst. Br. Geogr., 20:141–158.

BLALOCK, H. M. (1960): "Social Statistics," New York: McGraw-Hill.

BLAUT, J. M. (1959): Microgeographic Sampling: A Quantitative Approach to Regional Agricultural Geography, Econ. Geogr., 35:79–88.

BOURNE, L. S. (1969a): Land Use Succession in Urban Areas: A Study of Structure and

Change, *Proc. Assoc. Am. Geogr.*, 1969 *Conf.*, *Ann Arbor, Mich.*

BOURNE, L. S. (1969*b*): A Spatial Allocation Land Use Conversion Model of Urban Growth, *J. Reg. Sci.*, **9**:261–272.

BOWDEN, L. (1965): Diffusion of the Decision to Irrigate, *Dep. Geogr.*, *Res. Paper 97*, Chicago: The University of Chicago.

BOYCE, D. E. (1965): The Effect of Direction and Length of Person Trips on Urban Travel Patterns, *J. Reg. Sci.*, **6**:65–80.

BOYCE, R. B., and W. A. V. CLARK (1964): The Concept of Shape in Geography, *Geogr. Rev.*, **54**:561–572.

BROWN, K. M. (1971): Regional Differences in Efficiency: Implications for a Model of Regional Income and Growth, *Geogr. Anal.*, **3**:354–360.

BROWN, L. A. (1968*a*): Diffusion Dynamics: A Review and Revision of the Quantitative Diffusion of Innovation, *Lund Stud. Geogr.*, Lund, Sweden: Gleerup.

BROWN, L. A. (1968*b*): "Diffusion Processes and Location: A Conceptual Framework and Bibliography," Philadelphia: Regional Science Research Institute.

BROWN, L. A. (1964): The Diffusion of Innovation: A Markov Chain Type Approach, *Dep. Geogr.*, *Discuss. Paper 3*, Evanston, Ill.: Northwestern University.

BRUNN, S. (1968): Changes in the Service Structure of Rural Trade Centers, *Rural Sociol.*, **33**:200–206.

BUNGE, W. (1962): "Theoretical Geography," Lund, Sweden: Gleerup (2d rev. and enl. ed., 1966).

BURTON, I. (1963): The Quantitative Revolution and Theoretical Geography, *Can. Geogr.*, **7**:151–162.

BURTON, I. (1960): Types of Agricultural Occupance of Flood Plains in the United States, *Dep. Geogr.*, *Res. Paper 75*, Chicago: The University of Chicago.

BUSH, R. R., and F. MOSTELLER (1955): "Stochastic Models for Learning," New York: Wiley.

CAREY, G. W., L. MACOMBER, and M. GREENBERG (1968): Educational Demographic Factors in the Urban Geography of Washington, D.C., *Geogr. Rev.*, **58**:515–537.

CARROTHERS, G. A. P. (1956): An Historical Review of the Gravity and Potential Concepts of Human Interaction, *J. Am. Inst. Plann.*, **22**:94–102.

CASETTI, E. (1969): Why Do Diffusion Processes Conform to Logistic Trends? *Geogr. Anal.*, **1**:101–105.

CASETTI, E. (1966*a*): Analysis of Spatial Association by Trigonometric Polynomials, *Can. Geogr.*, **10**:199–204.

CASETTI, E. (1966*b*): Optimal Location of Steel Mills Serving the Quebec and Southern Ontario Steel Market, *Can. Geogr.*, **10**:27–39.

CASETTI, E., L. KING, and D. JEFFREY (1971): Structural Imbalance in the U.S. Urban-Economic System, 1960–65, *Geogr. Anal.*, **3**:239–255.

CATTELL, R. B. (1966): Psychological Theory and Scientific Method, in R. B. CATTELL (ed.), "Handbook of Multivariate Experimental Psychology," pp. 1–18, Chicago: Rand McNally.

CATTELL, R. B. (1952): "Factor Analysis," New York: Harper.

CERNY, J. W. (1971): Display of Trend Surfaces, *Geogr. Anal.*, **3**:268–272.

CHAYES, F., and Y. SUZUKI (1963): Geological Contours and Trend Surfaces: A Discussion, *J. Petrol.*, **70**:507–538.

CHORLEY, R. J. (1964): Geography and Analogue Theory, *Ann. Assoc. Am. Geogr.*, **54**:127–137.

CHORLEY, R. J., and P. HAGGETT (eds.) (1967a): "Models in Geography," London: Methuen.

CHORLEY, R. J., and P. HAGGETT (1967b): Models, Paradigms and the New Geography, in R. J. CHORLEY and P. HAGGETT (eds.) (1967a), "Models in Geography," London: Methuen.

CHORLEY, R. J., and P. HAGGETT (1965): Trend Surface Mapping in Geographical Research, *Trans. Proc. Inst. Br. Geogr.*, **37**:47–67.

CHURCHMAN, C. W., R. L. ACKOFF, and E. L. ARNOFF (1957): "Introduction to Operations Research," New York: Wiley.

CLARK, C. (1951): Urban Population Densities, *J. Royal Stat. Soc.*, **A114**:490–496.

CLARK, P. J., and F. C. EVANS (1954): Distance to Nearest Neighbor as a Measure of Spatial Relations in Populations, *Ecology*, **35**:445–453.

CLARK, W. A. V. (1965): Markov Chain Analysis in Geography: An Application to the Movement of Rental Housing Areas, *Ann. Assoc. Am. Geogr.*, **55**:351–359.

CLIFF, A. D., and J. K. ORD (1972): Testing for Spatial Autocorrelation among Regression Residuals, *Geogr. Anal.*, **4**:267–284.

CLIFF, A. D., and J. K. ORD (1971): Evaluating the Percentage Points of a Spatial Autocorrelation Coefficient, *Geogr. Anal.*, **3**:51–62.

CLIFF, A. D., and J. K. ORD (1969): The Problem of Spatial Autocorrelation, in A. J. SCOTT (ed.), "Studies in Regional Science," London: Pion.

COCHRAN, W. G. (1953): "Sampling Techniques," New York: Wiley.

COCHRAN, W. G., F. MOSTELLER, and J. W. TUKEY (1954): Principles of Sampling, *J. Am. Stat. Assoc.*, **49**:13–35.

CONKLING, E. C., and M. H. YEATES (1974): "An Introduction to Theoretical Economic Geography," New York: McGraw-Hill.

COX, K. R. (1968): Suburbia and Voting Behavior in the London Metropolitan Area, *Ann. Assoc. Am. Geogr.*, **58**:111–127.

CROXTON, F. E., and D. J. CROWDEN (1955): "Applied General Statistics," Englewood Cliffs, N.J.: Prentice-Hall.

CURRY, L. (1972): A Bivariate Spatial Regression Operator, *Can. Geogr.*, **16**:1–14.

CURRY, L. (1966): A Note on Spatial Association, *Prof. Geogr.*, **18**:97–99.

DACEY, M. F. (1969): A Hypergeometric Family of Discrete Probability Distributions: Properties and Applications to Location Models, *Geogr. Anal.*, **1**:283–317.

DACEY, M. F. (1968): A Review on Measures of Contiguity for Two- and K-Color Maps, in B. J. L. BERRY and D. F. MARBLE (eds.), "Spatial Analysis: A Reader in Statistical Geography," pp. 479–495, Englewood Cliffs, N.J.: Prentice-Hall.

DACEY, M. F. (1964a): Modified Poisson Probability Law for Point Pattern More Regular Than Random, *Ann. Assoc. Am. Geogr.*, **54**:559–565.

DACEY, M. F. (1964b): A Family of Density Functions for Lösch's Measurements on Town Distribution, *Prof. Geogr.*, **16**:5–7.

DACEY, M. F. (1962): Analysis of Central Place and Point Patterns by a Nearest Neighbour Method, *Lund Stud. Geogr.*, *Ser. B*, **24**:55–75.

DACEY, M. F. (1960): The Spacing of River Towns, *Ann. Assoc. Am. Geogr.*, **50**:59–61.

DANTZIG, G. B. (1963): "Linear Programming and Extensions," Princeton, N.J.: Princeton.

DANTZIG, G. B. (1951): Maximization of a Linear Function of Variables Subject to Linear Inequalities, in T. C. KOOPMANS (ed.), "Activity Analysis of Production and Allocation," New York: Wiley.

DAVIS, J. TAIT (1971): Sources of Variation in Housing Values in Washington, D.C., *Geogr. Anal.*, **3**:63–76.

DAY, R. H. (1970): A Theoretical Note on the Spatial Diffusion of Something New, *Geogr. Anal.*, **2**:68–76.

DAY, R. H. (1963): "Simple Methods of Estimating Certain Non Linear Functions with Emphasis on Agricultural Data," *U.S. Dept. Agr.*, *Agr. Handbook* 256.

DELENIUS, T. (1957): "Sampling in Sweden, Contributions to the Methods and Theories of Sample Survey Practice," Stockholm: Almgvist and Wiksell.

DELURY, D. B. (1950): "Values and Integrals of the Orthogonal Polynomials up to $N = 26$," Toronto: University of Toronto Press.

DORFMAN, R., P. A. SAMUELSON, and R. M. SOLOW (1968): "Linear Programming and Economic Analysis," New York: Wiley.

DRAPER, N. R., and H. SMITH (1966): "Applied Regression Analysis," New York: Wiley.

DURBIN, J., and G. S. WATSON (1950, 1951): Testing for Serial Correlation in Least Squares Regression, *Biometrika*, **37**:409–428, and **38**:159–178.

FARIS, R. E. L., and H. W. DUNHAM (1939): "Mental Disorders in Urban Areas," Chicago: The University of Chicago Press.

FICKEN, F. A. (1961): "The Simplex Method of Linear Programming," New York: Holt.

FISHER, R. A., and F. YATES (1943): "Statistical Tables for Biological, Agricultural and Medical Research," 3d ed., New York: Hafner.

FORD, L. R., and D. R. FULKERSON (1962): "Flows in Networks," Princeton, N.J.: Princeton.

FOUND, W. C. (1970): Towards a General Theory Relating Distance between Farm and Home to Agricultural Production, *Geogr. Anal.*, **2**:165–176.

FREUND, J. E. (1967): "Modern Elementary Statistics," Englewood Cliffs, N.J.: Prentice-Hall.

FRIEDMAN, M. (1940): A Comparison of Alternative Tests of Significance for the Problem of *m* Rankings, *Ann. Math. Stat.*, **11**:86–92.

FRUCHTER, B. F. (1954): "Introduction to Factor Analysis," New York: Van Nostrand.

FUCHS, V. R. (1962a): "Changes in the Location of Manufacturing in the United States Since 1929," New Haven, Conn.: Yale.

FUCHS, V. R. (1962b): Statistical Explanations of the Relative Shift of Manufacturing among Regions of the United States, *Papers Proc. Reg. Sci. Assoc.*, **8**:105–126.

GARRISON, W. L. (1960): Spatial Structure of the Economy, Part III, *Ann. Assoc. Am. Geogr.*, **50**:357–373.

GARRISON, W. L. (1959a): Spatial Structure of the Economy, Part II, *Ann. Assoc. Am. Geogr.*, **49**:471–482.

GARRISON, W. L. (1959b): Spatial Structure of the Economy, Part I, *Ann. Assoc. Am. Geogr.*, **49**:232–239.

GARRISON, W. L., et al. (1959c): "Studies of Highway Development and Geographic Change," Seattle: University of Washington Press.

GARRISON, W. L., and D. F. MARBLE (1958): Analysis of Highway Networks: A Linear Programming Formulation, *Highway Res. Board Proc.*, **37**:1–17.

GEARY, R. C. (1954): The Contiguity Ratio and Statistical Mapping, *Inc. Stat.*, **5**: 115–141.

GETIS, A. (1973): On Clustered Point Patterns, in M. H. YEATES (ed.), "Proceedings of the 1972 Meeting of the IGU Commission on Quantitative Geography," Montreal: McGill-Queen's Press.

GETIS, A. (1964): Temporal Land Use Pattern Analysis with the Use of Nearest Neighbor and Quadrat Methods, *Ann. Assoc. Am. Geogr.*, **54**:391–398.

GINSBURG, N. (1961): "Atlas of Economic Development," Chicago: The University of Chicago Press.

GODLUND, S. (1961): Population, Regional Hospitals, Transport Facilities, and Regions, *Lund Stud. Geogr.*, Lund, Sweden: Gleerup.

GOLANT, S. M. (1971): Adjustment Process in a System: A Behavioral Model of Human Movement, *Geogr. Anal.*, **3**:203–220.

GOLANT, S. M., and I. BURTON (1970): A Semantic Differential Experiment in the Interpretation and Grouping of Environmental Hazards, *Geogr. Anal.*, **2**:120–134.

GOLDMAN, T. A. (1958): Efficient Transportation and Industrial Location, *Papers Proc. Reg. Sci. Assoc.*, **4**:91–106.

GOLLEDGE, R. G., and L. A. BROWN (1967): Search, Learning and the Market Decision Process, *Geogr. Ann.*, **49B**:116–124.

GOULD, P. R. (1970): Is Statistix Inferens the Geographical Name for a Wild Goose? *Econ. Geogr.*, **46**:439–448.

GOULD, P. R. (1969): Methodological Developments Since the Fifties, in C. BOARD et al. (eds.), "Progress in Geography," vol. 1, London: Arnold.

GOULD, P. R. (1963): Man against His Environment: A Game Theoretic Framework, *Ann. Assoc. Am. Geogr.*, **53**:290–297.

GREER-WOOTTEN, B. (1972): A Bibliography of Statistical Applications in Geography, *Assoc. Am. Geogr.*, *Tech. Paper* 9.

GRILICHES, S. (1957): Hybrid Corn: An Exploration in the Economics of Technological Change, *Econometrica*, 25:501–522.

HADLEY, G. (1962): "Linear Programming," Reading, Mass.: Addison-Wesley.

HAGERSTRAND, T. (1967): On Monte Carlo Simulation of Diffusion, in W. L. GARRISON and D. F. MARBLE (eds.), "Quantitative Geography, Part I: Economic and Cultural Topics," *Dep. Geogr., Stud. Geogr.*, 13, Evanston, Ill.: Northwestern University Press.

HAGERSTRAND, T. (1953): "Innovations forloppet ur Korologisk Synpunkt," Lund, Sweden: Gleerup; translated and postscript by A. PRED (1967): "Innovation Diffusion as a Spatial Process," Chicago: The University of Chicago Press.

HAGGETT, P. (1968): Trend Surface Mapping in the Comparison of Intra-regional Structures, *Papers Proc. Reg. Sci. Assoc.*, 20:19–28.

HAGGETT, P. (1965): "Locational Analysis in Human Geography," London: E. Arnold.

HAGGETT, P. (1964): Regional and Local Components in the Distribution of Forested Areas in Southeast Brazil: A Multivariate Approach, *Geogr. J.*, 130:365–377.

HAGGETT, P. (1963): Regional and Local Components in Land Use Sampling: A Case Study from the Brazilian Triangulo, *Erdkunde*, 17:108–114.

HAGGETT, P., and C. BOARD (1964): Rotational and Parallel Traverses in the Rapid Integration of Geographic Areas, *Ann. Assoc. Am. Geogr.*, 54:406–410.

HANNERBERG, D., T. HAGERSTRAND, and B. ODEVING (1957): "Migration in Sweden: A Symposium," *Lund Stud. Geogr.*, ser. B, 13.

HARBROUGH, J. W., and F. W. PRESTON (1968): Fourier Series Analysis in Geology, in B. J. L. BERRY and D. F. MARBLE (eds.), "Spatial Analysis," Englewood Cliffs, N.J.: Prentice-Hall.

HARING, L. L., and J. F. LOUNSBURY (1971): "Introduction to Scientific Geographic Research," Dubuque, Iowa: Wm. C. Brown Company Publishers.

HARMAN, H. (1960): "Modern Factor Analysis," Chicago: The University of Chicago Press.

HARTSHORNE, R. (1959): "Perspective on the Nature of Geography," Chicago: Rand McNally.

HARVEY, D. W. (1969): "Explanation in Geography," London: E. Arnold.

HARVEY, D. W. (1967): Models of the Evolution of Spatial Patterns in Human Geography, in R. J. CHORLEY and P. HAGGETT (eds.), "Models in Geography," pp. 577–588, London: Methuen.

HIDORE, J. J. (1963): The Relationship between Cash-Grain Farming and Land Forms, *Econ. Geogr.*, 39:84–89.

HITCHCOCK, F. L. (1941): The Distribution of a Product from Several Sources to Numerous Localities, *J. Math. Phys.*, 20:224–230.

HODGE, G. (1971): Comparisons of Urban Structure in Canada, the United States, and Great Britain, *Geogr. Anal.*, 3:83–90.

HOEL, P. G. (1960): "Elementary Statistics," New York: Wiley.

HOHN, F. E. (1964): "Elementary Matrix Algebra," New York: Macmillan.

HOLZINGER, K. J., and H. H. HARMAN (1941): "Factor Analysis: A Synthesis of Factorial Methods," Chicago: The University of Chicago Press.

HORTON, F., and P. W. SHULDINER (1966): The Analysis of Land-Use Linkages, *Highway Res. Board Bull.*

HOWARTH, R. J. (1967): Trend Surface Fitting to Random Data—An Experimental Test, *Am. J. Sci.*, **265**:619–625.

HULTQUIST, J., J. HOLMES, and L. A. BROWN (1971): CENTRO: A Program for Centrographic Measures, *Dep. Geogr., Discuss. Paper* 21, Columbus: Ohio State University.

IKLÉ, F. C. (1954): Sociological Relationships of Traffic to Population and Distance, *Traffic Quart.*, **8**:123–136.

ISARD, W., et al. (1960): "Methods of Regional Analysis," New York: Wiley.

JENKINS, M. A., and J. W. SHEPHERD (1972): Decentralizing High School Administration in Detroit: An Evaluation of Alternative Strategies of Political Control, *Econ. Geogr.*, **48**:95–106.

JOHNSTON, R. J. (1970): Latent Migration Potential and the Gravity Model: A New Zealand Study, *Geogr. Anal.*, **2**:387–397.

JUDGE, G. C., et al. (1964): "Spatial Structure of the Livestock Economy," Washington, D.C.: USDA, North Central Region Research Bulletin, No. 157.

KAISER, H. F. (1960): The Application of Electronic Computers to Factor Analysis, *Educ. Psychol. Meas.*, **20**:141–151.

KANSKY, K. J. (1963): Structure of Transportation Networks, *Dep. Geogr., Res. Paper* 84, Chicago: The University of Chicago.

KEMENY, J. G., J. L. SNELL, and G. L. THOMPSON (1966): "Introduction to Finite Mathematics," Englewood Cliffs, N.J.: Prentice-Hall.

KEMENY, J. G., and J. L. SNELL (1960): "Finite Markov Chains," Princeton, N.J.: Van Nostrand.

KENDALL, M. G. (1955): "Rank Correlation Methods," London: Griffin.

KENDALL, M. G. (1939): The Geographical Distribution of Crop Productivity in England, *J. Royal Stat. Soc.*, **102**:21–48.

KERLINGER, F. (1964): "Foundations of Behavioral Research," New York: Holt.

KING, L. J. (1969): "Statistical Analysis in Geography," Englewood Cliffs, N.J.: Prentice-Hall.

KING, L. J. (1962): A Quantitative Expression of the Pattern of Urban Areas in Selected Areas of the United States, *Tijdschr. Econ. Soc. Geogr.*, **53**:1–7.

KIRKLAND, J. S. (1969): "Housing Filtration in Kingston 1953–1968," unpublished M.A. thesis, Department of Geography, Queen's University, Kingston, Ontario, Canada.

KNOS, D. S. (1962): "Distribution of Land Values in Topeka, Kansas," Lawrence: Center for Research in Business, University of Kansas Press.

KRUMBEIN, W. C. (1967): "Fortran IV Computer Programs for Markov Chain Experiments in Geology," *Lawrence, Kansas State Geol. Surv., Computer Contrib.* 13.

KRUMBEIN, W. C., and F. A. GRAYBILL (1965): "An Introduction to Statistical Models in Geology," New York: McGraw-Hill.

LABER, G. (1969): Determinants of International Travel between Canada and the United States, *Geogr. Anal.*, 1:329–336.

LATHAM, J. P. (1964): Comment upon Note by Haggett and Board, *Ann. Assoc. Am. Geogr.*, 54:410–411.

LATHAM, J. P. (1963): Methodology for an Instrumented Geographical Analysis, *Ann. Assoc. Am. Geogr.*, 53:194–209.

LAWLEY, D. N., and A. E. MAXWELL (1963): "Factor Analysis As a Statistical Method," London: Butterworth.

LEACH, E. D. (1966): "The Northern Colonial Frontier, New York: Holt.

LEE, D. B. (1967): "Analysis and Description of Residential Segregation," Ithaca, N.Y.: Center for Housing and Environmental Studies, Cornell University Press.

MACKAY, J. R. (1958): The Interactance Hypothesis and Boundaries in Canada: A Preliminary Study, *Can. Geogr.*, 11:1–8.

MACKINNON, R. D. (1970): Dynamic Programming and Geographical Systems, *Econ. Geogr.*, 46:350–366.

MACKINNON, R. D., and M. J. HODGSON (1970): Optimal Transportation Networks: A Case Study of Highway Systems, *Environ. Plann.*, 2:267–284.

MANDELL, P. I., and L. G. TWEETEN (1971): The Location of Cotton Production in the United States under Competitive Conditions: A Study of Crop Location and Comparative Advantage, *Geogr. Anal.*, 3:334–353.

MARBLE, D. F. (1964): A Simple Markovian Model of Trip Structures in a Metropolitan Region, *Papers, Reg. Sci. Assoc., West. Sect.*, 2:150–156.

MARBLE, D. F., and J. D. NYSTUEN (1963): An Approach to the Direct Measurement of Community Mean Information Fields, *Papers Proc. Reg. Sci. Assoc.*, 11:99–109.

MASSAM, B. H. (1972): The Spatial Structure of Administrative Systems, *Assoc. Am. Geogr., Comm. Coll. Geogr., Resour. Paper* 12.

MASSAM, B. H. (1971): A Test of a Model of Administrative Areas, *Geogr. Anal.*,3: 403–409.

MASSEY, F. J., JR. (1951): The Kolmogorov-Smirnov Test for Goodness of Fit, *J. Am. Stat. Assoc.*, 46:70.

MATÉRN, B. (1960): "Spatial Variation," *Medd. Statens Skogsforskningsinst.*, 50(3).

MAYFIELD, R. C. (1967): A Central Place Hierarchy in Northern India, in W. L. GARRISON and D. F. MARBLE (eds.), "Quantitative Geography, Part I: Economic and Cultural Aspects," *Dep. Geogr., Stud. Geogr.*, 13, Evanston, Ill.: Northwestern University Press.

MCDONALD, G. T. (1968): Trend Surface Analysis of Farm Size Patterns in Ontario and Quebec, *Cent. Urban Community Stud., Res. Rep.* 8, Toronto: University of Toronto.

MCNEE, R. B. (1967): A Proposal for a New Geography Course for Liberal Education, in "New Approaches in Introductory College Courses," Washington, D.C.: Association of American Geographers.

MCQUITTY, L. L. (1957): Elementary Linkage Analysis for Isolating Orthogonal and Oblique Types and Typal Relevancies, *Educ. Psychol. Meas.*, **17**:207–229.

MEYER, D. R. (1972): Geographical Population Data: Statistical Description Not Statistical Inference, *Prof. Geogr.*, **24**:26–28.

MILLER, R. L., and J. S. KAHN (1962): "Statistical Analysis in the Geological Sciences," New York: Wiley.

MILLS, F. C. (1955): "Statistical Methods," New York: Holt.

MOELLERING, H., and W. R. TOBLER (1972): Geographical Variances, *Geogr. Anal.*, **4**:34–50.

MORAN, P. A. P. (1950): Notes on Continuous Stochastic Phenomena, *Biometrika*, **37**:17–23.

MORLEY, C. D., and J. B. THORNES (1972): A Markov Decision Model for Network Flows, *Geogr. Anal.*, **4**:180–193.

MORONEY, M. J. (1965): "Facts from Figures," Baltimore: Pelican Books, Penguin.

MORRILL, R. L. (1967): The Movement of Persons and the Transportation Problem, in W. L. GARRISON and D. F. MARBLE (eds.), "Quantitative Geography, Part I: Economic and Cultural Topics," *Dep. Geogr.*, *Stud. Geogr.*, 13, Evanston, Ill.: Northwestern University Press.

MORRILL, R. L. (1965): The Negro Ghetto: Problems and Alternatives, *Geogr. Rev.*, **55**:1–18.

MORRILL, R. L. (1963): The Development of Spatial Distributions of Towns in Sweden: An Historical-Predictive Approach, *Ann. Assoc. Am. Geogr.*, **53**:1–14.

MORRILL, R. L., and R. EARICKSON (1969): Problems in Modelling Interaction, in K. COX and R. GOLLEDGE (eds.), "Behavioral Problems in Geography," *Dep. Geogr.*, *Stud. Geogr.* 17, Evanston, Ill.: Northwestern University Press.

MORRILL, R. L., and W. L. GARRISON (1960): Projections of Interregional Patterns of Trade in Wheat and Flour, *Econ. Geogr.*, **36**:116–126.

MORRILL, R. L., and M. B. KELLEY (1970): The Simulation of Hospital Use and the Estimation of Location Efficiency, *Geogr. Anal.*, **2**:283–300.

MORRILL, R. L., and F. R. PITTS (1967): Marriage, Migration, and the Mean Information Field: A Study in Uniqueness and Generality, *Ann. Assoc. Am. Geogr.*, **57**:401–422.

MURDIE, R. A. (1969): Factorial Ecology of Metropolitan Toronto, 1951–1961, *Dep. Geogr.*, *Res. Paper* 116, Chicago: The University of Chicago.

MURPHY, R. E., and J. E. VANCE (1954): Delimiting the C.B.D., *Econ. Geogr.*, **30**:189–222.

NAIR, K. R. (1954): The Fitting of Growth Curves, in O. KEMPTHORNE et al. (eds.), "Statistics and Mathematics in Biology," pp. 119–132, Ames: Iowa State College Press.

National Research Council Ad Hoc Committee on Geography (1965): "The Science of Geography," *NAS-NRC*.

NEFT, D. S. (1966): Statistical Analysis for Areal Distributions, *Reg. Sci. Res. Inst.*, *Monogr.* 2.

NELSON, H. J. (1955): A Service Classification of American Cities, *Econ. Geogr.*, **31**: 189–210.

NEWLING, B. E. (1969): The Spatial Variation of Urban Population Densities, *Geogr. Rev.*, **59**:242–252.

NORCLIFFE, G. B. (1969): On the Use and Limitations of Trend Surface Models, *Can. Geogr.*, **13**:338–348.

OLDS, E. G. (1938): Distributions of Sums of Squares of Rank Differences for Small Numbers of Individuals, *Ann. Math. Stat.*, **9**:133–148.

OLDS, E. G. (1949): The 5 % Significance Levels for Sums of Squares of Rank Differences and a Correction, *Ann. Math. Stat.*, **20**:117–118.

OLSSON, G. (1967): "Distance and Human Interaction: A Review and Bibliography," Philadelphia: Regional Science Research Institute.

OLSSON, G. (1965*a*): "Distance and Human Interaction," Philadelphia: Regional Science Research Institute.

OLSSON, G. (1965*b*): Distance and Human Interaction: A Migration Study, *Geogr. Ann.*, **47**:3–43.

ORCUTT, G. H., et al. (1961): "Microanalysis of Socioeconomic Systems," New York: Harper & Row.

PEARCE, D. W. (1971): "Cost-Benefit Analysis," London: Macmillan.

PITTS, F. R. (1967): MIFCAL and NONCEL: Two Computer Programs for the Generalization of the Hagerstrand Models to an Irregular Lattice, *Dep. Geogr.*, *Tech. Rep.* 7, Evanston, Ill.: Northwestern University.

PITTS, F. R. (1965): HAGER III and HAGER IV: Two Computer Programs for the Study of Spatial Diffusion Problems, *Dep. Geogr.*, *Tech. Rep.* 4, Evanston, Ill.: Northwestern University.

PORTER, H. (1964): "Application of Intercity Intervening Opportunity Models to Telephone, Migration and Highway Traffic Data," unpublished doctoral dissertation, Department of Geography, Northwestern University; available through University Microfilms, Ann Arbor, Mich.

RACINE, J. B. (1971–1972): Modèles Graphiques et Mathématiques en Géographie Humaine I, II, and III, *Rev. Géogr. Montréal*, **25**:323–358; **26**:7–34, 321–332.

RAVENSTEIN, E. G. (1885, 1889): The Laws of Migration, *J. Royal Stat. Soc.*, **48**:167–235; **52**:493–496.

RAYNER, J. N. (1967): Correlation between Surfaces by Spectral Methods, in D. F. MERRIAM and N. C. COCKE (eds.), "Computer Applications in the Earth Sciences: Colloquium on Trend Analysis," *Computer Contrib.* 12, Lawrence: University of Kansas Press.

REES, P. H. (1971): Factorial Ecology: An Extended Definition, Survey, and Critique of the Field, *Econ. Geogr.*, **47**(2)(*Suppl.*):220–233.

REVELLE, C. S., and R. W. SWAIN (1970): Central Facilities Location, *Geogr. Anal.*, **2**:30–42.

RHODES, E. C. (1940): Population Mathematics, *J. Royal Stat. Soc.*, **103**:362–387.

RIDDELL, J. B. (1970a): "The Spatial Dynamics of Modernization in Sierra Leone," Evanston, Ill.: Northwestern University Press.

RIDDELL, J. B. (1970b): On Structuring a Migration Model, Geogr. Anal., 2:403–409.

ROBERTS, M. C., and K. W. RUMAGE (1965): The Spatial Variation in Urban Left-Wing Voting in England and Wales in 1951, Ann. Assoc. Am. Geogr., 55:161–178.

ROBINSON, A. H. (1962): Mapping the Correspondence of Isarithmic Maps, Ann. Assoc. Am. Geogr., 52:414–425.

ROBINSON, A. H. (1956): The Necessity of Weighting Values in Correlation Analysis of Areal Data, Ann. Assoc. Am. Geogr., 46:233–236.

ROBINSON, A. H., and L. CAROE (1967): On the Analysis and Comparison of Statistical Surfaces, in W. L. GARRISON and D. F. MARBLE (eds.), "Quantitative Geography, Part I: Economic and Cultural Topics," Dep. Geogr., Stud. Geogr., 13, Evanston, Ill.: Northwestern University Press.

ROBINSON, A. H., L. B. LINDBERG, and L. W. BRINKMAN (1961): A Correlation and Regression Analysis Applied to Rural Farm Population Densities in the Great Plains, Ann. Assoc. Am. Geogr., 51:211–221.

ROBINSON, G., and K. J. FAIRBAIRN (1969): An Application of Trend Surface Mapping to the Distribution of Residuals from Regression, Ann. Assoc. Am. Geogr., 59:158–170.

ROGERS, A. (1969a): Quadrat Analysis of Urban Dispersions, I: Theoretical Techniques, Environ. Plann., 1:47–80.

ROGERS, A. (1969b): Quadrat Analysis of Urban Dispersion, II: Case Studies of Urban Retail Systems, Environ. Plann., 1:155–171.

ROGERS, A. (1967): Theories of Intra-urban Spatial Structures: A Dissenting View, Land Econ., 63:108–112.

ROGERS, A., and R. MILLER (1967): Estimating a Matrix Population Growth Operator from Distributional Time Series, Ann. Assoc. Am. Geogr., 57:751–756.

ROSE, H. M. (1970): The Structure of Retail Trade in a Racially Changing Area, Geogr. Anal., 2:135–148.

RUMMEL, R. J. (1970): "Applied Factor Analysis," Evanston, Ill.: Northwestern University Press.

RUMMEL, R. J. (1967): Understanding Factor Analysis, J. Conflict Resolut., 2:444–480.

SAUER, C. O. (1952): "Agricultural Origins and Dispersals," New York: The American Geographical Society.

SCHAEFER, F. K. (1953): Exceptionalism in Geography: A Methodological Examination, Ann. Assoc. Am. Geogr., 43:226–249.

School Mathematics Study Group (1961): "Introduction to Matrix Algebra," New Haven, Conn.: Yale.

SCOTT, A. J. (1971a): "Combinatorial Programming, Spatial Analysis and Planning," London: Methuen.

SCOTT, A. J. (1971b): An Introduction to Spatial Allocation Analysis, Assoc. Am. Geogr., Comm. Coll. Geogr., Resour. Paper 9.

SCOTT, A. J. (1970): Location-Allocation Systems: A Review, *Geogr. Anal.*, **2**:95–119.

SHACHAR, A. (1966): Some Applications of Geo-statistical Methods in Urban Research, *Papers Proc. Reg. Sci. Assoc.*, **18**:197–206.

SHEVKY, E., and W. BELL (1955): "Social Area Analysis: Theory, Illustrative Applications and Procedures," Stanford, Calif.: Stanford.

SHEVKY, E., and M. WILLIAMS (1949): "The Social Areas of Los Angeles: Analysis and Typology," Los Angeles: University of California Press.

SIEGEL, S. (1956): "Nonparametric Statistics for the Behavioral Sciences," New York: McGraw-Hill.

SIMMONS, J. W. (1964): The Changing Pattern of Retail Location, *Dep. Geogr.*, *Res. Paper* 92, Chicago: The University of Chicago.

SIMONNARD, M. (1966): "Linear Programming," Englewood Cliffs, N.J.: Prentice-Hall.

SMITH, D. A. (1963): Interaction within a Fragmented State: The Example of Hawaii, *Econ. Geogr.*, **39**:234–244.

SNEDECOR, G. W. (1946): "Statistical Methods," Ames: Iowa State College Press.

STEINER, R. (1957): Some Problems in Designing Samples of Rural Land Use, *Yearb. Assoc. Pac. Coast Geogr.*, **19**:25–28.

STEVENS, B. H. (1961): Linear Programming and Location Rent, *J. Reg. Sci.*, **3**:15–25.

STEWART, J. Q. (1950): The Development of Social Physics, *Am. J. Phys.*, **18**:239–253.

STEWART, J. Q. (1942): A Measure of the Influence of Population at Distance, *Sociometry*, **5**:63–71.

STEWART, J. Q. (1941): An Inverse Distance Variation for Certain Social Influences, *Science*, **93**:89–90.

STEWART, J. Q., and W. WARNTZ (1958): Macrogeography and Social Science, *Geogr. Rev.*, **48**:167–184.

"Student" (1908): The Probable Error of a Mean, *Biometrika*, **6**:1–25.

SUITS, D. B. (1957): Use of Dummy Variables in Regression Equations, *J. Am. Stat. Assoc.*, **52**:548–551.

TAAFFE, E. J. (1962): The Urban Hierarchy: An Air Passenger Definition, *Econ. Geogr.*, **38**:1–10.

TAAFFE, E. J., B. J. GARNER, and M. H. YEATES (1963): "The Peripheral Journey to Work: A Geographic Consideration," Evanston, Ill.: Northwestern University Press.

TAAFFE, E. J., R. L. MORRILL, and P. R. GOULD (1963): Transport Expansion in Underdeveloped Countries: A Comparative Analysis, *Geogr. Rev.*, **53**:503–529.

TAYLOR, P. J. (1971): Distance Transformation and Distance Decay Functions, *Geogr. Anal.*, **3**:221–238.

TEGSJÖ, B., and S. OBERG (1966): Concept of Potential Applied to Price Formation, *Geogr. Ann.*, **48**:51–58.

TEITZ, M. B. (1968): Toward a Theory of Urban Facility Location, *Papers Proc. Reg. Sci. Assoc.*, **21**:35–51.

THOMAS, E. N. (1968): Maps of Residuals from Regression, in B. J. L. BERRY and D. F.

MARBLE (eds.), "Spatial Analysis: A Reader in Statistical Geography," pp. 326–352, Englewood Cliffs, N.J.: Prentice-Hall.

THOMAS, E. N. (1960): Areal Associations between Population Growth and Selected Factors in the Chicago Urbanized Area, *Econ. Geogr.*, **36**:158–170.

THOMAS, E. N., and D. L. ANDERSON (1965): Additional Comments on Weighting Values in Correlation Analysis of Areal Data, *Ann. Assoc. Am. Geogr.*, **55**:492–505.

TINLINE, R. (1970): Linear Operators in Diffusion Research, in M. CHISHOLM et al. (eds.), "Regional Forecasting," pp. 71–91, London: Butterworth.

TOBLER, W. R. (1970): Selected Computer Programs, Ann Arbor: Department of Geography, The University of Michigan.

TOBLER, W. R. (1969): Geographical Filters and Their Inverses, *Geogr. Anal.*, **1**:234–253.

WALKER, H. M., and J. LEV (1953): "Statistical Inference," New York: Holt.

WARD, D. (1969): The Internal Spatial Structure of Immigrant Residential Districts in the Late Nineteenth Century, *Geogr. Anal.*, **1**:337–353.

WARNTZ, W. (1965): "Macrogeography and Income Fronts," Philadelphia: Regional Science Research Institute.

WARNTZ, W. (1959): "Towards a Geography of Price," Philadelphia: Regional Science Research Institute.

WATSON, J. W. (1955): Geography: A Discipline in Distance, *Scott. Geogr. Mag.*, **7**:1–13.

WERNER, C. (1968): The Role of Topology and Geometry in Optimal Network Design, *Papers Proc. Reg. Sci. Assoc.*, **21**:173–189.

WHEELER, J. O. (1970): Transport Inputs and Residential Rent Theory, *Geogr. Anal.*, **2**:43–54.

WHITTLE, P. (1954): On Stationary Processes in the Plane, *Biometrika*, **41**:434–449.

WILKIE, R. W. (1973): The Process Method versus the "Hypothesis Method": Nonlinear Analysis in an Argentine Interdisciplinary Case Study of Peasant Spatial Perception and Behavior, in M. H. YEATES (ed.), "Proceedings of the 1972 Meeting of the IGU Commission on Quantitative Geography," Montreal: McGill-Queen's Press.

WILLIAMS, J. D. (1954): "The Compleat Strategyst," New York: McGraw-Hill, Revised 1965.

WILSON, A. G. (1971): A Family of Spatial Interaction Models, and Associated Developments, *Environ. Plann.*, **3**:1–32.

WILSON, A. G. (1970): Inter-regional Commodity Flows: Entropy Maximizing Approaches, *Geogr. Anal.*, **2**:255–282.

WILSON, A. G. (1969): The Use of Analogies in Geography, *Geogr. Anal.*, **1**:225–233.

WILSON, A. G. (1968): Models in Urban Planning: A Synoptic Review of Recent Literature, *Urban Stud.*, **5**:249–276.

WOOD, W. E. (1955): Use of Stratified Random Samples in a Land Use Study, *Ann. Assoc. Am. Geogr.*, **45**:350–367.

YATES, F. (1949): "Sampling Methods for Censuses and Surveys," London: Griffin.

YEATES, M. H. (1972a): The Congruency between Housing Space and Social Space and Some Experiments concerning Its Implications, *Environ. Plann.*, 4:395–414.

YEATES, M. H. (1972b): Modelling the Social Geography of Urban Areas: A Canadian Example, in W. P. ADAMS and F. M. HELLEINER (eds.), "International Geography," pp. 852–854, Toronto: University of Toronto Press.

YEATES, M. H. (1969): A Note concerning the Development of a Geographic Model of International Trade, *Geogr. Anal.*, 1:399–404.

YEATES, M. H. (1965): Some Factors Affecting the Spatial Distribution of Chicago Land Values, *Econ. Geogr.*, 41:57–70.

YEATES, M. H. (1964): A Multivariate Analysis of Some Aspects of the Economic Geography of Florida, *Southeast. Geogr.*, 4:11–20.

YEATES, M. H. (1963): Hinterland Delimitation: A Distance Minimizing Approach, *Prof. Geogr.*, 15:7–10.

YEATES, M. H., and B. J. GARNER (1971): "The North American City," New York: Harper & Row.

YEATES, M. H., and T. G. NICHOLSON (1969): Spatial Association and Its Measurement, in "Computer Aided Instruction in Geography," *Assoc. Am. Geogr., Tech. Paper* 2, pp.115–139.

YEOMANS, K. A. (1968a): "Introducing Statistics: Statistics for the Social Scientist, 1," Baltimore, Penguin.

YEOMANS, K. A. (1968b): "Applied Statistics: Statistics for the Social Scientist, 2," Baltimore: Penguin.

YULE, G. U. (1925): The Growth of Population and the Factors Which Control It, *J. Royal Stat. Soc.*, 88:1–58.

ZANGWALL, W. I. (1969): "Non Linear Programming: A Unified Approach," Englewood Cliffs, N.J.: Prentice-Hall.

ZIPF, G. K. (1949): "Human Behavior and the Principle of Least Effort," Cambridge, Mass.: Addison-Wesley.

NAME INDEX

SUBJECT INDEX